After the Fall

After the Fall

*New Yorkers Remember September 2001
and the Years That Followed*

Edited by
Mary Marshall Clark,
Peter Bearman,
Catherine Ellis, *and*
Stephen Drury Smith

THE NEW PRESS

NEW YORK
LONDON

Requests for permission to reproduce selections from this book should be mailed to:
Permissions Department, The New Press, 38 Greene Street, New York, NY 10013.

Published in the United States by The New Press, New York, 2011
Distributed by Perseus Distribution

LIBRARY OF CONGRESS CATALOGING-IN-PUBLICATION DATA

After the fall : New Yorkers remember September 2001 and the years that followed /
edited by Mary Marshall Clark . . . [et al.].
p.   cm.
ISBN 978-1-59558-647-6 (hc.)
1. September 11 Terrorist Attacks, 2001—Personal narratives.
2. September 11 Terrorist Attacks, 2001—Social aspects.   I. Clark, Mary Marshall.
HV6432.7.A38125 2011
974.7'10440922—dc22   2011012833

The New Press was established in 1990 as a not-for-profit alternative to
the large, commercial publishing houses currently dominating the book
publishing industry. The New Press operates in the public interest rather
than for private gain, and is committed to publishing, in innovative ways,
works of educational, cultural, and community value that are often deemed
insufficiently profitable.

www.thenewpress.com

Composition by dix!

Printed in the United States of America

2   4   6   8   10   9   7   5   3   1

Contents

About the Transcripts

This anthology of September 11, 2001, stories is based on oral history interviews conducted by Columbia University's Oral History Research Office in collaboration with the Institute for Social and Economic Research and Policy. Some of the subjects were interviewed once, others multiple times over the course of several years. Some interviews were relatively brief; many lasted for hours. The interviews were recorded and later transcribed.

All of the interviews presented here have been greatly condensed from their original lengths. Our goal is to provide as wide a range of narrators and experiences as possible within the word limits of a single volume. The stories presented here were edited to suit the demands of the printed page while staying true to the core of each storyteller's particular voice and narrative. Verbal mannerisms that are tolerated by the ear can clutter and clog a written sentence; a thicket of small obstacles, such as "you know" and "I was, like, saying," has been cleared to allow ideas, details, and events to travel more easily.

In some of these narratives, separate interviews are combined to provide the most coherent or complete recollection of events. These are indicated by dates that are joined into one interview heading. In other cases, selections from second and third interviews are set apart to reveal how the person's reflections and reactions changed over time.

The original interviews and their complete transcripts are available at the Columbia University Oral History Research Office in New York City. The website is: http://www.columbia.edu/cu/lweb/indiv/oral/index.html.

Oral History Research Office
Columbia University
801 Butler Library, Box 20
535 W. 114th St., MC 1129, New York, NY 10027
Phone: (212) 854-7083
oralhist@libraries.cul.columbia.edu

Brief Time Line—September 11, 2001

7:59–8:42 A.M. (EDT): Nineteen terrorists are aboard as four American passenger airliners take off on transcontinental flights. The hijacked planes are carrying 246 passengers and crew.

8:46 A.M.: American Airlines Flight 11 crashes into World Trade Center Tower One.

8:50 A.M.: A New York Fire Department battalion chief who witnessed the crash establishes an initial command post in the lobby of Tower One.

9:03 A.M.: United Airlines Flight 175 crashes into World Trade Center Tower Two.

9:37 A.M.: American Airlines Flight 77 crashes into the Pentagon.

9:59 A.M.: Tower Two collapses.

10:03 A.M. (approximately): United Airlines Flight 93 crashes near Shanksville, PA.

10:29 A.M.: Tower One collapses.

5:21 P.M.: Seven World Trade Center collapses.

Over the course of the day some 25,000 New Yorkers evacuated lower Manhattan. More than two hundred fire units and more than one hundred ambulances responded.

Some three thousand people died in New York, Pennsylvania, and Washington, D.C.

Sources: The 9/11 Commission Report; Fire Department of New York / McKinsey and Co. report; news reports.

Acknowledgments

Oral history is created through multiple authorship. The two main authors are the narrators, who tell their stories, and the interviewers, who listen. But there are many others who ensure that the words spoken are transcribed, reviewed for accuracy, sent back to narrators for their own editing, and cataloged, indexed, and deposited into permanent archives. There are also those who preserve digital media, securing it for the future, preparing aural and video files for dissemination. All of these steps are essential for ensuring the long-term survival of archives like the September 11, 2001 Oral History Narrative and Memory Project and related oral history projects we undertook in the long aftermath of September 11, 2001. In the deepest sense, all of these participants are also authors of the archive. We can name some, but not all, of the people, organizations, and funders who supported the creation of an archive of nearly one thousand hours of testimony, six hundred of which at this time of writing are fully accessible to the public.

First, and foremost, we must thank our funders. Those include: the National Science Foundation, the Rockefeller Foundation, the New York Times Foundation's Neediest Fund, and very importantly, Columbia University itself. People who made that funding possible include James Neal, Director of the Columbia Libraries; Jonathan Cole, then Provost of Columbia; Lynn Szwaja of the Rockefeller Foundation; and Jack Rosenthal of the New York Times Foundation, who also directed the New York Times 9/11 Neediest Fund. There were those who inspired, supported, or participated in the creation of the September 11, 2001 Oral History Narrative and Memory Project including Robert Smith, our co-principal investigator, responsible for supervising interviews with Mexicans and Latinos; Kenneth Jackson, Manning Marable, and Patricia O'Toole, faculty at Columbia who supported the idea of the project early on; as well as Margaret Crocco of Teacher's College; Alessandro Portelli, whose oral history of Rome at a time of crisis inspired our belief that we could attempt to record a collective memory of crisis in New York; and Daniel Wolfe, who walked from lower Manhattan up to Columbia University on the day of September 11, 2001, to attend an oral history seminar because he believed oral history was important.

The staff of the Oral History Research Office who supervised the processing of the interviews and supported our interviewers include: Rachel Kleinman, our first project manager; Gregory Culler, project manager who oversaw the huge project of processing interviews into the archive; Jessica Wiederhorn, former associate director; Rosemary Newham, former assistant director and office managers Rachel Solomon, Kate Foster, Courtney Smith, and Jenny Dalbert. Most recently, Corie Trancho-Robie, our former assistant director, worked tirelessly to ensure that the final processing and preservation of our digital files took place. Charis Shafer, office manager, has made our transcripts and media files available to countless researchers. Credit for the creation of a permanent digital repository for the audio and video files goes to Stephen Davis and Janet Gertz of the Columbia Libraries, who saw to it that hundreds of hours of interviews recorded on mini-disks were transferred to high-resolution digital files. Len

Morris and his expert crew of Galen Films shot beautiful video interviews of a selection of our narrators in 2005.

Graduate research assistants who listened to large portions of hours we collected, checking transcripts, security legal releases, and writing catalog entries include: Margaret Bryer Gloria Colom, Nikki D'Errico, Whitney Krahn, Marilyn Krieger, Dave Loerke, Emily Long, Cynthia-Marie M. O'Brien, Jennifer Oh, Lucas Perkins, Courtney Smith, Shalini Tripathi, Rebeccah Welch, Ben Wright, and Grace Zhou. Undergraduate research assistants include: Patrick Alexander, Becky Besdin, Sam Daly, Devon Gallegos, Elizabeth Grefrath, Caronae Howell, Norly Jean-Charles, Neha Nimmagudda, and Min Jeong Yoon. Transcribers Rose Heridia and Deborah Lattimore, among others, devoted hundreds of hours to the careful translation of oral speech into prose. Russell Merritt accomplished the careful and slow work of cataloging the interviews. The Columbia Libraries and the Institute for Social and Economic Research and Policy at Columbia gave outstanding administrative support in managing complex budgets and reporting, including Kristine Kavanaugh, Joel Fine, Dana Connolly, and Leah Lubin. Beryl Abrams, associate general counsel at Columbia, provided invaluable advice about how to protect the rights of those we interviewed in many different contexts.

In the second round of our longitudinal project, Dr. Marylene Cloitre and her colleagues at New York University provided essential psychological services for our interviewers, and our narrators, relieving us of the burden of carrying the emotional weight of the archive alone. Also essential in that regard were psychologists Ghislaine Boulanger, Sharon Kofman, Elizabeth Hegeman, and Carole Tarantelli, as well as the psychiatrist Stanley Bone, who each contributed insights and support. Ronald Grele, former director of the Oral History Research Office, was always around to give friendly advice and go for a cup of coffee. Alessandro Portelli, though mostly in Rome, was nonetheless always present at times of important decisions and made it possible to talk about the project outside of the United States, a precious opportunity. Daily and essential support was provided by our families, who let go of ordinary life to let us pursue overwhelming amounts of work, most critically Micah King, who turned ten on September 18, 2001.

Lastly, because they are the most important, are our interviewers. We sat at their feet for the first months of our work as they reported from the field, in awe of what they were willing to undergo to build an archive of memory that would truly represent the urban complexities of the catastrophe and the city. They include: Gerry Albarelli, Carol Arber, Amber Baylor, Josephine Bellacomo, Laura Bleiberg, Emilyn Brown, Ann Cvetkovich, Sari Eckler-Cooper, Myron A. Farber, Nancy Fisher, Karen Frenkel, Rochelle Frounfelker, Sarah Gallogly, Grace Hechinger, Elizabeth Hegeman, Gina Herrmann, Lise Hilboldt, Marianne Hirsch, Kathleen Hulser, Maria Iacullo, Rory Jones, Temma Kaplan, Helen Kaplan, Valerie Kiesig, Nam Kim-Paik, Rachel Kleinman, Sharon Kofman, Samantha Knowlden, Julia Kraut, Alejandra Leal, Karen Malpede, Gerald Markowitz, Susan Meyer, Julia Miles, Sheena Morrison, Kristin Murphy, Joanna O'Brien (née Shea), Adele Oltman, Marilyn Pettit, Elisabeth Pozzi-Thanner, Naomi Rappaport, Claudio Rivera, David Rosner, Ellen Ross Yesenia Ruiz, Zohra Saed, Melanie Shorin, Jeremy Simon, Robert Smith, Suzanne Snider, Leo Spitzer, Amy Starecheski, Anne Sullivan, Ed Thompson, Tami Thompson, Nancy Vandevanter, Fride Vedde, Ayana Wellington, Sally Wendkos-Olds, Sharon Zane, and M'lou Zahner.

There is not enough space to list, and thank, our narrators, except to assure them that their memories and stories will live forever, teaching generations to come what it was like in the days, months, and years that followed the events of September 11, 2001, in New York City.

—Peter Bearman and Mary Marshall Clark

Introduction

Peter Bearman and Mary Marshall Clark

Oral history archives are repositories of living memory. The process of constructing them requires deep attention to the personal, cultural, and political identities of those we encounter in the intimate setting of the life story and the telling of that story through the prism of daily life. A guiding premise of the oral history archive is that one learns more "from traveling through a single land with a thousand pairs of eyes than traveling through a thousand lands with a single pair of eyes."* The land we travel through in this book is New York City in the aftermath—both immediate and long-term—of the spectacular attacks on the World Trade Center on September 11, 2001. And the eyes that we share are those of nineteen men and women whose experiences then and in the years following traversed their own paths to understanding what September 2001 and beyond meant for them.

The most singular natural effect of catastrophe is that it expels people out of daily life stories into a chaotic external space, an otherworldly space, where reality is experienced as something *other than* routine. In the case

---

* Marcel Proust, *Remembrance of Things Past,* Volume 5.

of the September 11, 2001, catastrophe, people were also thrust out of historical time: as the authority for making meaning of the events was quickly seized by the government and by media that too easily acquiesced to the Bush administrations's efforts to shape what the catastrophe meant. Defined almost purely in political terms, the events of September 11 and the days thereafter were described as unique and without historical precedent. This rendering of the attacks as an event without historical roots or cultural context immediately fixed in place the collective realm of memory and collapsed the experiences and suffering of thousands of individuals into the symbolic realm of the nation. The official narrative of September 11, 2001, quickly became a national narrative, and so it was no surprise that within less than twenty-four hours the event already had a title, "America at War," and a soundtrack.

The "otherness" and catastrophic non-reality of the months and years that followed in the political realm, from the pursuit of regime change to the hunt for imaginary weapons of mass destruction, was not mirrored in the everyday lives of people touched by the attack on the World Trade Centers. Against the background of 9/11, stripped of both time and context, the themes that structure the understanding of that time for ordinary and extraordinary New Yorkers may be surprising. But re-woven into the fabric of everyday life they should not be. There is of course the trauma of experiencing loss of life: of friends, family, coworkers, acquaintances, and strangers. There is also displacement—from neighborhood, workplace, and self, and from the strong immediate emotions of sadness, anger, and fear. But understanding has also meant reconfiguring the communities of identity one belongs to, building new ties and forms of social engagement, and new hopes and aspirations for the future. Perhaps most of all, it has meant learning to tell a new story: the story of how 9/11 did or did not shape what was to follow in real life. This book tells this story and, by doing so, attempts to capture the fabric of the real life of the city during these months and years, filling in both the sense of time and context that has been erased in the national narrative of "America at War."

Of the millions of people in New York on 9/11—students in their first week of classes, workers returning from their last vacation of the summer, tourists enjoying the cloudless morning, ordinary New Yorkers going about their morning routines—we have talked to just over six hundred. Some were in the World Trade Center towers when they were hit; others were just poking their heads out of the PATH station on their way into work from the suburbs; still others were the first responders whose ambulances and fire trucks raced downtown. Some were heading to work after dropping their children off at school. Some were in distant boroughs of the city, 9/11 brought to them only later in the day or throughout the first week, and into the months that followed. While not statistically representative of New Yorkers, they were substantively representative—hundreds of different eyes looking out from different standpoints, all on different trajectories.

We talked to them a lot and quickly. While others in the city were mobilizing food drives and pet rescues, in the first days following the attack we secured National Science Foundation, Rockefeller Foundation, and Columbia University funding to undertake a rapid field operation to collect, through oral history techniques, the early interpretations and experiences of those closest to the attack. As New Yorkers posted signs of missing persons in Union Square and shuttled food and emergency supplies to the makeshift stations set up for response and recovery on the Hudson waterfront, our project made its way across the city. Throughout, we were guided by the idea central to oral history: that everywhere people organize meaning through constructing and telling stories. One kind of story in particular, the life history, is particularly fecund with respect to its capacity to identify the meaning of events and memories of the past. These were the stories we focused on. Through building an archive of these stories, we believed we could help provide a basis for understanding the society in which people live—in this case, the nation's largest city, in the aftermath of the largest terrorist attacks ever launched on American soil.

For those who told us their stories—of being in the towers when the planes first hit, waking up in beds with views of the towers just blocks away, setting up their wares for sale in the shadow of the towers or in some distant borough of the city—the events of 9/11 were far too overwhelming to allow us or our respondents to pretend that an "ordinary" life history was possible to collect. This recognition came quickly: by the first few interviews we knew, and all of our interviewers felt intuitively, that an approach that focused first on 9/11 and then on the immediate aftermath was what everyone needed, interviewer and storyteller together. It was clear that documenting the meanings of events while the aftermath of the events was still unfolding, and while our own understanding of the complexity of the catastrophe and the suffering it caused was deepening, posed special challenges. The normal practices of oral history, from writing letters of invitation to those we planned to interview to having the luxury of time to do research, had no relevance to the situation we found ourselves in. Those normal practices serve as scaffolds for situating events and experiences in historical and cultural context. In their absence, the scaffold that was developed in this project was the life story as it unfolded in an extraordinary moment.

Stories have beginnings and middles and ends. The life story is told from an end that is both a moment in time and a standpoint. Looking back over the infinite number of prior events, experiences, thoughts, and emotions, the teller of the history selects just those events that can be arranged into a narrative, to get them from the *then* of some beginning to the *now* of telling. Seen this way, it becomes obvious that the life story changes over time, as the standpoints from which stories are told change. With this in mind, our initial idea was to collect life histories at multiple points in time—immediately after 9/11, and then a year or so later. We wondered whether we could observe how the impact of 9/11 led people to think of different events in the past as crucial to where they were now. And we wondered whether 9/11 would mark a turning point, a fork in the story, a new beginning of sorts. These were good analytical ideas, but they were impractical for the reasons already alluded to: the shock of 9/11 made it impossible to collect life histories in their pure form.

Yet there were advantages to the approach we developed. By embedding 9/11 into the context of people's life stories, it became clear that the opportunity we gave people to narrate their lives and their experiences of

September 11 simultaneously allowed them to construct a narrative that did not remove them from the time but instead allowed them to reenter it, and then reconceive it. In the midst of a sequence of events too difficult to grasp in their entirety, many of the descriptions that appear in this book are focused on a single element, a small fraction of the whole that in its precise description conveys both the beauty and horror simultaneously: the man in a blue suit falling with arms and legs crossed; an outstretched hand; curtains blowing in the wind where the planes first struck (later to be revealed as sheets, or cloth waved by people seeking help); Xerox paper raining down like confetti; furtive glances; quick words of comfort or caution. Only later does one realize that the enigmatic comment "it's not safe to go home alone," made to Debbie Almontaser, was the prescient understanding that sporadic harassment of those of Muslim faith would flare quickly on the streets. Amid the chaos of fleeing bodies and the blindness induced by the cloud of dust and debris that roared over those escaping the falling towers comes deep insight. In contrast to the official framing, the stories collected in this volume suggest a clarity of vision and understanding that is enhanced by multiple standpoints and views.

Against this background we quickly realized that we were not "interviewing" in the classic sense. We were acting as witnesses to those who were performing acts of witness about their own experiences and, equally importantly, about the experiences of strangers and friends they were connected to in the time of the catastrophe. In this time, the language that emerges after the silence of the catastrophe is the most important language for defining collective meaning and public memory. Experiencing the velocity and the richness of the river of words that flowed through the narratives we collected, one may be reminded of Foucault's statement that "language gives the perpetual disruption of time the continuity of space, and it is to this degree that it analyzes, articulates, and patterns representation such that it has the power to link the knowledge of all things across the dimension of time."[*] This changing of the catastrophe into words,

---

[*] Michel Foucault, *The Order of Things: An Archeology of the Human Sciences.*

into narrative structures and back into living time, is a central purpose of the archive.

CONSTRUCTING THE ARCHIVE

In the weeks after 9/11 in which we first created the September 11, 2001, Oral History Narrative and Memory Project, we planned to interview three hundred people representing very different communities of origin and proximities to the event, including those who we suspected would be most effected in the aftermath. We interviewed a wide variety of people: direct witnesses to the events—rescuers, educators, and workers—who were close to the site; those who were affected by the aftermath economically, politically, and culturally, including communities of Muslims, Sikhs, and immigrants from various parts of the Middle East; as well as professionals who responded to the multiple urban crises that emerged from the events over time. The idea was to interview people close in time to the event, in 2001 and early 2002, and to return to them a year or more later so that we could mark the ways in which their interpretations of their experiences evolved and developed over time.

We were aware that we had a unique opportunity to allow those we interviewed to define the meaning of the events and aftermath in their own terms. As oral historians, we were fascinated by the opportunity to construct an archive that might contribute to the public formulation of the meaning of the catastrophe's aftermath—one that was based on the individual life stories of real witnesses, who could testify to the shifting meanings of the experience of suffering. What was the meaning of this historical reversal, for those who were born here and had lived here for generations, versus what it meant for those who had recently come here? How did the meaning and definition of the 9/11 trauma differ for those who had experienced historical violence, and understood the meaning of being targeted prior to their arrival? What did it mean to the many Afghans, Pakistanis, Egyptians, and others who were targeted again? What did 9/11 mean to those who were stateless? How did these meanings differ across generations, ethnicities, nationalities? In short, what would the events of 9/11 come to mean, at different moments in time, for different persons in different places?

In oral history archives, narratives are formulated through the performance of the life story as part of a larger cultural and historical story, weaving back and forth from the narrative of the individual to the historical and social. Fortuitously, we insisted that our interviewers begin by collecting the life stories of those we interviewed, giving them equal valence to the descriptions of the events and aftermath of 9/11. We deliberately named the project "The September 11, 2001, Oral History Narrative and Memory Project," to let those we interviewed know that they had a role in constructing the memory of September 11 through constructing the archive, as well as to let those we interviewed know that their stories would form the bases for historical interpretations. Our thirty interviewers often began their interviews by saying to their narrators: "As you tell us your stories, imagine that they will form the basis for how people understand this time fifty or sixty years from now." This had the double effect of reminding people of the permanence of the archive at a time during which it seemed that everything was fragile and ephemeral, and of their ability to shape the long-term memory of the event. While it was difficult for many we interviewed in September and October 2001 to do more than to try to reformulate their sense of what actually happened on the day of 9/11 itself, by November and December, people were using the interviews to retell their life stories and begin to integrate the effects of the event within the narratives of their lives and the lives of those they witnessed. As time passed, the nature of the interviews also changed.

As we began to complete interviews within the communities of those who were targeted in the aftermath, and experienced tremendous cultural alienation out of their anxieties as recent immigrants or refugees, we saw how interlaced the trauma of the event was with the trauma of the aftermath. In the case of Pakistani father and son Zaheer and Salmaan Jaffrey, the mourning was divided. The son, who believed his disabled father must be dead (since he hadn't heard from him for ten hours and the father's walk down from the seventieth floor would have been so difficult), later described his terror over the political aftermath of 9/11 in immigrant and Muslim communities as greater than his terror that his beloved father was dead. The father matter-of-factly described his descent from the seventieth floor as uneventful (he had suffered worse and longer in war) but told of an unabated sorrow over his son's fear about leaving his neighborhood for months following the event.

Memory for others was polluted by irrational guilt. One of our most brilliant narrators and, later, interviewers—an Afghan American poet and candidate for a degree in comparative literature—described the paralysis she felt upon immediately hearing about the event as a "guilt that she couldn't locate" and that prevented her from writing poetry for at least two years after the event. She did a series of interviews with Afghan American women of her generation describing the ways in which they were reconstructing their own cultural narratives, using for the first time the link between "Afghan" and "American" to signify the duality in identity they now felt.

For those trapped in the area of the site of the destruction, the acts of survival and rescue were complicated by the narratives of patriotism and heroism that were superimposed by the theme of nationalism and sacrifice. Those who died were at the top of the hierarchy, endowing the families of Americans who died and suffered and those who supported them with the largest role in defining the public task of constructing appropriate museums and memorials at the site, which would exclude the stateless workers who had also died because their families couldn't risk exposure. The heroes who survived were also placed in a hierarchy that began with the firefighters and worked down toward the paramedics, and then the ironworkers and engineers who had to dismantle the wreckage. Many of those we talked to at times resented this hierarchy of suffering; but, more important, they described the acts of survival and rescue as complicated by their reality of needing to abandon someone in order to survive as the towers began to collapse. These were the stories that the unreal histories of heroism performed in the media excised.

The haunting stories we collected began to coalesce around certain themes that were not being covered in the media. One was that the reality of exposure to the catastrophe was far greater than was being reported. These reflections on the event and the course of events flowing from it—seemingly inexorably—gave rise to reflections largely ignored in the public discourse increasingly dominated by the imaginary; reflections about what it meant to be a member of a community, to be a New Yorker, a Muslim in New York, or a Dominican in New York after 9/11. To what communities and in what networks did one belong? What was different and what remained the same? What did it mean to reenter the everyday routines? It was the desire to capture these reflections and thoughts that motivated the creation of this archive.

Many of our first respondents were eager to participate in multiple rounds of storytelling one or more years later. How had the time gone? What effect did 9/11 have on them, on their sense of identity—on who they were and what they stood for? Close to one decade later, as the macro-cultural discourse changed in unexpected ways after 9/11, so things changed for those living in the city. In the stories collected here we see some of these changes—but of course, not all.

June 2011

1.

James E. Dobson

Paramedic

Interviewed by Ed Thompson (11/1/01) and Gerry Albarelli (3/6/03)

James Dobson was born in 1952 and grew up in Astoria, Queens, New York. His father was a chef, and his mother and sister worked at St. John's Hospital Center in Queens. Dobson has worked as an ambulance paramedic since he was nineteen years old. He is married with two grown children. On September 11, 2001, Dobson and his partner, Marvin Bethea, began their day at 7:00 A.M. by responding to a medical emergency. After delivering a patient to Mt. Sinai Hospital in Astoria they received a radio call that a plane had hit the World Trade Center. They were told to drive to the Fifty-ninth Street Bridge, which leads into Manhattan, and wait for instructions. They met up there with a lieutenant from the Emergency Medical Services and soon headed over the bridge.

NOVEMBER 1, 2001

So as we're on the bridge going over to Manhattan, I'm in the tech seat and my partner Marvin Bethea is in the front seat. We had a student in the back who is in the paramedic class. As we're just about coming into Manhattan we find out that another plane hit the other tower. So the student says to me, "Oh my God. Terrorists."

Marvin says, "Yes, it's terrorists." He was on the phone trying to talk to his girlfriend, and she was watching TV.

Then the student says to me, "Anthrax." I look at him, and he's a young man who has two children.

I turn to him and I say, "Well, it's too late now. We're on our way in."

We hit Broadway, and we're looking up like everybody else, and the problem was that no one was moving. You had people going into stores buying cameras to take pictures of the fire. No one realizes that because the fire is half a mile up in the air that they are in danger. It seems so far away. It's just like a stampede of people coming through. Everything is so tight and narrow [in that part of town] and they're trying to keep people away. But the most they can keep people away is a block, and that's on Broadway.

So we're down there about five minutes and we're looking around. And they've got us on a side street and we see shoes all over the place. And I looked down and there is someone's telephone. And I said, "Oh my God. What's going on here?" Even though we knew what was going on, it just seemed, like, odd.

So then the lieutenant says, "Okay. We're going to go, and they are going to do on-the-scene triage, right on the site." They're setting up a triage area on Fulton and Church streets, which is the east side of the towers. I get out right away, and I go down to the corner of Fulton and Church, and there it is all patients. They have all these people sitting along Church Street in chairs. And there are all vehicles, and it has got to be a hundred, maybe two hundred people, just like milling around.

So I try to take charge because that's what I am supposed to do. I start treating people. I start telling the EMTs, "Get me this. Get me that." And we're tagging people, and when you tag people you tear off how critical they are, and if you leave the tag on and it's black, that means you're not going to take care of them. They're dead. But we're taking care of all the people that's coming out.

Six firemen are carrying a lady out on a door, and they said, "She just fell down an elevator shaft." It was a young lady, probably about twenty-five to thirty. She is laying on the board, she is alive, she's all bruised up and everything, and she's moaning and groaning. So a doctor came over. I don't know where he came from, but he was just a regular doctor in plain clothes. He says, "I'm a doctor. Let me look at her." So as he's looking at her he says, "She's all right. Just put her on a stretcher and take her."

I said, "No. No. Doctor, don't worry about it, I've got it." So I took out, like, all precautions for spinal injury, and I put her on a backboard and cervical collar and stuff like that, and I put her in the ambulance. I told the firemen [who] brought the lady out, "Okay. I've got this. I can handle this." I said, "You just go back in and get more people." And these are the kinds of things that bother you, what you said to people, because I'm sending them back in to their deaths. I didn't know that at the time. And they would have went back in anyway. But after it's all over it just plays on your mind.

So then all [of a] sudden they bring me out another unconscious person, and this is a man about [in his] forties to fifties. They say, "He's been unconscious for, like, thirty minutes." I'm down on one knee and I'm taking his blood pressure. And then all of a sudden I hear the noise, and it sounds like an avalanche. So I look over my right shoulder and I see it coming down. So, you know, I had to run. I started running and I'm saying, "I can't outrun this. I know I can't outrun it. This is like a mile-high building. Where am I running to?"

So what we do is, on our ambulances, when you go to any kind of disaster you leave the windows open. So the windows were open in the ambulance, the lights were on, the engine's running, because you want to hear other sirens that are coming so you don't have a collision. So I get in the back of the ambulance, and as I'm going by, there's an EMT from the city there. Big, tall, blond-headed guy. I don't know his name. And I say, "We've got to get in the ambulance."

Now, his ambulances are locked. So he goes, "Okay. Okay." He jumps in the back with me. And we have a cubbyhole that goes from the back to the front, but because of my size I don't fit through that too well. And I know the windows are open. I weigh three hundred pounds, and I'm six foot three. I don't fit through that little hole.

Okay. So now I'm in the back, he's in the back, and we're just grabbing people and pulling them into the back of the ambulance, screaming and yelling and everything. And you hear this terrible roaring sound that's coming down. So now I go through the cubbyhole and I'm trying to close the windows because there is smoke coming in. It was really ground-up cement and it's just coming in. I scream to him, "Close the back door!"

So the ambulance is swaying and everything. Everything starts getting black. It goes pitch, pitch black. And I say, "Oh, Jimmy. This is not good. This is not good. I'm going to get buried alive here." I'm talking to myself in my mind, and I said, "This is a bad way to end a career." So I hit the switch for the lights in the back, and the air conditioner, because right now we already have like an inch of silt all over everything inside. So all you hear is all these explosions, and everything got black. And then all of a sudden you see the orange ball of fire go by. Now, the orange ball of fire, I don't know if it was from the building or from a vehicle that blew up.

Now, we have me in the back, we have four ladies and a gentleman and the EMT. There are seven of us in the back of the ambulance. So I tell them, "Okay. Everybody calm down now. We are going to have to work together." I turned the main tank of oxygen on and I hooked them up with oxygen masks, and I said, "We're going to do like skin divers do. We're going to buddy-breathe. You breathe a little bit and pass it on to the next person to breathe a little bit."

So I'm looking out the front windshield in the dark. It was black for so long, and then all of a sudden I saw it got a little lighter, a little lighter. So I open the side door, and when I came outside the ambulance there must have been like a foot of paper, debris. Everything to the left of us was all destroyed. And all the people I took care of were all swept away. They were all gone. So now I take the people that could get out of the ambulance and I am heading up the block with the EMT. I turned around, and for some reason I went back to the ambulance because it was still running. Everything is destroyed but this ambulance. I mean every vehicle is destroyed. For some reason it wasn't.

So, I said, "Okay. Let me see if I can move this thing." So I started driving the ambulance and it is moving. I said, "Oh man. Bonus." So as I go up the block they are banging on the side of the doors. People are starting to come out of the buildings where they sought refuge and they're opening the side doors. Five or six people jump right in. The back door's open, the side door's open, I'm behind the steering wheel. I've got no partner because at the time Marvin was working up the block, so I didn't know if he was dead or alive. The student was gone. So I'm by myself. I go up over Broadway and there is a lieutenant from the city there, and I say, "I've got six patients in the back. I'm going to go to Bellevue hospital."

So I start driving. I'm looking at the East River and you can see the clear blue sky. So I'm driving toward the clear blue sky, and I go down about three or four blocks, I don't know how many, and I make a left-hand turn and all of a sudden when I go up about a block all of these people are in medical outfits and there are stretchers on the outside. I pull over. I said, "It's better than no place. It's like an oasis." I open the back door, and all of these people are taken out on stretchers into [New York University Downtown Hospital].

So I bring the people in there and you see all the burned people, all the people that came to that hospital first. The staff was getting overwhelmed. They don't have stretchers. So I turn around, and they ask me, "What's going on out there?"

So I say, "It looks like the tower, one of the buildings came down."

They are saying, "Are you sure you're all right?"

And I say "Yes. I'm okay." So I'm there, and I have to admit I said to myself, "I'm safe now. I'm safe now." And I said, "No, but I've got to go back. I've got to go back." So I take the ambulance and I go back. The only place I know to go is back to where I started. So I go down Fulton and I go all the way down to the end. I thought maybe my partner Marvin's there. So I go back down there and I see there's a young doctor there. This is the part that was really upsetting. He was a young doctor, good-looking kid, about twenty-five, and there's a black man laying there, and he's bleeding from his mouth, his nose, he's having a hard time. He's breathing still, and he's moving the right hand. And there's another gentleman with him.

So I get the stretcher and the backboard. In the meanwhile there is a man, who looked like a Spanish man, but they had, like, chalk all over them; everything is kind of odd because everything is in black and white. Nothing has color anymore. So when we looked at the guy bleeding, it made it more vivid because you could see the red. So I get the backboard to the doctor and this other gentleman. There is steel on this man's lower legs and the other man wasn't moving; he was unconscious. First I grab the steel, I go to yank it, and it was twice as heavy as I thought. It was bent like a pretzel. So I try with all my might and I'm just teetering, and it slides off his legs. So we get him up and we put him on the stretcher, just laying flat on the stretcher because I have no more backboards. We put the other man on the seat and all of a sudden this lady comes out of nowhere who has—she's a black lady and she's completely gray—but she's not talking. She's just walking like she's a zombie. So I put her in the side of the ambulance door. One man who is dressed in a suit helping the doctor had a policeman's badge, a detective's badge, hanging out of his pocket. So he jumps into the ambulance past the lady and sits on the jump seat. So I just took the same mask that we were buddy-breathing and I put him on the oxygen. So I have the oxygen on both of them and I say to the doctor, "Come with me to the hospital, Doc."

He says, "You really need me?"

I said, "I've got no one back here. These two people are critical. They're dying."

He says to me, "Okay."

And then the police officer speaks up and he says, "Don't let this fool you." He shows me the badge. He says, "I'm a PA."

I said, "PA? Port Authority?"

He goes, "No. No. A physician's assistant for five years." He says, "I've got your back."

So the doctor says, "He's got your back. I'm going to find more people." So he goes around the corner and he's gone. I get in the ambulance and I drive. I don't go more than five or ten feet and the PA tells me, "I have no oxygen back here." He says to me, "I can't breathe." So I stop the ambulance and I look inside and [the oxygen tank] says two thousand, that's the normal pressure. Now I'm getting a little worried because these people are dying back here. He's pulled the hose off the patient's mask, and it's all bloody, and he's got the hose in his mouth and he's telling me he can't take the pain in his chest. He's having a heart attack on me. So the guy I'm going to rely on, he's critical. He's lying all over everything and he's like, "I can't breathe. I can't take the pain."

I just look over my shoulder, and I'm ready to call for the doctor, and the second building right in front of me starts coming down. So now I run around and we're going to leave that doctor, and I know he had to die. He didn't make it because he went around that corner, over the metal, everything else, and there's no way of running. He can't even run. So it's like I have to leave him too.

So I start riding the ambulance up Fulton back to where I started. I'm just hoping that it doesn't stall. I'm trying to outrun [the collapse]. I'm jumping over the curbs because there's police cars just abandoned, and vans abandoned, impeding me getting to safety. So I'm jumping over the sidewalks and you see people just holding against buildings and laying on the floor. And the second building comes down. It's nothing but black smoke. Just black, black, black smoke. So now I get on the side of the Brooklyn Bridge and now I'm going down back to the hospital. They ask me, "What have you got?"

I say, "I've got two crushed people from the first tower coming down, and I got this lady, and I've got this police officer who looks like he's having a heart attack."

[*Dobson delivers his patients and, fighting back fear, turns his ambulance back toward Ground Zero.*]

I'm getting just two blocks in, three blocks in, and people were just—I had policewomen running down the block screaming, "I'm going to die! I'm going to die!" People who were probably seasoned firemen and policemen, they all thought they were dying. They thought this was the end of the world. I was putting them in the back of the ambulance and now I'm like a shuttle bus. I'm just going up, grabbing like four people, back to the hospital. I kind of looked funny in my mind because I'm the only one going back and forth with this little shuttle thing, but I'm the only one who got out of that whole triage area.

I think it's the fourth or fifth time that I take a different route, and now I go up a different block, and I'm saying, "Well, maybe I can get closer to where the people are trapped." It's now like an hour and a half. I'm missing Marvin, I'm missing the student, and I go up and I get almost to Broadway. There are these firemen and policemen and they're in the street. And then there is no one around. It is so quiet. And if you look[ed] down the street all you saw was the black smoke and a fire. It looked like hell in front of you.

A police officer says, "Don't go no further because if you go further up, the street's starting to get mushy from the intense heat, the subway's there, and you may wind up in the subway."

So I say, "I've got to go up one more block. I've just got to go up one more block to check it." And I go up one more block and there's Marvin in the smoke looking up at this black wall of smoke and fire and flame with a cell phone to his ear. I don't even think the cell phones worked that day but he had it to his ear, looking, and he was just mesmerized. He sees me and I see him. So I get out, and he runs to me and I run to him and we hug each other. I say, "We made it. We made it, Marvin." So he gets in the ambulance. I make a U-turn and I say, "Marvin, where's the student?"

He said, "I don't know."

I say, "Oh no, we lost the student. Well, at least you're alive."

So now I've got to go up to the towers. I don't think I can just make a U-turn, and now I've got to go right where they are squirting the water. So now I'm driving off, and you're driving over things, but, you know, you're seeing body parts, and you're seeing stuff like that, and you feel that you are running over stuff, but you're not paying attention to what you are running over. You don't want to pay attention to what you're running over.

[Dobson and his partner start heading down to a rescue staging area by the Staten Island Ferry.]

So now the firemen come down the block and one guy tells Marvin, "I can't see. I can't see." So we put him in the back and Marvin starts flushing his eyes out. Marvin flushes out the fireman's eyes and we were telling him, "Stay with us. Your eyes—maybe you can't [see]."

The fireman says, "No. No. I'll be all right. I've got to turn around. I've got to go back." And he gets out of the ambulance and he walks back. He's going to fight the fire again. Oh man, some people are so brave.

So now we're going back toward the Staten Island Ferry and there is a young black man, an EMT from the city, and he's standing on the corner. He's looking up and he just has this weird look on his face. So I stop. I say, "Hey, you. What are you doing?"

He says, "I'm guarding the body parts."

I said, "Guarding? Guarding the what?"

He says, "I'm guarding the body parts." He has a red bag at his feet that we use for contaminated things. He must have put body parts in there.

So I said, "Oh no. No. You don't have to do that today. You don't have to do that now." I said, "Come with me." And as I get out of the ambulance to get him he runs down the block, just runs. You know, [I think] his mind snapped. He just ran. So I said, "Okay. This is not a day to chase people. Let's go back to the ferry."

[At about 3:00 P.M. Dobson and his partner are released for the day. They head back to their base in Queens.]

I went up the FDR Drive and it was such a nice day, I didn't drive fast. I went all the way up to the Triborough [Robert F. Kennedy] Bridge. As I'm coming over the bridge a truck driver looks at us, he beeps the horn, and he hands us a container of soda. It was a full container of soda, and I'm like, "Oh, thanks," and I take a big, big drink. I give the drink to Marvin. And it was like the greatest soda. I was like a little kid. It was such a treat. It was so good.

We finally got back to Saint John's. It was about four fifteen. All the people were on the ramp. I got out of the ambulance and they looked, and they were like, "Oh my God! Oh my God!"

And I said, "Oh, this piece of junk." [Laughter] This piece of junk cab got me through this, and I gave it a big kiss. I gave it a big kiss. [Laughter] Then they made us shower outside and then I just went home.

[Later I told Marvin] it's kind of strange. We both survived and we know people that passed away there. But not the student who was with us that day. I wondered the next couple of days, "Why did I survive? If I ran the opposite direction, to my right, I would have died with everybody else." And you can't figure it out. Then you talk to people, and people said, "It wasn't your time. It wasn't your time."

Are you the same, Mr. Dobson, since September 11, or has your life changed in any way?

Yes, it's changed. It's changed. The one thing that's changed the most is, like, what's going on now in Afghanistan. Even after this happened and they started talking about retaliation, I'm more of a pacifist than ever. I'm a Republican—but what I saw that day, the devastation, I could not see us doing to other people. Life is too cheap then; it doesn't mean anything and there's no reason for it. Their people did not attack me, Jimmy Dobson, or the American people per se. They attacked the corporate world. They killed people, yes, but they want to show that the United States can't fight against their religion and all that stuff.

MARCH 6, 2003

[*In New York City, some ambulance crews are part of the Fire Department of New York. Other crews are associated with hospitals, private ambulance companies, and volunteer ambulance corps.*]

After September 11 I went right back to work. Marvin did the same thing. I was like, "Oh, I can handle this. I can get through this." It's like getting on a horse and riding again. I think it was the wrong thing now. It's been very hard since then to go to work. It's because every day we get hit with a different paper saying how to treat biological warfare, chemical warfare. Now they're issuing gas masks to all the ambulance drivers. Like the other day they closed down the Whitestone Bridge when I'm working, and it had something to do with terrorism. They put us all on alert.

I get mad. I talked to one captain from EMS, the fire department sector. He said, "Oh, we lost two [people]." We didn't lose two. We lost eight people. We lost two that were involved with the fire department. But the other six people were on the ambulance that died too. It's just that it's kind of a thankless job that you do.

No one really cared about us. I mean, me and Marvin, we weren't invited to anything. They had concerts in the city and all the firemen, policemen went. They had concerts and they went all over the country. They even went to Hawaii. They went to Florida. And we weren't invited to anything. We were unknown.

Now, they know we were down there. They sent us. They knew the names of who were down there. And I try to tell people, "You had policemen working that day at Ninety-sixth Street and First Avenue, who are considered heroes. Okay? You have people [like me] at Ground Zero when the buildings come down, and people don't even know them from Adam."

It's very hard to live your life that way and then be kind to other people, on top of it. People don't realize—every day, ambulance drivers save people's lives. Policeman doesn't save a person's life every day. A fireman doesn't save a person's life every day. Ambulance people save people's lives every day. Yesterday I had a call, baby dying. I saved that baby's life. If I was a fireman, I'd be on the front page news. If I was a policeman, I'd be on front page news. When they hear ambulance people do it, "Oh, that's their job."

So when you don't get any recognition, and then with the dual [ambulance] system, if you do not belong directly to the fire department you're completely disinvolved from anything. They had one day where they had the [search] dogs come [to the U.S. Open] and they honored the dogs, but they didn't honor the EMS people.

We had one nice thing that happened to us. Fort Scott, Kansas, on the anniversary, on the day of 9/11, sent us a package and it had letters from kids and all that. They sent this package and there was a brochure in there and it was their Octoberfest. So we're sitting in the office and we said, "You know, this was so nice. We should fly there and tell them in person how nice it is." So for our own sake, we went. We bought tickets. We called them up and said we were going to come out there and visit the school and all that stuff, to thank the kids for the letters and the people there being so nice. So we went out there and they did a ceremony for us, and gave us a certificate from Fort Scott and they took us around the town. But it was our idea. They didn't say, "Come on down."

I don't think I could really say I'd get through a lot of this without the help of my wife, Linda. She's been wonderful. Linda—I mean, she's my true love and she's been so good to me over the years. When this all happened, I would have mood swings. I would get very angry. I would get depressed and cry. She put up with a lot of this stuff and then she decided, "You need help. You can't do this on your own. It's too long now." And she really did talk me into going to a psychiatrist and I've been doing a lot better. So after talking to the doctor and all, he told me I had post-traumatic stress [disorder] and depression from it. So I've been going to him about four months and it's been much better.

Take me through those months leading up to three or four months ago. You said you were angry.

Well, you get angry. Just simple things like driving a car. I went to get a bag down near Queens Boulevard where I work. I'm with Linda. I'm with my daughter and I'm in the car. There's a lot of traffic, so everybody's edging, pushing their way in. A young guy pulls out with a Honda. I'm letting him go but I'm close to him. So his window's open. He says, "Hey! You!"

So I said, "Hey, you."

He says, "You nearly hit my car!" He didn't curse. He didn't say nothing else.

So what I yelled back to him is, "I'll hit your car if I want to hit your car." Now right away it's confrontational.

My wife's saying, "Jimmy, calm down, calm down."

"No. This is not right." So now I maneuver away and I just pull the car near a fire hydrant. And I get out. He can't go nowhere, this guy, and I walk up to him. Now, I'm pretty big. I'm three hundred pounds and I'm six foot four, six foot three. I go up to the side of the car, and he's looking at me. I say to him, "Now what are you going to do?" And I spit on him. I spit right on him, to provoke him, trying to get him to get out of the car. My daughter's like, "What are you doing?" And then I went in, I got the bag. I come back out and I spit on him again. Then I get in my car and drive away like nothing's happening. Now, that's abnormal. So that's like an altercation, where it's not me.

And then I was having nightmares and she would wake me up at night, my Linda, and she'd say, "Jimmy, Jimmy." Then she would hold me. She would hold me like I was an infant. She'd hold me at night and [say], "You're going to be all right," and she'd stroke my hair or something. I remember having nightmares where buildings are collapsing, falling, people screaming. I had dreams of mass destruction and the strange thing I found was I was having dreams of giving up. I remember one dream where everything was going bad. And then all of a sudden you felt the heat. It was like a nuclear bomb went off. Like I was dying in my dream but it was okay and I didn't have to wake up. I wasn't frightened. And that's strange because it's a nightmare. It's part of the post-traumatic stress; that's what the doctor said to me.

You think about death a lot. You think about what happens after death, where you go. Why did I live after September 11? Why did other people die? The way I look at death, I tell my daughters, if no one died there'd be no room for new people. It's part of life. And I've been around death since I'm twenty, so that's like thirty-one years now I've been around people dying. It's still like the unknown. I don't want to die. And I hear it all the time from old people, "Oh, don't get old." And I usually say back to them, "Well, there's only one alternative to not getting old and I don't want to do that."

So I think about it. Does it scare me? No, not really. Do I want to die? No. But I do think about it.

2.

Mary Lee Hannell

Director, Human Resources,
Port Authority of New York and New Jersey

Interviewed by Myron Farber (12/4/01 and 3/4/03)
and Mary Marshall Clark (6/22/05)

*Mary Lee Hannell was born in 1960 and grew up in Latham, a small town
in upstate New York. Her father was a florist—the fourth generation in his
family to sell flowers for a living. After college, Hannell went to work for the
Port Authority of New York and New Jersey. She got her start in the Human
Resources department and quickly made her way up through management.
The Port Authority, which owned the World Trade Center, was headquartered
in the North Tower of the World Trade Center. In 1993, Hannell had just
stepped out of the building for lunch when a terrorist bomb exploded in the
World Trade Center's parking lot.*

*In 2001, Hannell was the executive adviser to the chief administrative
officer of the Port Authority. She worked on the sixty-seventh floor. Hannell is
now director of Human Resources for the Port Authority.*

DECEMBER 4, 2001

It was a fairly ordinary day for me, which means that before I even get to the office, I've put in a whole day's worth of work with three small children. It's getting them ready and getting them prepared for school and getting them off to school. I remember it being a beautiful, crisp day. I got to work early and I had just gotten off the elevator and walked into my office. I heard a gigantic boom, one which moved the building significantly. I was thrown to one side. I remember hearing the building kind of creaking. So I came out of my office and asked if anyone had any idea what that was. There was a woman who was around the corner from me who started screaming, because she was on the side of the building where she actually saw the plane hit the building. She was very worked up and started running around, screaming, "A plane has hit the building!" So I gathered some people. I walked to my boss's office and when I got there I picked up the phone and dialed my husband's number. I said, "A plane has hit the building."

He said, "How do you know?"

I said, "One of the women here saw it. A plane's hit the building."

He said, "Just go down the stairs. Don't wait. Just go down the stairs. We'll meet outside."

Then I said to my boss, "There's smoke in the corridor. I think we need to go now."

He said, "Yes, let's just go." We tried to calm this one woman down because she was really hysterical. But we very clearly made a decision: we need to leave now. There was another gentleman on the floor who was a retired policeman and he said, "Let's take a quick look to make sure everyone's out of their offices." So we did that and got everybody together. Went out into the corridor and opened the door and held it open and made sure that everybody moved through. We waited for two women who went back to get their handbags—and if I've learned anything, it's never go back to get anything because you never know how much time you have—and started downstairs. There were no public address announcements. There was nothing to say, "Go." There was nothing to say, "Stay." There were no fire alarms going off.

Got on the stairs. No smoke. But a very chemical smell, a very, very intense smell that caught you in your throat. I stayed with this policeman and with one of the staff people that works for me. People were very orderly walking down the stairs but there were people who were afraid. Some had walked down the stairs in the 1993 bombing. Some were just afraid. So what we were doing is keeping up a dialogue, joking around, laughing, reassuring people. There was a woman with us who had asthma. The more upset she got the harder it got for her to breathe. Then there was this gentleman who had been burned. So a couple of us kept up a running dialogue with people to try and keep people calm. We kept saying, "Look. We're on the forty-fifth floor. We're making great progress." Whatever it took to make people keep moving. We'd also say, "Don't worry. We have a lot of time. We have as much time as it takes, because if it takes eight hours to get out of the building, it takes us eight hours to get out of the building." There was never, ever, for one moment, a thought that the building was going to collapse, ever.

The stairway was actually very crowded but we were moving. I can't believe it would have been as orderly or as calm had people really thought that there was a problem. We didn't know, while we were in the building, that the second tower had been hit because you couldn't feel it or hear it in the stairwells. My husband knew because he looked at his pager as he was going down the stairs, and he has something from one of the news services that feeds in headlines. Then he knew it was a terrorist attack as he was going down the stairs. But I did not. Oddly enough—and what he yells at me all the time about—is that he ended up getting out of the building ahead of me, even though he was above me, because I waited for a couple of people to go back and get some things. So we were continuing down, having these conversations. Everything is going fairly smoothly until we hit about the thirties. There was a very elderly woman who works for the Port Authority in our records area. She has a tremendous amount of difficulty walking and she takes one stair at a time. So everything started to back up. About the thirtieth floor we start to encounter smoke. So it's a little harder to breathe. People who are already very tentative are even more tentative now. Some people started to cry. Some people start to worry. We're still doing, "The lights are on. It's fine. Don't worry. We're already on thirty. We're more than halfway down. We're going to be fine."

People are taking handkerchiefs out, taking off jackets, and giving them to other people so you could put something in front of your mouth. One of the jokes we had, a funny joke, was one of the women had her gym bag with her. She had not yet gone to the gym. So she had a pair of shorts. She had a tee shirt. She had socks. She had a sports bra. She handed all of her clothing to people, including the sports bra, which was clean, she assured us, to people to put them over their mouth so that you had something over your mouth, so you could breathe. The woman who was asthmatic started to panic and started to breathe even more heavily. So as we were going down the stairs, as we would pass a door, we would open it where we could. If there was fresh air we'd say to her, "Come over and breathe. Just breathe the air. Close your eyes. Breathe. Don't look." Because some of the floors had fire alarms going off. Some had some kind of liquid. I don't know if it was jet fuel or [if] it was elevator hydraulic liquid. But, "Breathe, and you're going to be fine."

At floor twenty-seven we passed a man who was in a wheelchair, a very heavy wheelchair. He has at least one person with him and he's just sitting there. He's not moving. He was one of the people we passed that did not make it out of the building because he wouldn't let people carry him down. He wanted to take his chair with him. He had some other medical issues that the chair helped him with and he was worried. So his friend stayed with him and neither of them made it out of the building.

Did it bother you that you were going past this man?

Yes, it did. But there didn't seem to be anything I could do. There wasn't anything I could reasonably do.

So are you with anyone you know at that point?

I'm with a woman named Eileen Dalton, who works for me, and I'm with a couple of other Port Authority people that I know.

Was it crowded in these stairways?

Yes, once you got to twenty-seven it was crowded enough that there were periods of time when you were no longer moving. So you were just waiting. You were stopped, and you were just waiting. Then, as you start to hit these areas where you're waiting, people start to get a little antsy. There starts to be some yelling. "We've got to move. You've got to move. We've got to get out of here," from above us. People starting to say, "Just keep moving. Just keep moving. Don't stop. Don't stop."

So I started to yell up the stairs, "We've got to wait. Don't keep coming. Just stop where you are. There are people ahead of us but we're moving. So just stay where you are and take a rest. As long as we're stopped, take a rest." Because these stairways were very hot. So by this time, after about an hour, it's very hot. You're sweaty. Your clothes are clinging to you. Now there's smoke. It's a little harder to breathe. There are women who are going down the stairs in bare feet because they had high heels on and their feet hurt so badly that they took their shoes off and held them in their hands. There's water pouring down the stairways. A little at first, trickles, and as you go down farther, more water, more and more water. So you're starting to say to people, "Hold on to the railings. It's slippery. Be careful."

Then at about twenty-two you start to see firemen and paramedics. Everyone, as far as I could hear, says the same thing to them, which is, "There's a man in a wheelchair on twenty-seven."

The paramedic says, "Yes, we know. We're going to get him."

Everyone moved to the right so that the firemen and paramedics can come up the stairs. By this time, the firemen, in particular, are huffing and puffing because now they've already walked up twenty-five flights of stairs with forty or more pounds of equipment on. The stairs are hot. They're congested there. So they're huffing and puffing but they're going. So I felt a little better about the man in the wheelchair because I was convinced that now that the firemen knew where he was, and the paramedics, that they could help.

The next thing I remember is we get to the very last staircase and there's an open door. We step out on what's called the mezzanine. The mezzanine overlooks the plaza of the World Trade Center. It looked like a movie set. It was covered in debris. There were fires. The windows had blood on them. There was something that I was staring at. I stared and I stared and I stared—until I realized it was a body, unrecognizable. It looked like a rag doll that someone had thrown. But my first reaction was, it's a movie set. It's not real. It's a movie.

We worked our way around the mezzanine past all of this. There were body parts everywhere and piles of burning debris. I remember thinking, "I don't understand why there are so many bodies." I didn't know the second tower had been hit. I didn't know any of those things. So the first reaction was, it's not real. Then it's realizing what you're looking at. I don't understand what happened but I know we're in trouble and we've got to get out of here.

I came across the mezzanine and standing there was our chief operations officer. There was an escalator that went down. The escalator was off. He was encouraging people to move down the escalator, just trying to get people to move as quickly as possible down the escalator. Walked down the escalator and at the bottom of the escalator the last couple of steps were completely filled with water. The sprinklers were going off. There's glass all over the floor and there was water coming down. There were people standing there telling you where to go. "Go out this way. Go out this way."

A woman came up to me and she grabbed my hand. She said, "Are you Mary Lee Hannell?"

I said, "Yes."

She said, "I am so-and-so." I didn't recognize the name. She said, "Have you seen my husband?" Her husband worked on the sixty-eighth floor and worked for my boss. She said, "Have you seen him?"

I said, "No, but I'm sure he's okay. I'm sure he got out." She stopped and she wouldn't walk any further. She kept looking back and I was afraid that she'd wait for him. I said, "You know what? You can't wait for him because he won't find you. What if he goes out a different exit? Why don't we just keep moving? You're going to find him. He's fine."

She said, "Okay." So I held her hand for a while and dragged her down to the retail area of the concourse, where there were people who were yelling, "Hurry! Hurry! Hurry! Let's go! Let's go! Let's go!" She started running. We came around the corner and there was another Port Authority person there, who's the director of financial services. He said, "Go up the stairs. Go back up the stairs. Just go." Passed him, went up the stairs and came out onto Church Street, which is where Borders bookstore was. There was a fireman there yelling, "Move. Don't look up." So, of course, everyone stopped and looked up. "Don't look up. Don't look up. Keep moving. Keep moving." So we went a little ways and turned around and looked up.

I thought, "Gee, that's weird. How'd the fire move from one building to the other? It must have skipped over somehow." This is what I actually thought. It must have skipped over to the building. I don't know how that happened. So then I'm still with Eileen [my co-worker]. Crossed the street and there was my boss standing there. He hugged me and he hugged Eileen. He said, "I'm so happy to see you."

We decided to start walking down Fulton Street but we were not in a big hurry because we figured, "We got out of the building. They'll put the fire out. I wonder how many months it'll be before we go back in? Let's see, last time [after the 1993 bombing] it was February to April. Let's see how long it'll take this time." Get to the corner of Fulton and Nassau streets. Which is about two blocks. We're kind of milling around because I'm looking for my husband now. Looking, looking, looking. I don't see anything. I hear this tremendous sound, like this low rumbling sound, but really, really loud. We turned toward the building—and the problem with being on Nassau and Fulton streets is, as close as you are to the Trade Center, and as tall as the buildings are, you can't see them because the other buildings near you obscure the view.

But all of a sudden we see this huge cloud of gray. It puffs up and then it starts to puff toward you. I remember thinking at that moment that there's a scene in an Indiana Jones movie, *Raiders of the Lost Ark*, I think, and there's a large boulder that starts to come down and Harrison Ford starts to run from it. All I could think of is this huge boulder coming down at me, and thinking, this is like a Godzilla movie. This isn't real. This can't be happening. Godzilla's going to step up next with a piece of the building and we'll be done.

It's moving very quickly, this dark gray cloud. I'm with my boss and with Eileen. We grab hands and we run across Nassau Street to the next intersection, as though that would help. We know that we can't outrun it. So my boss tries a couple of doors to get inside and they're locked. Then the three of us just turned our backs, held hands, and just closed our eyes, because I think we thought the building was falling on us. That was the second time where I thought I might die. You're holding hands. You're completely engulfed and you're breathing whatever it is: concrete, glass, who knows what else. Just pulverized stuff but it's everywhere. So every time you take a breath you're inhaling it. You can't see anything because it's gone dark. So we just stood there. I don't even know how long we stood there. I remember when the cloud was coming toward us hearing people scream. But when the cloud engulfed us, I kept thinking—this probably wasn't accurate—but my impression was that it was very quiet, almost like being in a snowstorm when it's very, very quiet and the snow's just falling around you.

The three of us just stood there until it had subsided enough—I don't even know how long it was—that we could see maybe a foot in front of us. My boss, who's got a great sense of direction, said, "Let's just keep moving. Let's move east and then uptown. So we'll head toward the South Street Seaport and then we'll move uptown." I couldn't see anything because I wear contacts. Every time I opened my eyes I had more of this garbage [in them]. So I just hung on until we emerged from this stuff. As we were walking people had their car doors [open] and the radios turned up. People were in the street, listening and talking about what happened. There was a woman who came up to me and she said, "Were you in the World Trade Center?"

I thought, "Gee, that's really strange. How did she know I was in the World Trade Center?" I said, "Yes."

She said, "God bless you. I'm so glad you're okay," and she hugged me. I said to my boss, "How did she know I was in the World Trade Center?"

We keep going. We get to what we find out later is the Department of Water for the city of New York. A man comes out and says, "The three of you need to come here."

I said, "No, that's okay. We're just going to keep going."

He says, "No, no. You need to come here. I have a men's room and ladies' room and you need to come in. I want you to take all your clothes off and shake them out. I want you to wash yourself off."

It wasn't until then, when you looked in the mirror, that you realized you were covered from head to toe in gray stuff. We'd been wet from going under the sprinklers and so the stuff stuck. So we went in and shook our clothes. I washed out my contacts, did all that stuff. Tried a phone but I couldn't get through on the phone. Paged my husband. Couldn't get to him. Left a page but nothing else. Then we kept going. We were really thirsty so we decided to stop at a bar. They had one of these huge flat-screen TVs and that's when we saw what happened. That was the first time we actually saw replaying of the plane into the building, and showing the building collapsing. This was about twelve thirty. I remember looking at my watch and saying, "I need to call school to find out about my kids." I don't know where my husband is; I don't know when I'm going to get home. Somebody's got to take them. There was a pay phone, so I stood in line and then called school. This is, again, one of those times when I really knew that things were bad. The secretary at school, who I know very well, answered the phone. I said, "Hi. This is Mary Lee Rocha." She went crazy, screaming and crying. I'm going, "What's the matter? What's the matter?" And she's screaming. She must have screamed for five minutes.

She finally said, "I can't believe you're alive!"

And I thought, "What are you talking about?" Then it kind of started to seep in: Wow. Maybe there are people who didn't make it out. There are people who are not okay.

I said, "I don't know when I'm going to get home."

She said, "Your father called and he and your brother and your sister-in-law are on their way down [from Latham] to pick up the children."

I said, "Great. I just need to know that they're safe because I don't know when I'm going to get there."

She said, "I've had phone calls from other families who want to take your kids." I guess everyone knew that we worked for the Port Authority, or worked in the World Trade Center. She said, "So they're okay."

I said, "What do they know?"

And she said, "We've not told anyone anything."

And I said, "Okay. Are you going to tell them?"

She said, "No. We're not going to tell them what happened. We're going to allow people to pick their kids up early but we're not going to tell them what happened."

I said, "Well, please make sure that if something happens, and they find out, please make sure that they know I'm okay."

So she said, "All right."

[*Hannell and her two colleagues eventually caught a ferry to Weehawken, New Jersey, and later found people to drive them home.*]

I arrived home at about eight o'clock to a whole houseful of people. My husband got home an hour ahead of me. So he was there, my dad was there, my brother and my sister-in-law, her two kids and then my kids, and a neighbor who came wandering out when they saw us there. So then I think I had Chinese food finally, after I had a shower. That was my day.

How did your children react to all this?

The three of them are definitely at different stages. The phone call I made in the bar was to school because I knew that I wasn't going to get home in time to get them and I didn't know where my husband was. I chose not to think that he didn't make it out. I chose to think he did, but that I didn't know where he was.

[I've] come to find out my son has a first-year teacher this year. She's brand-new. On that morning she received a cell phone call from her sister, in the classroom, talking about the World Trade Center. So he heard, "Terrible incident, something awful happened." Then she took a survey of the kids whose parents worked at the World Trade Center. So he raised his hand. Then he went to the lunchroom and he overheard the lunch ladies say that the Twin Towers had collapsed. So he sat down with his food and he told his friend, "I think my parents are dead." Then he came back to the classroom. Parents started showing up at school to take their kids out of the class. So kids were disappearing, and there he sat, and there he sat, and there he sat. He has a friend named Eric, and Eric's grandfather came to pick him up. His grandfather said, "Eric, come on. We're going to go home."

He said, "I can't leave."

The grandfather said, "What do you mean, you can't leave? Mom told me to bring you home."

Eric said, "I will not leave my friend Andrés because he thinks his parents are dead, and I refuse to leave until someone comes to get him and I know he's okay." [Cries]

My dad and my brother and sister-in-law got there about two thirty. The school called my son down to the office and he thought, "Oh, this is great. This is wonderful." He ran as fast as he could because he said, "I know that my parents are going to be there." When it was my dad Andrés said, "Now I know they're dead." No matter what they told him, he didn't believe them. It wasn't until he spoke to me on the phone, and he spoke to his father on the phone, that he finally let himself believe that we were okay. To make matters worse, since we had been told that the students [hadn't been told] anything, it wasn't until about three weeks later, when we were just having a really hard time with him—he was really not himself, he was angry, he was really emotional—that he finally told me this whole story. We got him a counselor and she was really wonderful. But I went back to the teacher afterward and I said, "How is it possible that all the students in school knew that this child thought his parents are dead and you didn't?"

And her comment was, "Well, I thought he looked kind of distraught but I didn't know what to say. So I didn't say anything."

What makes me angry is that now I've got a ten-year-old who went trick-or-treating, who wants to know how we can be sure we'll be safe when we ring that person's doorbell. What if that person takes out a gun and shoots us? He wants to know if we don't come home one day, who do he and his brother and his sister get to go live with? And will they be safe? And will they have enough money? And will they have to leave all their friends behind?

MARCH 4, 2003

What role has the Port Authority played in the cleaning up of the World Trade Center site?

We did have a project manager who was in charge at the site and a group of people who worked with him, because it was a site that we still owned. So even though some of the cleanup was directed by the city of New York, the Port Authority still had a great role in how that was accomplished. Our own [deceased] folks were there to be recovered. So we played a fairly low-key, low-profile role, but an important one nonetheless. My role was limited to the unfortunate task of keeping an accounting of remains that were recovered and identified, and making sure that the liaisons that we had who were working with families were notified, and that the senior staff here was notified as quickly as possible. So I spent a good portion of my weekends and Monday mornings wondering who they had found over the weekend, and what family we were going to be able to go to and let them know that we had recovered the remains of their loved ones. I don't know if it was more painful to tell people, "There's no trace," or to tell people that, after months and months and months, we've recovered someone.

I know that for me, personally, there was one person who was lost in the Trade Center. Her name was Debbie Kaplan. She worked for my husband for a number of years. Very Orthodox Jew. And there was no memorial service because her parents, who felt very strongly about this, felt that they weren't able to carry out a memorial service until something of her was found. And so I remember my husband—this was probably four or five days before Christmas—asked me what I wanted for Christmas. I said what I wanted was for them to find her. And they did. They found her remains and the family was very, very grateful. And there're so many people, still, who don't have that closure.

This experience of 9/11, I have to say, is something that grows over time, because I think that early on I was in a lot better shape than maybe I am now. Even though it's not as raw and it's not as prevalent. I mean, at one point I think we all felt like we were swimming with our heads just barely above the water with regard to this whole World Trade Center disaster. What happens, I think, over time is you rethink so much of the what-could-have-beens and the, "Boy, I made that decision, not knowing how important that decision was." That creeps up on you. It's really powerful and it's sometimes tough to manage.

Tell me about your home life. Is it changed at all as a result of the World Trade Center disaster?

There was a time there where we were coming home, where every day we were heroes [to our kids] because we walked through the door. It was, put everything down, stop everything you're doing, "Mom and Dad are home. Let's give them hugs and kisses." And very clingy. So that's gone back to normal.

Are you ever stumped by their questions as to what to do or how to view things?

I was certainly stumped by my daughter. We were out at an Italian restaurant one night and she said to me, "I need to ask questions. Can I ask questions?"

I said, "Absolutely, we have time for questions. Go ahead."

And an hour and a half of questions [followed] about the World Trade Center. "How many people were there on the planes? What were their names? Can I see pictures of them?" But the question she asked me that stumped me was, "Why did people jump out of the building? Why did they jump? Didn't they know they were going to die? Why would someone ever do that, Mommy? Why would they do that?" And I have to admit that I sidestepped it. I told her that we don't really know why, but maybe some of them fell rather than jumped. Because I can't explain to an eight-year-old that jumping out of a building was better than whatever it was they were facing inside the building.

How long after the event did she ask those questions?

It was months. Months. I was not as aware as I probably should have been of how much she was thinking about it. I do remember her saying she never wanted to see any of it on TV. Apparently what happened [on September 11] is, when they came home with my brother and my sister-in-law and my dad, the television was on and she saw it over and over and over again. So her policy is, "I don't want to see it anymore. I don't want to talk about it until I'm ready to talk about it."

[A few months later.]

I wish I could remember when it was, but it had to be before February or March of 2002, because that's when my mother-in-law left, and I think she was still there at the time. Actually, what we had to do was we went and found the *New York Times*, and there happened to be a spread in the *New York Times*, and it had all the photographs and the names.

My husband brought her home and we found the paper and we sat her down. She sat on his lap and she would point to the picture and she'd say, "Who's that, and what's his name? Who's that, and what's his name?"

These are the portraits of grief that the Times *ran?*

No. This was an article about the hijackers. This was about the hijackers she wanted to know, the nineteen. She will occasionally ask me about [people we knew who died]—because she recognizes names of people that we work with, so she'll say, "Daddy, is Greg okay?"

And he'll say, "Yes."

"Mommy, is Lou okay?"

"Yes, he's fine." And she did stumble upon Neil Levin [the deceased executive director of the Port Authority], and I had to say, "No. He's not okay." So she really took a long time with that.

JUNE 22, 2005

How long have you worked for the Port Authority?

Eighteen years. I can't believe it's eighteen years. I had actually intended on only staying for ten but then I had a great opportunity at the Port Authority, so I stayed. After 9/11, I decided I would stay until the dust settled. And it's not quite settled yet.

What have been the physical aftereffects for you and your colleagues?

One was that, because I wore contacts and was engulfed in that cloud, I developed a fairly severe eye infection. The other thing that happened to me was this cough. It took about six months to get rid of the cough. I would cough all the time. The other thing that happened, and it periodically comes back, is I would be asleep—and either it really happened or I would dream it would happen—but I would feel as though as I had stopped breathing. I would sit bolt upright in bed, to get a breath, because I couldn't breathe. But not like in asthma, like where you're wheezing to catch your breath. Just, I'd stop breathing. It happened to me a couple of times on the PATH train. Where I would fall asleep and I'd be woken up because I had stopped breathing.

Certainly the psychological aspects of 9/11 are the most difficult, I think, and they're the hardest to get a grip on. People at work were doing simple things like pouring your coffee, pouring your milk into your coffee, putting the milk on a hotplate, putting the coffee in the refrigerator, having a meeting, and then something would trigger a name and people would fall apart and just cry.

You still work for the Port Authority and the Port Authority's still in charge of those buildings, so there's not really a way you can separate from all of that.

No, there's not. It's pretty much with you all the time. And then there are just silly things—I think a week before the most recent 9/11 anniversary we were riding [the] PATH, and you're a little antsy anyway. We get on the PATH train and there is a bag sitting on the floor. It's a Victoria's Secret pink-striped bag and there's a man, kind of standing near it. The next stop he gets off and the bag is just sitting there. So I say to my husband, "Go check out the bag."

He says, "Somebody left their bag."

I said, "No. I'm not staying on this car, unless you go check out the bag." So he goes over, and he comes back.

And he says, "Somebody left their lunch."

I said, "How do you know it's their lunch?"

He said, "There's a banana on top."

I said, "What's under the banana?"

He said, "It's a napkin."

I said, "Did you pick up the napkin?"

He says, "No. What do you think? It's an atomic banana? Give me a break. It's somebody's lunch!"

I said, "I'm moving out of this car."

You're left with a bunch of silly things—in the best light, silly things. In a bad light, really serious things that you have to deal with all the time.

In terms of the lingering effects, in terms of your own family and your sense of your future, how would you describe that, aside from work?

In some cases—and glamour is the wrong word for it—but that's how some people come at me with questions, like, "Ooh, you were in the World Trade Center? Wow! Can you tell me about it?" And the answer's always, "No." Because there's nothing glamorous about it. I keep saying to people, there aren't words big enough, or deep enough, or sad enough to really express to you what it was like. You don't want me to be able to give that to you. You don't want me to be able to kind of put that burden on you. And it is a burden.

Is it lonely?

You know, it's something that a lot of my friends talk about, that it is lonely. I think the difference for me is that my husband also went through it. And so the two of us can talk about it and kind of be on the same wavelength about it, and have an understanding about it. It's definitely a club. It's not a club you can join, it's not a club you want to join, but it's a club you're in, or you're not. If you're not in the club, people don't want you asking questions and pretending to be in the club. You're not in the club.

Do you ever miss the buildings?

Yes, I do. And my husband definitely misses them. He keeps saying that he thinks the buildings are actually just out for cleaning and that they'll be returned to the spot soon. He looks forward to that happening every day.

That's the only building that I ever worked in, my entire Port Authority career.

You really just want to go back to September 10. You just want everything to be the same. One of the things I remember about that morning was how blue the sky was. It was brilliantly blue, no clouds. It just had that little chill in the air that you get in the fall. It was absolutely perfect out. And now, every time I see that kind of sky, that's what I remember. I remember September 11.

3.

Somi Roy

Film and Media Curator

Interviewed by Gerry Albarelli

Somi Roy is a New York–based film and media curator specializing in Asian, Asian American, and nonfiction films. Roy was born in 1956 in the northeast Indian state of Manipur. His mother was the youngest daughter of King Churachand. Roy's father was the first Western-trained surgeon in Manipur. Roy moved to New York in April of 1982 and attended State University of New York at New Paltz. He is an exhibition curator for major museums and also works for public television. Roy has also been a curator and program officer at the Asia Society. On September 11, 2001, Roy was at his apartment in lower Manhattan.

MAY 6 AND MAY 9, 2005

I was born in Imphal, which is the capital of Manipur. People often ask me, "Where do you come from?" And I say Manipur. And I wait for the silence that follows. Usually there is a silence. There's very little knowledge about this area, even in India. It's on the border of Burma. It's a very small, discrete culture. People are of mixed Tibetan and Burmese ancestry, and throwing in a bit of—depending on how far you want to go back—the Mon and the Khmers and the Thais and so on. So that's where I grew up.

Tell me about your mother and father.

My mother was the youngest daughter of the king of Manipur at the time, the maharaja. She was the fifth of five daughters. Her mother, much to her rage, never produced a son to be an heir to the throne. Her mother had various stepchildren, recognized as children of the king. Although her mother was the official queen, a stepbrother became the king of Manipur. She comes from a very high-status family that traces its genealogy to the first century A.D. She married my father who came from a family that was beneath her station. And so she promptly got disowned and thrown out of the family for fifteen years. They actually eloped to Calcutta from Manipur. And my father's family was not good enough because they could only trace their ancestry to the fifteenth century, and that simply would not do in isolated Manipur, which is the center of the cosmos, you see? But his family was a very academic family, and his father—my grandfather—was perhaps the first Western-trained physician. My father was the first Western-trained surgeon [in Manipur]. So I grew up in a family very aware that we were different, that people kind of looked at us all the time. My mother's a bit of a society lady at that time, and my dad is a very successful surgeon.

Your mother was a society lady? Tell me what you mean by that.

Oh, we had a lot of parties at home, dinner parties. I mean, now in retrospect, it was because there are no restaurants there. The way people entertain each other is to go and eat at each other's houses and drink themselves silly and so on. Everyone looked to Jackie Kennedy. My mother had subscribed to *Home and Garden* and *Ladies' Home Journal* and I saw pictures of Coca-Cola and apples even before I tasted or drank any of that. So I got exposed to a lot of Western culture. We had the first oven and she used to make birthday cakes for me. We were the only family to have birthday parties in a culture that simply did not even keep records of people's births.

Did you have servants?

Servants, yes. We had lots of servants. Even today. For one thing, it's a feudal kingdom and so there are all sorts of social stations and social categories and different words to use when you're addressing someone of a certain stature. And different vocabularies, like the Japanese do. You can't use the same word for sleep or for eat, depending on who you're talking to. So we had servants and we had a couple of housemaids and boys, and we had a cook and a driver and a gardener.

So do you want to talk about September 11, is it okay?

Things never really quite die; you never quite lose people in your lives. I remember on 9/11 I was living in a loft downtown in the South Street Seaport area and, of course, that was totally cordoned off. There was no power and there was this dust everywhere. For some reason I came back home almost every night, like a homing pigeon. I was [getting around] on my bicycle. I'd always hated cargo pants but I really found the advantage of cargo pants that summer. In the weeks after 9/11, I had the cell phone in one pocket and water in the other, and my charger, and flashlight, and my PalmPilot. I was totally connected. And there I was on my bicycle, going up and down the East River Park because that was the only route where you didn't have to go through a lot of police [road] blocks. But I used to come home every night and there was no power.

When you don't have power you wake up early. You become more diurnal; you wake up with the sun; you sleep with the sun. So I woke up very, very early one time. I remember my batteries were kind of running low on my cell phone and I was thinking of Jupiter. I missed him a great deal because he was the only person in New York, virtually in America, that I could speak my own language to. Every time I thought of a cheesy bilingual joke, who else could I call, you know? I'd call him and say, "How about this one?" And he would laugh quite appropriately and encouragingly. So I missed that.

And so I didn't know who to call. So just on an impulse, I took out my phone book, I looked [Petros] up in the phone book and there he was on Eighty-first Street, so I dialed the number and he picked up. And I said, "Petros?"

And he said, "Somi?"

I hadn't spoken to him in more than ten years, much less seen him. And immediately he said, "Is it Jupiter?"

And I said, "Yes, I'm sorry he didn't make it." And then I started crying. It was the only time I actually cried during that week. I was kind of too busy and too stunned about this whole thing. Jupiter was the guy who told me to stay on in America [when I had come for a visit]. He had said, "Oh God, it's easy, come on we'll just get you a college admission. Come to New Paltz and study your photography there. You don't have to go back [to Manipur]." And since I didn't have a job to go back to I said—I was young and I liked New York—I said, "Sure." So he was very close to me. He was a very important part of my life in those years. And after he got married we moved apart a little bit, but he saw me every few weeks because he used to work at the World Trade Center and I was on South Street. He used to come by after work [at Windows on the World] with fancy dishes, I don't know, something "Lorraine" or something "Crouton"—whatever they were preparing in the kitchen, you know.

I'd like to ask you to take me through the day of September 11, but before you do that, tell me a little more about Jupiter.

Jupiter was a couple of years younger than me. His father and my father had been friends since grade school. And his grandfather and my grandfather were the first generation of Western-trained physicians. His mother and my mother were also friends when they were kids. So we were family friends, his family and our family. We grew up together.

Jupiter had been in America about six months before I arrived, so he was showing me the ropes, trying to get me odd jobs, that kind of thing. And he was working as a waiter in a restaurant. And he was very good-looking. The girls were totally nuts about him. He looked up to me as an older brother. I was working at the Asia Society at the time and my program was getting quite popular in the city. I was in the public eye, and in the papers and in the press, and so he was very proud of me, I think, on some level. And there were only six Manipuris, I think, or maybe four, in New York. Four in the city, one in Poughkeepsie, and one up in Beacon—Jupiter. So there weren't a whole lot of people; we don't have a community here. So he was my community; he was my family because we all have to create our families here.

So I wake up September 11 and I go to work at nine. I'm always a little tardy. So around nine o'clock I said, "Let me check e-mail." And I had NPR on and I heard, "Oh, this plane has been flown into the World Trade Center." I said "Wow." So I turned on the TV in my bedroom and I was looking at it from my work space—I have a little office area, and the sound was down and I was watching. I was thinking, "What's going on over here?" And the doorbell rang. My assistant Brian was there. And people were running all over the place. I look downstairs and South Street is full of people running, some without shoes and with briefcases. We parked in my living room with the television, just watching it.

So the first thing I did on 9/11 was to just send an e-mail out to my entire address list. I said, "I'm okay." The lights didn't go off, the phones didn't go off, not until four or five in the afternoon, so I sent off an e-mail to people. And then I started getting phone calls. People I hadn't spoken to in years. This kid Scott that I had known and hadn't spoken to in years, he was the first one who called and said, "Are you guys okay?" I had no idea it was so big, even then.

Then I got a call from India, from this friend of mine who was a photographer, Pablo. He called me saying that Jupiter's brother, Laba, wanted to know whether Jupiter was okay. I said, "Oh, my God, Jupiter!" And I said, "He does work there [at the World Trade Center]. And he does go into work early." He used to sometimes go in at six in the morning to do breakfast. So I called [his wife] Nancy but I couldn't get ahold of her.

So finally my friend Sanjib called me. He said, "Yeah, [Jupiter] went to work this morning." I finally got ahold of Nancy. She was in the middle of this whole thing, with all her other fellow instructors at the Rockland Psychiatric Center that she worked in. They were gathering around just saying, "Everything's okay, calm down, surely something is going to turn up. So all that time I was on the phone, calling everyone who knew Jupiter. And so I really didn't watch TV very much or anything. My mental picture of 9/11 is really my computer and the telephone—I barely watched the TV.

Brian said, "Look at those people, walking home to Brooklyn." It was like the scene from *The Ten Commandments* with Charlton Heston leading people across the Sinai Desert. There was a stream of people walking across the Brooklyn Bridge. Endless. It was a stream without a break. And downstairs was another stream of people all covered in dust, all with briefcases half open, women with no shoes. They had to shut off the FDR Drive, so that was eerily empty. The sound was different, because usually we have this constant roar in the background of traffic.

Tell me about your next conversation with Nancy.

Nancy was very businesslike. That was her way of coping. She's a very together person. So we formed a team of people to look for Jupiter. And I went to my boyfriend, Tom, to his apartment on the Upper West Side. He had an old album of photographs and there was a picture of Jupiter and me clowning together. And so I took that, and I scanned it and I made a poster, with my cell phone number saying, "Jupiter Yambem. Last Seen in Tower One." We had to distribute those posters around town. I mean, there's this horde of people putting posters up. New Yorkers were amazing; everyone helped me. And I knew that deep down, rationally speaking, I knew that it was useless. You're going to recognize him with this lousy picture, a xeroxed picture? But it was just something to do, I guess.

We [gathered] DNA samples. We took his comb, his toothbrush, to turn it in [to the authorities]. So there was my friend Rajeshwar—this Manipuri guy who had just come to New York—Jeff, Nandan, myself, Tom, and Sanjib. We had faxes and faxes and faxes, lists of places where bodies were being taken. We just kind of fanned out.

And then on the fifth day, on Saturday, we got news that they'd found him. He was one of the first people to be found. Amazing! They found part of him, at any rate. And so a guy came to Nancy and said they'd found his body. And then, of course, the whole second week was completely different after that. His family kept calling me. My friend Laba, his older brother, kept calling me. My cell phone bill was $2,000, you know? Because I was getting calls from India. No one else seemed to be able to get calls except me. They seemed to be calling me only.

Jupiter's the youngest of five brothers, and so brother number three calls and said he's coming to the funeral, for the cremation. And I'm saying, "Don't come. There's nothing you can do, really." And then the funeral home wouldn't keep [Jupiter] any longer. They said, "This body's in really bad shape. It's against the law. We have to cremate him now. I'm sorry, we can't wait any longer."

And we said, "Please wait until Laba gets here. His brother's on his way, getting his visa right now, he's buying his ticket right now, let him come. Just wait until he gets here."

"No, no, we have to do it."

I think it was on the twenty-sixth of September. I forget the date. We had to have it that day. And so the morning of the cremation it's a beautiful day. September 11 was a beautiful day too. You must have heard from other people how lovely that day was. I remember Angamba, the third brother, the morning of the cremation. He's on the cell phone with me and he said, "I'm on the way." He was driving from JFK into Beacon where they had the cremation. I said, "You know we got to start." So he didn't quite make it to the cremation. Manipur is Hindu, so they wanted to have a Hindu ceremony there. They wanted the lighting of the fires to be synchronized. So I was holding up my cell phone. Laba's on the cell phone with me from Manipur. I was holding up my cell phone, and then the Catholic priest was saying, "A time to live and a time to die," or whatever he was reading. So I was holding it up to this reading, "The Lord Is My Shepherd, I Shall Not Want," reading the Psalms, and on the other side the Hindu ceremony was starting. So it was done by cell phone.

The box Jupiter's body was in was so small. The box was about the size of the top of that table, which is not more than three and a half feet long. For a guy who was five feet-seven inches. It really bothered me. So we were really emotional.

And then, this is another interesting story. I'm calling up one of Jupiter's friends. His name was Cherian. I said, "Cherian, I have bad news for you. Jupiter died."

And he said, "I have bad news for you too. My brother Joseph died."

I said, "What happened?"

He told me that Joseph, who lived up in Cambridge, Massachusetts, had flown in that morning to be at a breakfast that Jupiter had organized at Windows on the World. Three people came in from his office. They came in two cabs. One cab got stuck in traffic and they survived. But Joseph, he made it to the business breakfast. So Cherian says to me, "How come they found him?" Because they also found Joseph. How many people were found from the 150 at the breakfast? Like seven or eight bodies are found? And Jupiter was one of them and Joseph was the other?

So Cherian says, "Do you think they talked about us? Do you think Jupiter might have gone up to him and said, 'Are you from India? I'm from India too. Your name, Mathai, sounds familiar. Do you know Cherian?' So was the last conversation about you and me?"

I said, "I don't know, Cherian. Who knows?"

MAY 18, 2006

I was visiting my family in 2002 [in Manipur] and I'd heard that there was a play called *World Trade Center*. So I asked around if there was a way that I could see it. The play is performed by a traveling troupe, all male actors. You invite them to your home. You pay them about $150. They come on the day of the performance and you give the space to perform. The form of the theater is called *Shumaang Leela*, and *Shumaang* means courtyard and *Leela* means play. It's a courtyard play, the courtyard theater of Manipur.

This *Shumaang Leela* is performed primarily as an improvisational form. Traditionally what happens is the play is set on a theme. It's not written. It is usually performed by people who are not literate. So there are no lines to learn. They're given a situation and you have a story structure, a narrative structure, and the actors improvise around it.

World Trade Center falls on this category of *Shumaang Leela*. It is slightly modernized in the sense that a script that was actually written. But once the play has been directed, and has been put together by a director who's commissioned by the troupe, they perform as many as two or three times a day in the busy season, which is around Manipuri New Year, around the spring festival. And they can add to the play as they see fit. They can change the direction.

So this play was written by a guy called Ranjit Ningthouja who was about thirty years old at the time. He's from the provinces. It was directed by Birjit Ngangomba who is fairly well known, and then they took it on the road. So when I asked about the play, they were really booked. They were very popular. So they asked me to come to a show in a village called Tentha, which is about an hour from the capital city of Imphal. So we drove down. It turned out to be a performance that had been paid for by the local Communist Party. They sang some songs about hammers and sickles and had a good bout of traditional Manipuri wrestling called *mukna* before the show. Then they sang a few patriotic songs, and then the play.

So I was there and they announced—I don't know how they did this research—"Here in the audience we have Somi Roy, who is from New York, who actually knew Jupiter Yambem, who has inspired this play. Jupiter and Somi lived in New York and Jupiter was attacked in the World Trade Center in Tower Number One. Somi, who lives just a few blocks away, watched the towers fall. And now, after the death of his friend, he is left all alone in New York City."

It was very touching, because—did I tell you that one of the last conversations I had with Jupiter was when he wanted to come by and see me? I had called him and told him I'd just come back from Manipur. So I called him and said, "Hey, listen Jupiter, your brother sent a few things for you. Come by and pick them up, okay? I haven't seen you and we'll hang out." So he called me—he usually worked the morning shift and was done by like two o'clock in the afternoon. He called me on a Saturday and he said, "Can I come over now?" I lived on South Street, about a ten-minute walk from the World Trade Center. And I said, "Ah, no, I'm taking a nap. Don't come now, come some other time." And that's the last time I spoke to him. It's been kind of a source of regret that I didn't see him again.

So I go to this play about him. It was the story of a beautiful Afghan girl who meets an American boy called Steven at NYU, at the arch. I asked the writer later, "Now how did you know NYU has an arch?"

He said, "Oh, I didn't know. But here when you want to meet your girlfriend you have to go and stand by the gate, because the girl's college won't let you in. And you wait for the classes to get out and you wait at the gate. That's where we all meet our girlfriends. So I presumed that since New York would have a university it would be called New York University. Then New York University must have a gate, and obviously that's where people there would meet, because obviously that's how people do meet everywhere around the world."

The hero is an assistant to Jupiter. The main character, Steven, is an assistant banquet manager, as Jupiter was the banquet manager. So the story is that Steven and his wife get married on the eleventh of September 2000.

In 2001, on 9/11, Steven is in his office and he gets attacked. The planes come. His wife is on the cell phone with him, celebrating their wedding anniversary by singing songs to one another on their cell phones. This is because *World Trade Center* belongs to that subgenre of *Shumaang Leela* called *Isei Leela*, which means "song drama." It's basically a melodrama. It combines comedy and drama. It's a popular form of entertainment. It's the only professional kind of theater in Manipur. There's a lot of singing because they have to compete with the Bollywood films that come to town. This form evolved sometime in the 1980s.

World Trade Center was an *Isei Leela*. Reshma, the Afghan girl, and Steven are singing songs to one another when they are attacked. Now as it turns out, Steven's younger brother, Albert, is an officer in the American army. So Albert goes off to war in Afghanistan. Then Reshma decides that she wants to go to Afghanistan to visit her father. The play moves back and forth between New York and this unspecified place in Afghanistan where an Afghan clan couple are dancing and courting one another, much to the disapproval of the local Taliban. The woman has to keep her face covered and the man has to wear a beard. There's a lot of resistance that the characters show to the edicts of the Taliban, the pious edicts of the Taliban.

But on the other hand, this is where Osama bin Laden is hiding out, in the same village. So we see Osama bin Laden celebrating the success of the attacks on the World Trade Center. This being Manipuri *Shumaang Leela*, Reshma happens to be Osama's cousin. So she goes to Afghanistan and her dad says, "Did they chase you out, my daughter?"

And she says, "No, no, no, they didn't chase me out. I just came to see you. But I need to tell my cousin, stop this war."

So she is pleading for the end to this violence that is taking place. In the meantime they are attacked by the Taliban. And then the GIs come. There are a lot of extended battle sequences. And then she dies at the hands of the Taliban, but in the arms of none other than her brother-in-law, who happens to be posted in Afghanistan. She entrusts her baby to her brother-in-law and asks him to bring the baby up in a world of peace and harmony where there are no battles between people over race and creed and religion.

Ultimately, what happens is that the presentation of the World Trade Center and 9/11 boils down to just one person. Here is this huge catastrophe, this big political event, this big war, and in Manipur it boils down to one person, only as it affected one man. One line in the play is, "America can't be all that bad. After all, it gave one of our kids a decent job and a decent livelihood. His countrymen must be very proud of him."

It was a very, very touching play because it uses the clout of *Shumaang Leela*—using populism, using entertainment—to provide first the political background and education. So here you are being brought up-to-date on something that's happening in the world outside, re-creating it, re-imagining it, and reformulating it according to local perceptions. But what has interested people here in America [about the play in Manipur] is the benign picture of America that was presented. America as the good guy. And why was that, people keep asking me all the time. "Why is the picture of America so good?"

Well I have my theories, my own hypothesis. One is that Manipur has no contact with America outside of the media. There are no tourists there. The visa for India is not valid for Manipur. You would have to get special permission. It's a militarized zone and so there's no tourism there. There are no sweatshops. There are no McDonald's. None of the detriment of corporate American globalization actually exists there, except for the images. And what are the images that are being shown of America abroad? They come either from Hollywood, or they come from Madison Avenue, or they come from CNN interspersed with advertising from Coca-Cola, and Tums, and Pampers and whatever. America's the land of plenty. America's the land of democracy. There's no word for "white man" in [Manipur]. There's that little interaction. It's probably the most isolated civilization in the world today. So their picture of America is going to be different.

And the other reason is that it's sentimental. They're playing to the crowd. After all, it's the land where Jupiter got his job. This is the land that gave Jupiter a livelihood and respect. This is the land where he married and had a child. So we're not going to demonize America. America has stood for democracy. The same in India. For all its problems, India's basically a democracy. So people do give it that. America does believe in democracy. It is a democratic country after all. That is important.

4.

Donna Jensen

Computer Programmer, Manager

Interviewed by Gina Hermann

Donna Jensen was born in 1959 and raised in the small upstate New York town of Somers. Jensen's parents were math and science teachers in the local schools. Jensen earned a BA in classical philosophy from the State University of New York, Purchase. In the early 1980s, Jensen began to teach herself computer programming, eventually becoming a senior technologist at Viant, a health care payment processing company. Her office was on the thirty-eighth floor of the World Trade Center's North Tower. At the time of the terrorist attacks, Jensen was in her apartment in Battery Park City near the World Trade Center.

NOVEMBER 16, 2001

I was supposed to be [at work] at eight thirty and just through a total fluke I woke up at eight seventeen. That in itself was very strange because usually I put my alarm clock right next to my ear, and I turn it on. This is the only time in my life where the alarm clock was right next to my ear but it was off. It had turned off and that never happened before. Since I live right here, my commute to the World Trade Center was literally a two-minute walk through my courtyard and across the street. So I ran around trying to get ready. I had *The Today Show* on, which I usually have on in the morning. I was all ready to leave, and usually the last thing I do before I leave is flick off the TV and head out the door.

So I was all set to go and the TV suddenly turned to static, for an instant, and then resumed its normal programming. I heard a sound, what sounded like someone slamming one of the doors down the hall. Then after a few minutes of normal programming they showed a picture of the World Trade Center and they said, "We have reports that a plane has just hit the World Trade Center." So I immediately switched off the TV. I ran to the phone and called my mother because she knew—obviously she knows where I live, and she knew I was working in the Trade Center, and it had hit the tower where I was supposed to be working. I told her, "Turn on the TV. Don't worry, I'm okay." And I ran out.

In the lobby downstairs people were looking out the window. People had seen it go in. Even before I went outside, people were telling me that it was a large commercial jet, not just a little airplane. I went outside to the courtyard. I walked out into the little grassy park. I could see a slit, a horizontal slit in the building, in the World Trade Center. From the grassy park the two Trade Center towers took up the whole sky. Again, we were just several hundred feet from the towers and the sky was an unbelievably deep, deep beautiful blue with not a cloud. The towers were that light, silver color. From behind the tower, I could see the beginning of flame but not much flame, just a horizontal slit, in the tower. The aluminum was curling away from the slit.

I thought, "Well, gee, I should page my boss and tell him I'm going to be a little late." I had my bag and my briefcase and all my stuff, my business dress. I didn't think anything, other than property damage, would happen. I know what it looks like on TV: plane hits—and boom. There's a big flame. That isn't what I saw. I saw a hole. It looked controllable, and there wasn't that much flame yet. I watched for a while, and then I decided not to call my boss, that he'd probably understand if I was late. Then I decided to go get my camera. All I can tell you was that it was not voyeurism and that I was not being cavalier, but things, wonderful things, happen around here all the time. I woke up early one morning last spring and saw an ultralight flying down the river leading a "V" formation of geese on a migration path. Just a few weeks before September 11 a guy had flown a parachute into the Statue of Liberty and dangled there for a while. Amazing things happen here but no one gets hurt. I also remembered when the Empire State Building had been hit by a plane. I'd seen pictures of that. At the time, on September 11, I thought no one was hurt in that either.

So I came in [and] I heard another sound, like a door slamming, and grabbed my camera and ran downstairs. Again, I didn't think it was another plane at all. I just heard another door slam, and ran down, and ran again into our little courtyard. Others of my neighbors were standing there and they said it was another jet. I spent a lot of time talking out loud to myself, and I remember saying then, "It's not an accident." The North Tower, the whole top of it now, was great balls of flame. But in the South Tower, the one that had just been hit, it was a perfect little slit. Perfect horizontal little slit. There was no piece of a plane sticking out. The planes had gone all the way in. Again, believe it or not, I still did not think anyone would be hurt and I stood taking pictures of the towers and planes. One of the most interesting things was that Xerox paper was flying all over the place around both of the towers, coming out where the windows had been. The windows in the towers were sealed, but from all over the towers, especially the upper halves of them, Xerox paper was billowing out. There was a steady, constant fall of the Xerox paper. But every once in a while a huge, like, globe of it, like a nova, would come out of one of the windows, thousands of sheets, just billowing in a sphere outward.

I decided to get a closer look. So I walked toward the Trade Center through my little courtyard and to our little street, South End Avenue. A lot of people were standing there watching. I began to see very large pieces of debris come out, especially of the North Tower. The South Tower now had lots of flames coming out, but the North Tower was in bad shape. The aluminum spans were twisting out and a lot of heavy debris was falling from the North Tower. I saw a sheet waving high up there in the tower. I remember trying to remember whether any of the offices had curtains. I just remember thinking it was very strange. There was this curtain or sheet waving out of the tower. But I didn't think anything of it. I didn't realize what it really was until I saw images like that on the news, that it was someone waving a towel or something, who was trapped.

I stood watching the debris come down. Debris was coming down sort of near us. I looked at what I thought was a piece of debris, and it wasn't. It was a person. He was a young man. Remember, I was very close. I could see him very clearly. He was thin and he had a white shirt with long sleeves and a black tie and black pants and a belt and dark hair. He was facing in my direction. He was coming down headfirst with his arms up and his legs just out a little bit. I thought he looked so nice. He had gotten up that morning and put on those clothes and he looked so nice. He wasn't struggling at all. He just sailed down. I watched for an instant and then I had to turn away. I'd never seen anyone die before. I turned away and turned toward the wall behind me. I retreated back to the courtyard. I wasn't sure what to do. That changed everything. I put my cap on my camera. There was no more picture taking. That changed the tone of the whole thing.

By this time it was getting very noisy. The fires were roaring loud and the smoke was getting a little smelly. The South Tower was having very bad flames come out of it and bigger debris was falling. I retreated back into the courtyard and went back through the little glass lobby of my building. I wasn't sure what to do. I went in the front and out the back way of the lobby toward the Hudson River where there's a little park just for tenants and a little path down to the esplanade. So I walked on that path. I don't know why I did that but I wanted to not look back in the direction of the towers. I walked on that path to the esplanade, and there was a fireboat there with big fire hoses coming out, and I thought maybe they were feeding water up to the firemen trying to fight the fires at the towers. I walked up the esplanade just a little north to where there's a marina, and there was a crowd of people standing there watching the towers. Again, that was a very good vantage point for the towers. More debris was falling and big pieces of twisting metal were coming out of the north building and paper was billowing out, especially of the north building. A whole crowd was there watching.

I watched the debris come down. Then my eyes fixed on one of the pieces of debris, and it was a man. He was heavyset, and he had thick black hair and [a] navy blue suit on. He was almost in a sitting position. His body was in a V shape. He was bent at the hips, and his legs were upward, and his head was upward, and he was looking at the sky and not struggling at all. He just came down as if he were sitting down looking at the sky leaning backward. The crowd said, "Oh." I wanted to get away from them after that very quickly. There was something in the way they said "Oh" that made it clear to me they were watching people come down. It wasn't an "Oh" of shock. It was something else. It was an "Oh" of, "Another one."

So I went out again into my courtyard. I wanted to get closer to the Trade towers. I didn't know what to do. I felt I wanted more information. I wasn't able to make any decision about what to do. I talked a lot out loud to people. People were different. Some people were in a daze. My friend Susan, it was as if she wasn't registering anything. I remember saying to her at one point, "They must've used accelerants," because the flames were so massive, as massive as the Trade towers were. The flames were billowing out and covering them. But Susan didn't respond, and a lot of people were like that. They stared. They didn't respond. Then they would slowly wander off. Some people were sipping coffee, staring up at it. The only people that were voyeuristic about it were the crowd down by the marina. They were excited, watching the people come down.

What went through your mind when you saw the first person fall, aside from what you're telling me about how nice he looked?

First, my heart jumped. My heart started pounding. The first thing that went through my mind was how beautiful he was.

What explanation did you give to the fact that he was jumping?

I wasn't able for days to give any explanations. A lot of what I saw, most of what I saw, I still don't know how to interpret. My brain stops. It doesn't have the pathways to make meaning out of what I saw. [Now] I seek out other people who were there and who witnessed people jumping. I seek them out and I always try to ask them whether they saw any of the jumpers struggle, and no one saw anyone struggle. The fact that they didn't struggle makes a huge difference to me. In a situation like this, you have to make huge decisions in an instant, huge decisions. After a week or so after September 11, I came to a conclusion about the jumpers. By jumping they were taking their lives back. By jumping, they were taking control over their lives again and that's why they didn't struggle. They didn't jump out of panic. They didn't jump out of fear. They jumped because that was how they took their lives back. I think that's why it was so beautiful. When I saw that first man fall, he was so graceful and so beautiful and so courageous.

Someone explained to me that if a person jumps they die long before they hit the ground. Did anyone say anything like that to you?

I had heard that years ago. I don't think that's true.

Would it make a difference to you if they were?

On a practical level I'd be relieved for them, that their suffering was over sooner, that they didn't feel pain. But the honor of what they did would not decrease. When the victims' families tour [Ground Zero], when the

National Guard is there, they stop what they're doing and they salute the victims' families. That's how I feel, because of the honor and the courage of the people who jumped. [Cries]

I can still see them. I can still see them. And just think about the magnitude of what they had to do. That the only way they could take their lives back was to jump eighty floors. Don't forget that the sun was shining on them. There was still that beautiful blue sky, and that man with his white shirt, it was pure white. It was still such a beautiful day.

So, once again, I decided to start walking toward the towers to see what I could find out. Since I was right next to the Six Hundred Building, I couldn't see the towers. Suddenly there was this huge roaring sound. It sounded exactly like a big plane coming from that direction, from the east where the towers were. People starting running past me in the opposite direction. But I kept walking toward it. But this roaring sound got really loud and I heard machine-gun fire coming toward me from the other side of the building. It was this rat-tat-tat-tat-tat-tat-tat-tat, this snapping sound but in perfect rhythm, this loud, cracking, snapping sound. I turned around and ran. I suddenly realized that there were other planes coming and that this was a fighter plane, and it was chasing me, and it was gaining on me. I ran like hell back toward the lobby and other people were running back toward the lobby. I thought, "Okay. Should I stop here and kind of plaster myself next to this wall?" And I thought, "No, don't do that because the strafing will get you." So I kept running. I had this image from the trailer from the *Pearl Harbor* movie that had just come out where there's this guy running and there's this Japanese fighter plane chasing him and strafing him. That's exactly how I felt, and it was gaining on me. This guy ran past me and I yell out to him, "What's happening?" He said, "The World Trade Center's falling."

I, at that point, was not making decisions about what was real and what wasn't real. I still thought it was an airplane strafing people and coming toward us. At the same time, I began to have images in my mind of the Trade Center like a huge tree toppling down onto us. I ran into the little glass room of the lobby and ran out the other side onto the little path. I dropped the lens cap of my camera and spent a millisecond thinking about trying to pick it up. Just to the left was a little back wall for the lobby. For a second I stood against that, thinking, "Okay, if the Trade Center falls it'll just crush this wall and I'll get crushed with it." Every single one of these decisions I was trying to make, first of all, happened within less than a minute. And every single one of these decisions I was consciously thinking, "Okay, which one of these decisions is a fatal mistake?" Because there was a right way and there was a wrong way. Should I run or should I shield myself with this wall? I thought, very consciously, "After this all happens, are people going to say, 'and that's when Donna made her fatal mistake by leaning against that wall'?" Every few seconds I had to make a decision of should I keep running or should I brace myself here and would that be the fatal mistake? Because there was no in-between. Then I decided to keep running, away from the building, away from the towers, and toward the river.

I remember a man, an older man, dragging a little child by the hand toward the lobby and toward the Trade Center. I thought he was crazy. I started talking to myself and I said, "This way. This way." I ran down [this] path behind my building, and then there's the esplanade, and on the other side of the esplanade is the Hudson River. I'd got to the river and I'd outrun it. Things were still clear at the river but I could still hear this roaring behind me. People were on the esplanade, crowded and running around. I started to run to my left, south, down the river. But there was this huge wall of brownish-gray smoke. It was billowing, but almost in sped-up motion. People think of billowing as kind of slow and cloudy and nice. But it must have been twelve stories high, this billowing wall of solid brown. That's when I thought, "Well, I can't run that way." So I started to run north and saw exactly the same thing billowing out from the other side by the marina where the people had been standing, just billowing. This was the first time I was scared because I realized there was nothing I could do. I couldn't run any farther. There were people bunched on the esplanade and I knew it was going to hit me. Whatever happened, I knew it was going to hit me.

So I knew there was nothing I could do. For the first time, really, I was in very bad danger of dying. So there was a park bench there, right by the esplanade. I held on to its railway and I bunched up my sweater and put it over my mouth, and I knelt down, because I had heard that in smoke you're supposed to stay low. I didn't want to get down too far, though, because people were running around and yelling and I didn't want to get trampled. As I knelt down, just before I closed my eyes, I realized there were people actually sitting on the park bench that I was kneeling next to, just sitting calmly, looking out at the river. I'll never forget the backs of their heads just sitting there. I knelt down, closed my eyes, and it hit me. I could feel the debris hitting me. I could feel the roar. I could hear just this roaring sound and crackling, burning sound and people yelling on all sides of me. I kept my eyes closed for a few moments, and then I opened them, and I couldn't see anything. It wasn't black. It was opaque, brown-gray, completely opaque. I closed my eyes a little then and really was very skeptical that I was going to live. I could feel the debris hitting me from above. I could hear it hitting on the sides and in back of me.

Then something very strange happened. I realized I could breathe. I still had my hand up to my sweater, with my sweater bunched in front of my mouth. But I realized I could breathe. In fact, I realized I could breathe very easily. To show you how not completely rational I was, I started doing deep breathing exercises to try to calm my heart down, which was very silly, but I did, to try to calm myself down since I still couldn't move and people were still jostling and crowding and yelling and mostly just screaming. As it cleared, and I could still breathe, I began to feel that I probably would live. I still couldn't see much. My eyes were scratched and, I'm sure, very red. But finally I could begin to see shadows in front of me, silhouettes in front of me. What I saw, I saw shadows of people going over the railing of the esplanade and jumping. So, without thinking, I got up and jumped. As I was standing over the esplanade, I saw below me the fireboat and there were firemen there. They were saying, "Jump. Jump. We'll catch you." I did. It was a far jump too. Sometimes I go and look at where I jumped and it's a far jump. But I did, and they caught me. One of the firemen—a few of them caught me, but one of them held on to me, and he just hugged me.

I said, "I'm all right," but he continued to hug me. I realized he needed to do that. He knew he wasn't catching me anymore. He just needed to hug me, so we hugged each other for a while. Then I detached myself so he could help other people.

Starting on that morning, I became a very visceral person, which is part of the reason I can't do my job anymore. I have terrible trouble abstracting, thinking, drawing conclusions. I'm getting better, but that morning and for the first weeks afterward I was at my worst. During that whole time I was running and thinking about the possibility of making fatal mistakes. That was a big turning point in my whole relationship with what was happening. I didn't draw any conclusions about whether it was a plane or whether it was the World Trade Center falling or both or neither. It was, in a way, like dream theory says, that completely contradictory things exist side by side and it was that. I think when I saw the billowing stuff come around me I still did not draw conclusions because I had the image in my mind of the falling Trade Center as a tree. So I was expecting to be hit from above by big pieces of shiny aluminum. Of course, we [now] know that what I was in and ultimately covered by was the impact explosion of the Trade Center going down from its base. It was almost like an inverted mushroom cloud. It mushroomed out from its base. When I was in the midst of it, I was living in this funny kind of binary universe where I live, not live, live, not live. I couldn't even abstract it beyond that.

When I mentioned earlier about how I felt the honor of the courage of the people who jumped, what I was thinking about were the times I was running from the courtyard into my lobby and then through my lobby into the esplanade and very consciously making instantaneous life-or-death decisions. What I do know is that the people who jumped were going through that also. They had to make a life-or-death decision. Go or no go. I can understand that. I can understand making the biggest decisions you'll ever make and having an instant to make them and yet having them be rational and integrated decisions. I know that's what they faced and I know and I saw what they did in response to having to make that decision. The way they chose to go is the only way they could take back their lives. It's the only way they could *do* something, and even though that doing would lead to death, doing was life. Taking action was life.

What would the alternative have been?

Standing there. Doing nothing. Crying. Panicking. Waiting.

Burning.

Burning. So I understand how deeply rational and deeply human they were in what they did and how deeply courageous they were.

I'll go [back] to the fireboat. I was standing on the deck when we were heading out and this beautiful old man just stared at me, and I stared at him. I think he was Chinese. He was Oriental. He just looked at me and he said, "We were lucky."

I said, "We were lucky."

He said, "We were lucky." Again, it was just this incredibly meaningful conversation. To be getting away from New York was so important. I still couldn't see very well and the air was still terribly smoky, even though we must have been about a third into the river. I was standing next to a guy, and finally he was able to point out to me that there was only one World Trade Center tower. I could finally see that there was just one there, and that was horrible. As I watched, the top of it was black smoke now. Then the black smoke started dripping, like black liquid. Someone yelled, "The second tower's coming down." And someone started taking pictures and I took one more picture. The big, black, melted liquid started going straight down. I felt like I was watching the end of the world. I felt two thousand souls gasping. And I felt that very consciously. I knew that all of my colleagues who had been in the Trade Center were dead. For the rest of the afternoon I was getting pages [from co-workers], people saying, "Can you see the rest of the team? Do you know where the rest of the team is?"

I just answered, "No." I didn't have the heart to page back. I was sure they were all dead. But when the tower came down it was almost audible. I felt the gasp of the two thousand people. I don't want to get Christian here but, like, this exhalation of two thousand souls just becoming nothing.

[*The fireboat took Jensen and the others to the New Jersey shore. She found refuge there at a hotel. The place was full but a guest shared her foldout couch with Jensen. Then followed a seven-week odyssey when Jensen stayed with a friend and in hotels, applying for emergency aid, dealing with insurance claims and FEMA, researching the health consequences of living near Ground Zero, and finally moving back into her apartment in lower Manhattan.*]

I haven't been able to work. I've had two episodes of physiological panic attacks where, just out of the blue—for no reason—I've been suddenly in a cold sweat, and shivering, and my heart was pounding. I see what I saw that day playing out in front of me. I see it constantly and vividly. Since this was also my neighborhood that was destroyed, I've had many situations where images come to me. If you say, "I need to go buy this certain magazine," and you might just see in your mind's eye for an instant that newsstand on your block where you go to buy your magazines. I'll do that and then I'll realize my magazine stand was at the base of the World Trade Center. Not only is it not there now, I think about what I saw when the Trade Center came down. It's nothing. It's pulverized. My Radio Shack, it's pulverized. My Duane Reade. I'm reminded constantly, I pull out old bags, and they have receipts in them from stores that don't exist anymore. But since I've been able to get sleep that's been better.

One thing that has happened that I've had great trouble with is a couple of instances of guilt. It's not just guilt. I'm Italian. I know guilt. This is a strange feeling of searing, self-loathing guilt. It was a horrible, murderous self-fury. So now I'm taking pictures.

Of what?

The wreckage from every angle. I'd like to take pictures of people but right now the wreckage, this historical document kind of aspect of it, not because I really want to but I'm really afraid if I don't that horrible guilt demon will revisit me.

What's that guilt about?

I don't know. I saw a psychiatrist when I realized I was doing bizarre things, like e-mailing the transcripts of the 911 calls to my friends with a jovial little note, like walking until I just drop, just trying to walk myself to exhaustion. I could not tell what was real, what was not real, what was sane, what was not sane. She told me I had survivor guilt. She said people who didn't see it, who weren't there, who had watched it on TV, wouldn't have survivor guilt. That surprised me because the people I had known who had seen it on TV—in some ways I felt so sorry for them. Because they had to be passive in it. At least I had been an actor in it. At least I had saved my life. I had done things I was proud of. I felt sorry for the people who had only seen it on TV because they couldn't do anything.

　　Some other changes: I don't care about my job at all. I really just don't care. But one thing that's interesting is that I'm not afraid of things. There's so much I'm not afraid of, especially when I was high on adrenaline. Staying in Queens, there are some thugs who would hang around on street corners and I'd practically go up and taunt them. My feeling was "Hey, I outran the World Trade Center. I am not afraid of you." And I'm very much not afraid of things anymore.

Is that a good feeling?

Yes. I want to feel it more. I'm still kind of sleep-deprived. I think if I were less sleep-deprived I'd feel it more. But, yes, it's a great feeling. It's a little reckless. I shouldn't go taunting thugs in Queens. But it's a good feeling. Two other things that have really changed are that I can't be alone anymore. I was a very solitary person. I loved spending time alone. I loved traveling alone.

Do you have a partner in your life?

No. No. Believe me, I was extremely solitary. I loved it. I loved having a three-day weekend and not talking to anyone. I can't do that anymore at all, at all. Even this weekend. I don't have to go back to work until Tuesday and I'm very worried.

I imagine it must have been hard those seven weeks being a single person.

Being a single person without a family nearby. The closest people who took care of me were Red Cross and the hotel people who gave me my soap and shampoo every morning. That was very hard. That took a lot out of me. Like I said, I've just moved back in here. There's a strength you have from having a foundation, literally ground under your feet. To not have that for so long after having been shaken so badly took a lot out of me. There's going to be yet another struggle to let that part of me heal that has just begun.

But at the same time I was also a very silent person, and my silence was broken to a large degree. I've been writing letters to the editor. I've been talking to you. I never, never would have talked to an oral historian before. There's a certain kind of boundary around me that's not as strong or even there anymore. When I saw that first man fall I saw how beautiful he was. It's the first time I was ever proud to be a human being and it was right then that the boundary started falling completely. I don't know where that's going to go. It might not lead anywhere but I don't know.

Is there anything else that you want to say as part of your testimony?

Yes, there's one thing. I have friends who try to tell me to stop dwelling on [9/11]. First of all, that's very hard to do living here. But I think that it's very important to know that not everything that happened that day was bad and that this place is horrible now, but it's also sacred. It's becoming a sacred place. It's going to be, if it's not already, one of the holiest places. It's very beautiful now. Even in its destruction, it's so beautiful. It is not something to put behind us. There were so many beautiful things that happened that day. There were so many heroic things. There were so many brave people, simple people. To me, that was a day of miracles, and I don't know any rule that all miracles have to be good miracles. I think it started with two very bad miracles, but that whole day was full of miracles.

Daily life down here is significantly different than in any other part of Manhattan. Can you describe what was going on when we met on the corner of Chambers and North End Avenue? Right in front of Stuyvesant High School. When we came around that bend in the World Financial Center, there were policemen, soldiers, all kinds of personnel that I couldn't even identify.

Yes. At the southern corner of the marina, it's an important place for a few reasons. First, there's a police memorial there. There had been a police memorial but now there's also a makeshift tent of memorials to the police and also to the firefighters who died on September 11. Across from that, in what was a grassy area that's now pretty destroyed, there's a makeshift memorial to all the civilian victims. That memorial's been there pretty much from the beginning. It's full of teddy bears, it's full of flowers, and people are putting candles there now. And poems and pictures of the civilians. Many, many people go to that memorial now. What we saw today were a few things on top of that. We saw visiting soldiers. A lot of the soldiers we saw were from other armies and other countries. A lot of so-called official visitors.

But what has happened, and I've saved the most important thing I think for last, what has happened since September 11 is that the victims' families have been given full and regular access to Ground Zero. The Red Cross and other charity groups take them through as companions, take them through and let them visit Ground Zero and let them visit the ruins and stay there as long as they need to, as many times as they need to. We saw the victims' families today. They're given hard hats. Some of them, I think, emotionally can't walk and they're driven on little carts. The victims' families tour the Trade Center and then come across West Street onto South End Avenue where we were. Then right down that little incline to the memorial place. They carry teddy bears and flowers. It's a very solemn procession.

The victims' families are given great honor. When they pass everyone must stop. If you don't stop, the police and the soldiers will tell you to stop. Everyone stops and bears witness and lets them pass. I have seen on their faces such grief, especially the older people, the mothers, I guess, and the fathers. Their faces hang with grief. The National Guard always guards that entrance to South End Avenue because it becomes Ground Zero at that point. So it's a major checkpoint. When the victims' families come out of Ground Zero, the National Guard stands at attention on either side of the procession. [Cries] They honor them. I understand that completely. I understand that completely.

5.

Maria Georgina Lopez Zombrano

Street Vendor

Interviewed by Elisabeth Pozzi-Thanner

Maria Georgina Lopez Zombrano was born in 1942 in Bogotá, Colombia. She immigrated to the United States in 1967 when she was twenty-five. She worked as a caregiver for families in Connecticut and New York before she had to leave her position due to a retinal detachment that permanently impaired her vision. With help from the Commission for the Blind, Zombrano began to work as a food vendor at the federal office building at 90 Church Street, across the street from the World Trade Center. On September 11, 2001, she arrived at work at seven fifteen in the morning.

NOVEMBER 14, 2001, AND OCTOBER 28, 2003

I live in Queens, and I live in the Elmhurst. My work is in Church Street in front of World Trade Center, just across the street. I have to take two trains, G train or R train to lead me to Cortlandt Street, or I have to take E train until Chambers. But in the morning I take one hour and ten minutes. Because of my disability, I take longer. So I have to take the train by six o'clock in the morning to get to my work. I have a vending stand with candies, newspapers, sodas. Also, I have twelve machines all over the floors. I have candy machines and soda machines, coffee and snacks and sandwiches. That's why I have to start early in the morning, to fill the machines and to fix it sometimes because they broke during the night.

My customers usually people from Housing [Department], from Boston Property, from the post office, from Legal Aid. They are my customers, and people who pass by to go to the post office. So that I have all kinds of people.

You hardly see anything anymore. How do you manage with money, or how do you manage to know what kind of merchandise you are giving your people, the customer?

Most of the times people are very, very honest and they help with the bills. Also, I have a machine, and in case that I am not completely sure that they give me a bill that they told me, I put the bill into the machine and the machine let me know if the bill is one, five, or twenty. I don't change bills bigger than twenty.

But in that building people were very, very honest. Also, we order the merchandise in a specific order, so we know where the things are. I know where the sodas are by names and by sizes. In the vending stand I have no problem because people also are helping.

Sometimes I have to be strong because I can not feel ashamed or bad because I start making mistakes. I make a mistake because of my eyes, not because I want to do it.

Do you run your vending stand all by yourself?

No, I have a friend. The name is Julio. He's completely blind, but he's a good mechanic. He's helping me with the machines. He's the one who fixes everything. And he also helps to count the money.

September 11, what do you remember?

Oh, September 11 for me was one of the most worst days in my life. I was leaving home a little bit late because we work until late that Monday. So Julio decides to stay home because I don't need him that day because all my machines are fixed or full of candies and everything. My vending stand looked beautiful because we worked until late that Monday. So, Tuesday, he stayed at home.

I arrived at work around seven fifteen and I started working in my vending stand, putting all my goods together, my candies. Then I was going to my storeroom to put my table with all the cookies I place in my vending stand, when I heard a big bomb. There just was a big, a big moment—I don't know how to call it. Everything trembling. It sounded like it was a storm. Nobody knew what happened. All my things I have on the table fell on the floor, like twenty boxes. Everybody started screaming and said, "The airplane crashed into one of the towers of World Trade Center." No time to close my storeroom because everybody was screaming.

So I come back to my vending stand and I tried to call Julio. I told him, "Something is wrong. No, I don't know what is going on. People are screaming, but nobody knows what is in there. Everybody says something different—earthquake, hurricane, a terrorist." Meanwhile, I was talking with Julio, I was helping the lady—the second plane—

You were helping, can you tell me about the lady? What was that?

The lady came to me. I was talking on the telephone. The lady came to me and said, "Please, I need to speak with my husband. Give me your telephone." I immediately hung the phone and gave it to the lady. She was calling her husband because she has a little baby in the day care that they have in the World Trade Center. So she cannot call [the center]. The telephone call did not get through. She cannot hear anything about her baby. And she came back again for me to give [her] the telephone. I give it again, the telephone, and she called her husband again. And he said, "Unfortunately, our baby is dead." So she fell on the floor. She screamed. I tried to give her some water. I tried to help her.

People came to grab her and grab me, two ladies, and they took my telephone. I was so scared also, because all of the building was trembling and all the things I have, they are moving, and stuff like that was crazy. They closed my vending stand and ran. I have no idea where or who the ladies were. When I went out, there was a lot of smoke and a lot of stuff on the air and a lot of people screaming. And people don't know if they have to go into the building or if they have to come out because of all the different orders.

Who gave the orders? Do you know who the people were?

I have no idea. Some people outside of the building said, "Inside." So people ran inside. Other people said, "No, terrorists on the building." So people went outside. There were two different orders.

What did you think about your own safety? Did you have thoughts about what you wanted to do for yourself?

In the beginning, I was thinking to get into the corner because there was so much confusion. Everybody was running. The worst thing for me was going out with my stick without knowing where I have to go. So I say, "Well, I stay in the corner of the building and sit there and see what is going on or what I can do." Because I do not want to be on top of anybody.

So did you stay in the lobby or did you go out?

The three ladies lead me out by my hand and they say, "Come on. You can't stay here anymore. There are terrorists here. We have to go."

I say, "No, no, because I have to close. I have to grab my bag."

They say, "No, no, no. There's no time."

I take my stick because I have it in the corner. I just grab my stick. But my mind was in such a way that I can't think about my bag. I can't think about anything. I have no coins in my pocket. They bring me out of the building. Meanwhile, there was a lot of police, a lot of people who made orders. They don't let us move anywhere until the big balls of smoke, all the dust, all the glass, all the fire are coming. So people started running. The sky gets completely black. It was horrible. Do you know, I think about why the [streets] get [covered] with all kinds of glass, how far the glass [fell], because when I get to Chambers Street, I have to walk on top of the glass. My boots get broken because of the glass from the street. I didn't see that people had blood on their blouses and their arms and stuff like that.

They told me, "We have to run. Hold your stick." One lady took me from one arm, and the other lady took me from another arm. They run until Chambers Street because we cannot stay there because of [falling] glass. They say big balls of dust and big balls of smoke are falling. We get to Canal Street. At Canal Street people feel more safe and people were more calm.

I was thinking about what [happens if] these ladies go. What can I do? I cannot call Julio because the telephone doesn't work. I don't know if Julio is still home. I know there would be trouble if he ran to find me. I was not sure if he was still at home. I was not sure if he will come to pick me up. That was bothering me a lot. It scared me a lot.

These ladies talk to each other. One of the ladies says, "I have to go to Connecticut." The other one says, "I have to go to New Jersey."

So I was thinking, "And what about me?"

"Where do you live?" they asked me.

I say, "I live in Queens."

They say, "No, I won't let you go by yourself. We will stay here together. We will help you." But I don't want to go to Connecticut and I don't want to go to New Jersey. I don't know [those] people. I know I want to go home because I want to stay with Julio. I [also] have a feeling that if my store is [still] open, that somebody else could come and take the money or take my things from me. Everything I have is there. So all this is bothering me, but it was impossible to speak with anyone because everybody was so scared. People on the street say, "Hi, Maria. How are you feeling?"

I say, "My God, is terrible. I feel horrible."

They say, "Do you have money?"

"No, I have no money. I have no time to take my money." They give me coins. They give me a banana. They give me water. Everything that people have, they give me. Thanks to God, I meet some people I know. So one lady said, "I live in Queens also. Don't worry. I could bring you home."

Who was that lady? Did you know her?

Hilda. The name is Hilda and she lives in Queens. So we start walking again. I go with this lady. She says, "Don't worry. I will bring you home." She grabbed my arm, and we started walking again to Fourteenth Street because they told us in Fourteenth Street you could take a train.

How did you get the information about what was happening?

People with special megaphones in all the stations. Because we walked from one place to another to get a train. They say, "No, I'm sorry. There are no trains. There are no buses around here. You have to go to Fourteenth to Twenty-third. We went to Twenty-third. No. We went to Thirty-fourth. No. To Fifty-ninth. There were no buses, but there was a taxi. One taxi would take, like, five or six people. They bring us from Forty-second Street to Fifty-seventh Street in the same cab. They dropped us there, and we start walking again until Fifty-ninth because they said trains are working between Fifty-ninth and Queens. But when we went there, they say, "No. No trains. You have to walk."

So did you cross the bridge?

I crossed the bridge and I was nearby Queens Plaza, and there was a bus. For my friend, and me, the bus stopped and pick us up.

How long did it take you to get home? When did you get there?

At three o'clock, from nine twenty. At three o'clock I arrived home.

How was that, to come home?

Yes, so good. We cried for a long time, [Julio] and I, because I thought I would never see him anymore. I thought it was the end of my life because we are not safe anywhere until we arrive home. After we listened to the news and saw that everything was okay, we got calls from people in Colombia calling to see if I was okay or that Julio was okay. Many friends, many people were calling us with worry. All those people because—can you imagine how many people I knew that were working in the World Trade Center? One of my friends died. That was very difficult. Very, very difficult.

Now I have no job. All my things are lost. I have my money. I have some allowance that they give me, individually. I have coins that we save to buy some stuff that we needed at home. I lost my bag, but they gave me the bag the following Sunday.

Tell me about that.

My bag was inside of the vending stand and I thought I lost all my papers, and I thought I lost my passport also, because that day was election day so I had to bring the passport with me. I had my IDs, everything with me. All the things I have that were precious I have in there. So Sunday morning I was so scared about my bag because I lost my IDs. I lost my credit cards. I lost my bag, everything a woman keeps in a bag. So somebody else calls on the telephone and says, "Are you Maria Lopez?"

"Yes."

"I have a bag in my hands."

I say, "My God. What?"

They say, "Don't worry. Where do you live?"

They brought my bag to my house and I asked him who found it and how he brought it to my house, and he said, "No, I have a friend in the reserves, and he found your bag at the World Trade Center." I have no idea how my bag got to the World Trade Center. That I will never know. Nothing was missing from the bag. I found even the dimes and nickels, my bank card. But I have to obtain another one because I have no idea what's going on. But the money I have there. I have $60 in paper money.

Have you been able to go back at all to your vending stand?

Yes, that was another hard time because in the beginning, like for three or four weeks, they didn't let anybody go there. I was calling and calling, and they said, "No way. You cannot get in." I was calling and calling. They didn't let me until October 30. They called me and they told me that I could go there with specific people to pick us up and with a special paper to come into my building. A supervisor and a police lady came with me and Julio to my place and they gave us one hour to pick up what I needed. But it was a big, terrible thing to find my vending stand the way it was—everything on the floor, everything wet, smelling. The cash register was broken. All my books, my papers, my checks, everything on the floor, I have no idea what—

Could you rescue things that you still needed and that you could use?

Yes, I rescued my passport. I rescued my IDs. My social security card. Julio's social security card. Certificate that we are American citizens. My jewelry because I took it from home because I thought it was more safe in the vending stand.

In a special place?

Yes, and nobody knows it. They wouldn't imagine that I had my jewelry in that place. I found it all except one cross that my father gave me. He gave me that cross when I graduated. It was very valuable for me because it was my father's present, and for him it was very hard to get because he was poor and he saved all his money to get it for me. Also, I didn't find the paper money. In the cash register it was, like, $320, and $1,000 in dollar coins, and $1,000 in paper money. I didn't find it. It's lost.

Is anybody going to help you to—are you going to get anything back from that? Is there some insurance?

Yes, the Commission for the Blind are helping us with insurance. Yesterday we went there, and a special corporation is helping me with a loan. They are going to give me a loan, and if I need it, I will use it to buy my stuff again for my vending stand. I received $50 from the Red Cross, and I received $250 more from the Red Cross.

How do you sleep? Do you have dreams?

Oh, yes. Right now much better. But in the beginning, for some reason, I started dreaming that I have no hands. All the time I was dreaming that somebody else was cutting my hands. I dream about hands all the time. I am counting some money, and some hands come and take the money away from me, or a dream that somebody comes and cuts my hands. I have no idea why I am dreaming about hands. It scares me.

6.

James P. Hayes

Priest

Interviewed by Edward Thompson (10/25/01)
and Gerry Albarelli (4/2/03)

James P. Hayes is a Catholic priest at the Church of St. Andrew's in lower Manhattan. Hayes was born in 1949 and grew up in Manhattan. He attended St. Jean Baptiste High School. His novitiate was in Massachusetts. Hayes earned an MA in Divinity from the Jesuit School of Theology, Loyola University of Chicago. Hayes also holds an MA in psychology. He was ordained at the Church of Saint John Baptiste in New York City. Hayes has spent much of his career counseling inmates and sex offenders. He became the pastor of St. Andrew's in 1988. The church is approximately half a mile from the World Trade Center site.

OCTOBER 25, 2001

My ministry is basically outreach to the different [government] agencies here, particularly doing a lot of debriefing as tragedies had occurred with the Health Service Department at the FBI, particularly TWA [the crash of TWA Flight 800 in 1996] and prior to that, the initial bombing of the World Trade towers [1993].

A lot of the ministry here involves parishioners as well as people in the courts, people in the law enforcement community. It's a unique situation because you're in a church that ministers to the court system, the marshals, FBI, DEA [Drug Enforcement Administration], U.S. Attorney's Office. You have to be a regular priest who can minister sacramentally and pastorally. You also have to deal with people like the director of the FBI, the [federal] marshal, those people. We have the older Italians from Little Italy. They're still the staple of the older members of the community on weekends. The weekend community, also, is a very, very emerging and substantial group of young people. Five years ago we started an education program here in this church and we started with five students. This year, we're starting the enrollment at seventy-nine. The weekday crowd is basically lawyers, police officers, agents, that type of thing.

Now I'd like you to tell us about your observations on September 11.

Okay. That Tuesday I was just on my way downstairs. I live up on the third floor of the rectory at St. Andrew's. I had gotten a call from an FBI person right after the first explosion. I was right outside, going out of my room. The message was to get to that location, that a plane had hit the World Trade towers, and get there ASAP.

On the way down I grabbed the [sacramental] oils and on the way out of the front door I was informed that a car was waiting outside from the United States Marshal Service to drive me to that location. The driver, one of the marshals, drove me down to within about two or three blocks of the Trade towers, the difficulty being everyone was coming toward us.

The second plane had just hit and debris was falling down in the sidewalk and the street, after the explosion.

Before I got out of the car, in two different terms, he said, "Be careful and be safe." He said again just before I went toward the towers, to be careful and be safe. I went down to the street right by the Millennium Hotel on Church Street and I noticed that all the ambulances were converging right there. They were just setting up a triage center.

So I proceeded to walk toward a group of firemen. I believe they were from Rescue Five. Two police officers were trying to get their oxygen tanks on, and in the process they had dropped their handcuffs. I reached down and got the handcuffs and secured them for them, and the man in back of me said, "Okay. Let's go." So we went into the tower right by Borders [bookstore]. It struck me that everyone was coming out of one location. There was only one door at that area of the tower complex and everybody was streaming out. They were running. They were wet. They were hyperventilating. It struck me that there may be somebody stuck downstairs. There's a mall in the basement of the complex and because everyone was coming out of one door, I'm thinking maybe there's somebody stuck, fallen, hurt, trapped downstairs. So they went in. I followed them. They went down the escalator by Borders. They proceeded south toward the second tower and I proceeded to go west and was able to, within a matter of minutes, check every single store in the mall area to make sure that nobody was locked in, nobody was screaming, nobody was fallen down hurt.

I retraced my steps back out the same entrance and just before I came up the escalator—people, again, were still running out of the tower— another group of firemen came by. They were going in the same direction as the previous group, toward the second tower. I got out of the tower area by Borders with everyone else and then proceeded to go over to the Millennium Hotel in the front, where they had just set up the triage. People were cut and burned and severely wounded. Some people were hyperventilating. I remember one man. He was overweight, profusely sweating, and he just was stooping over. I asked him if he needed any help and he said no. He just looked up at the tower and he repeated twice, "My son's up there. My son is up there."

I proceeded to help a young doctor, a woman doctor, get some water, get some towels, get some blankets—they were coming out of the Millennium Hotel—and distribute them to the people who were outside the hotel complex. There was a man in the street. I don't know what street, Vesey or Dey Street, or something like that. He kept telling people as they're coming out of Borders to keep running toward Broadway, keep running toward Broadway. Then, all of a sudden, he yelled, "The tower is coming down!" I was facing the Millennium Hotel at the time and I looked over my shoulder and the tower was coming down.

Everybody at that point was running out of their shoes. They were literally sprinting like you had a target gun and you just shot in the air. They were jamming toward Broadway. We got everybody into the ambulances in a matter of, like, ten seconds. I just stood there. I was at the corner. I knew I couldn't go right because the glass in the Millennium Hotel would be coming down and I couldn't run that fast to catch up with everybody, who literally just kept running toward Broadway. I spotted a car, a little black car, about fifteen feet from where I was standing, and as the rumble came down I dove under the car like a baseball player.

Then all hell broke loose. All the metal, the concrete, the pellets of white, light fabric from the walls, and there was just a stream, a waterfall, of brown, black ash. And it just came down and came down and came down. It was like a waterfall that didn't stop for about eight or nine minutes. Then the black ash came. As the black ash came, it enveloped everything. The sky was colored black. The black ash sucked the oxygen out of the air. I could hardly breathe. Then I would open my eyes and it was black, and I'd close my eyes and it was still black. For a minute, I thought I had died. I said to myself, "This isn't too bad."

Then everything settled down. I got up from the wheel well of the car, started to brush myself off. This is about eight or nine minutes of the black soot that was coming into my mouth and sticking to my tongue and my mouth and nose and eyes. I started to brush myself off and I heard this guy coughing in the trunk end of the same car. It was a fireman. He brushed himself off. He handed me some gauze for my mouth and we just stood there. We didn't say anything. We didn't say a word to each other. We just proceeded to walk, shuffle, very slowly toward Broadway. There was nobody. There was no cry of "Help." There was no cry of needing assistance.

We got to Nassau Street and it was really eerie. He said he had to find his company. We shook hands. We hugged. He told me to be safe and be careful. He went south and I went north back to St. Andrew's. When I arrived, the deacon of the church was at the step of the stairs outside the church. He came over and he just grabbed me, and he brought me upstairs to the nurses who were here from the FBI. A good friend of mine, actually, who works in the bureau, she looked at me and she was terrified. I didn't know what I looked like. I didn't know whether I was cut or bruised on part of my body because you couldn't see the reflection because of all the dust and soot. We talked for a little bit. She said, "Go up and take a shower." I took a shower and I took about twenty minutes getting all the gook—I looked like something from outer space.

Yes. Some of the firemen, I understand, dove under their fire trucks, but the firemen were hit by the concrete.

Yes, I know. I know. I know.

That could have happened to your black car, but didn't.

Yes. Yes. It didn't.

Miraculously.

Miraculously. After I showered I went back out over to Worth Street, which is about four blocks from here, where there was a triage center, and then also in Foley Square. Later in the afternoon I went back down to the site, back down to Ground Zero, and I saw the fire trucks that you're talking about and police cars right by Borders. It was like they were too close to the building and nobody expected it was going to come down and come down so fast.

What was going through your mind when you were under the vehicle and everything had turned black?

I just hoped I would get out alive. It was like, "Well, it's going to come down. Am I going to be all right? Am I going to be fine?" I'm a pretty tough guy. I mean, I'm short and wiry, but I'm pretty tough, and that scared the shit out of me. Excuse my French.

We're at day forty-four now. Are you still shaken up by this tragedy?

Yes. Not so much. The recurring image for me is looking over my shoulder and having the tower, a 110-story tower, fall right behind me. I feel that I've been blessed, that God, in many ways, had saved me. That's one of the reasons why, after that incident, I went back out and ministered to the sick. We were the first group—there was a deacon, myself, and a minister who also happens to be a marshal—we were able that day to get a driver from the marshal service. We went to all the different potential morgues and there were no bodies. There were no bodies.

The next day we got a ride from another group of marshals up to NYU and went into a refrigerated truck and blessed the first forty bodies. And a lot of body parts. The reason for the morgue, for me, was because of my experience dealing with registered sex offenders who mutilated people, victims, I have a pretty decent background in medicine. And I think there was an unconscious feeling for me that God spared me, that God did really save my life. I could, with my experience, give something back to God. I was in a position—every day since the eleventh to about the thirtieth of September—to go down to the morgue at Ground Zero and bless every single body, body part, body bag that came in.

I've read and heard others say that this horror is the personification of evil, but also, there was something good that came out of it. How would you describe the good that has occurred?

I think the good has occurred from the get-go of going down to that pile and seeing thousands of people, thousands of people, searching for a brother. Ironworkers, carpenters, firemen, policemen, everybody raced to that location. That is an unbelievable experience, to be part of that. I didn't even think about not going back there. It was like I was saved, I took care of what I had to take care of, I changed, and I went right back out, rather than just staying in the rectory and making sure the church was okay.

They say that over 90 percent of the firemen who were killed were Roman Catholic.

Yes, sir.

And something like 85 percent of the police officers. So, in a sense, you were ministering to the injured and to the dead who were part of your faith, at least some of them. There were many thousands of others who were in the building who we have no idea what their faiths were.

Theologically, it might not have been the appropriate thing to do, but it was the right thing to do, to bless the body parts. The morgue was in such a frenzy because people would bring the body bag in, they would put it on a table, they would unzip it, we would bless the body part, they would go through the preliminary identification, zip the bag back up, and put it into a refrigerated truck. I think some of the horror of what human beings could ever do to somebody else—when you see a hand and nothing else, when you see two heads severed and nothing else. It's from the evil act. You're watching all of these people walk that pile and bless it. I think what this attack brought out is the real pinnacle of the human spirit, the highest point of a human being, a stranger, reaching out and helping another human being. And I think that's one of the Christian dictums, to lay down one's life for one's friend.

And in this case, I think, New Yorkers laid down their life for a stranger, somebody they didn't know. They knew their first name and that's it. Of all the things that people say about New Yorkers, I think that's really the core of what it means to be a human being and what it means to be a New Yorker.

I understand that there was great reverence and dignity and ceremony when a body part or a body was found by the firemen or by the policemen. Can you describe that?

Okay. Particularly with the firemen, they call each other "Brother." I witnessed that at the site. They would bring their brother in. There are some unwritten laws here that I soon learned, that they brought the body bag in and they were all there when the body bag was opened. They all took off their hats when their brother was blessed. Then the ME [medical examiner] would go through the identification process, very, very slowly. Then, after the identification is made and noted, the body bag was zipped up and the same firemen would bring their brother to their own ambulance. They didn't want anybody else's ambulance but their own [fire] house. They call them, I think, buses. They would stand there and they would wait and wait until the ambulance came. Then the person who would be opening up the bus, he would just yell, "Attention!" And everyone would take off their hat, a silent moment, salute, and then the bus would go and the firemen would go back out. Tremendous courage.

APRIL 2, 2003

[*Father Hayes has been a priest at St. Andrew's since 1988. He describes his work prior to 9/11.*]

Because I'm a therapist I did a lot of counseling. A lot of people from the police department, many people from the FBI came over. I think a lot of people thought that it was a safe place to be, because in any organization, be it the NYPD, the marshals, DEA, FBI, there's always going to be paper. There's always going to be a trail of paper following you. So if you see a therapist in-house there's going to be a report in your file. So you come over to Father Hayes, who's a therapist, get some therapy, move on with your life, deal with some issues, there's no paper. I was seeing forty clients a week.

So I did that for quite a long time. Was asked to do some debriefing after the first bombing of the Trade towers, debriefing of agents, supervisors. Mostly supervisors at that point, because of what they were seeing— body parts, rubble, tragedy. TWA Flight 800, that was extensive. I did a lot of debriefing of people. Many of the agents on-site at the crash had never seen a body part, and they had three hundred new agents come in, I think, two days before. They shipped every single one of them out to the crash site. So you can imagine the trauma of, "Dear Mom and Dad, my first assignment as an FBI agent in New York City is picking up what I think might be an elbow in the water."

How do you do that debriefing?

Telling them, first of all, that there's no recording, there're no notes taken, there're no judgments. Finding out who they are, what they did, what they saw, what it smelled like, how it's affected them, how it's affected their family. A lot of resistance, lot of resistance, because the basic question that you have to get to in this type of a session would be to find out what they took from the crash site. I believe every fireman, some police officers,

EMS not so much, but I think a lot of firemen, when they go to the site of a fire, they take something. It might be a little piece of wood, it might be a little rock, it might be part of a watch. It's a transitory object. It reminds them of that fire. So when TWA went down, one of the obvious questions I had to ask was, "What did you take?" Now, legally, that's pretty precarious because then you get the reaction, "I didn't take anything."

"Well, you have to take something. What did you take?"

"I didn't take anything. I'm a lawyer. I'm an FBI agent. I can't contaminate a crime scene."

"We're not talking about a crime scene. What did you take from the site?" And it was like pulling teeth until you finally got the answer. "I took this. Okay."

[I ask] what they do with it, where they keep it. Is there a ritual, is there like a little altar that they keep it in? Do they keep it in a box? It's all trying to help the person cope with seeing something that you, in the course of life, you're not expected to see and you're not prepared to see. It kind of hits you sideways.

You were mentioning before I turned on the recorder that you still think a lot about September 11. It is still with you?

Yes. November 1, I believe, was the last time I went down to the site. At that point this whole area was locked down. And I decided not to go down after November. I think it was the second [of November] because that was the day that most people who were at Ground Zero feared. It was the day that there was going to be a change from rescue to recovery. In other words, they weren't going to find any survivors. The rest of the work was going to be just picking up body parts.

I spent the first three weeks at Ground Zero every day for about ten to twelve hours a day, blessing body parts that were brought into the morgue at Ground Zero. That really does not bother me. What's been a recurring drama and trauma for me has been dealing with the part of the story that had become since then almost a daily wake-up. When we were down in front of the Millennium Hotel, this police officer had yelled, "The fuckin' building's coming down." I looked over my shoulder and I couldn't believe it. A 110-story building coming down right behind me. And we got the people in the ambulance and I froze. There was nowhere for me to go. The stuff was already coming down. The doors on the ambulance were closed. I looked around and simply saw a car like ten feet away, and dove under the car as the ash and the metal and glass came down. That's been part of the nightmare every day. I wake up almost every morning the past, I'd say a good year, I wake up in tears. It's almost like I am crying in my sleep, grieving, grieving over all the people whose only crime was showing up for work.

I had a very, very difficult time after November 2, because as I would be going to therapy, and I've been in therapy for many years—twice a week since September 11—I could not even look in that direction. I'd have to cross over Broadway and go to the West Side. Every time I would look at the lights and see the cranes and see that space, I would have to look the other way. It was almost like this nightmare and bad dream that I was part of, and I really grapple with that.

In my life, whenever there was something going on, there was always, like, a loose end. There was always something that I didn't do or thought I didn't finish. And that always for me was like a bugbear, the thing that just stuck out. And I came to realize that day, and the day after, and the first three weeks at Ground Zero, there were no loose ends, that we did well. We did very well. And that's very difficult for me to come to grips with because I'm always looking for the loose end, that we could have done something else, we could have done something different. And I think part of the reason of why I went to the morgue was like putting myself in that situation, rather than having somebody who had never seen a body part come on the scene and see this body part. They were very, very gruesome. I don't know if you've spoken to anybody else at any of those sites but the parts were gruesome.

I did not see one human body intact. I saw fingers, I saw hands, I saw a rock attached to a nose. I saw two heads together, hundreds of torsos.

Someone's intestines. I also saw a friend of mine from the bureau, John P. O'Neill. His body was part of the bodies that we dealt with. It was not so much the types of body parts—fingers, hands, legs, arms, noses, whatever—it was the amount. There seemed to be thousands of body parts, thousands of parts. All shapes, all sizes.

Interestingly enough, all the body parts were gray. So when they would come in we would be like, "It's gray. What is it? Is it a hand or finger?" Some of them are obvious. Some of them are like limbs, like a leg or a head.

Also there's no blood. There's a principle—I forget exactly what it is called—that if the human body is hit with a certain projectile at a certain velocity it automatically drains or evaporates all the blood. And you would think that in a crash site like that or a disaster there would be blood everywhere. There wasn't an ounce of blood. It was all gray lumps of flesh, cold, smelly.

What about this question, "What's next?" Is that on your mind?

I try to say to myself, "Okay. I am probably the luckiest man in God's green Earth from September 11. I did good work." But the other part of me says, "Okay, what's going to happen next? Are we going to be attacked again?" The whole object of terrorism is to make you crazy, make you terrified. In my case, I think the terrorists have succeeded because I'm thinking, "Okay, nuclear attack. What type of mask, what type of provisions do we have?"

What about your faith? Has 9/11 shaken you in some way?

In terms of my faith, I don't know. I know it's changed my homilies. The style is different. I'm more concerned about what's going on with people. I don't use the microphone. I walk back and forth in the aisle. Talk about fear that people have, fear that I have, fear of the war. Just trying to deal more on a feeling level. And maybe the bigger lesson perhaps that I've learned from this September 11 is to feel, to feel pain. Before September 11, I was trying to be somebody in control, trying to always make sure that everything was taken care of. And now I've learned that my own life is out of control. The end part of my life is out of my control. And I think what this September 11 has taught me is to really feel pain, feel pain of families.

How do you make sense of what happened on September 11?

Evil people doing evil things. People didn't have a chance. I remember speaking about this in one of the services over the year and I got this letter from some guy in the neighborhood. He was almost saying, "I heard your homily, and how could you dare say that these people are evil? How could you dare? We need reconciliation. We need compassion and forgiveness in our church, and how could you dare say that?" And he talked about just-war theory and all this crap. I didn't know how to respond. The only thing I could say to myself was, "I'll take you down to Ground Zero. That's evil. I'll take you down to the morgue. That's evil."

7.

Roberta Galler

Psychotherapist

Interviewed by Amy Starecheski

Roberta Galler was born in Chicago, Illinois, in 1936. At the age of ten she contracted polio and spent long periods of time in hospitals for surgery, as well as at the polio treatment center at Warm Springs, Georgia. Galler attended Northwestern University and began an MA degree at the University of Chicago. She left school to join the civil rights movement and work with the Student Nonviolent Coordinating Committee in Mississippi. Galler moved to New York in 1970. She was active in the anti–Vietnam War movement and later returned to school to become a psychotherapist. On September 11, 2001, Galler was at home in her Battery Park City apartment. Galler has post-polio syndrome and uses a motorized scooter.

MAY 17 AND JUNE 21, 2005

People will be listening to this interview forty or fifty years from now. If you could, just start out by telling us a little bit of your background, and how you got to be who and where you are today. Starting with your date and place of birth, that would be great.

I was born August 13, 1936, in Chicago, Illinois. My father was born in Russia, and my mother was born [here]. She was one of seven children; her family was from what was then Lithuania. Both parents grew up in Yiddish-speaking households, but were very [much] assimilated, and I grew up in an assimilated household. They were from lower-middle-class circumstances.

Did you grow up speaking any Yiddish?

I didn't. Although I could understand some Yiddish I didn't speak Yiddish at all. My parents' generation was very busy trying to become American. My grandparents were themselves poor but they took in many other people who were coming in after the war, and so we'd hear these veiled stories. I certainly remember through my childhood having nightmares about the Second World War, and nightmares about the Holocaust. I would have repetitive dreams of my parents taken off to concentration camps and me feeling like I shouldn't leave the house because if I'd stay there I could protect them. As I grew older and talked to a lot of my friends, it turns out we all had recurrent dreams like this. I mention this because some of that kind of imagery and dreams recurred during 9/11.

I know you got polio in 1946.

Well it was in the midst of a very huge epidemic. I had just turned ten years old. A very mundane little thing [happened]: I had gone to the store to buy what was then a glass of sour cream. It came in a little glass jar and I was running with this jar of sour cream. I tripped and I fell and I cut my knee on the glass that shattered. I think I had gotten a couple of stitches in my knee. I began to complain that my other leg was sore. They said it was because I was compensating for the sour cream incident, but in fact I was developing polio. I woke up one morning and I couldn't get out of bed. During the course of one day I had become paralyzed from head to toe. By the time I got to the hospital I was completely paralyzed.

[*Galler describes her experience of being sent to Warm Springs to recuperate.*]

The social scene was very startling at Warm Springs. It had been a place known for President [Franklin] Roosevelt's founding. He had died shortly before I had polio and so there was still a lot of the staff that was there. There were a couple of very significant incidents. One is that when I was applying to go to Warm Springs, my doctor—in writing the application letter for the sponsorship from the March of Dimes—refused to write a letter for me. He said he had written his quota for Jewish patients to go to Warm Springs. [So] I went to Warm Springs without the funding that my family really needed for me to go there. So I didn't have the modern equipment of an aluminum wheelchair. I had the old-fashioned, wooden one and felt the sense of being poor because I didn't have the equipment that other people had. The other thing was, although I was not such a practicing young Jewish person, I was among mostly young, white Christian girls in my room who had never met anybody Jewish before. I arrived with what was then in fashion, a Ouija board, and was regarded as a bit of a "Jewish witch." With some social consciousness— I'm not even sure where it came from—I was acutely aware that even in the land of Roosevelt there was no professional black staff. The only black people who were around were the servant class who did the laundry. Raising this question, even as a kid, was scandalous. I was a northerner raising these questions. I was Jewish, and I was in a wooden wheelchair as opposed to an aluminum wheelchair, and so I was a bit of an outsider.

And then less than ten years later as a young woman in college you found yourself very deeply involved with the civil rights movement. Could you speak about that?

Well, again, it was somewhat related to both disability and being Jewish. When I first went to college, to Northwestern, I told them that I was disabled and therefore I needed accommodation. When I arrived, I was told I had been assigned to a third-floor walk-up room. So I said I could not take that room in the dormitory they had assigned me. And then they were in a great quandary because they didn't have any "Jewish rooms" on the first floor. Therefore I was put into a wing that was all young Christian girls who were sorority girls. In putting me in the room they also had to change the roommate to make sure that I had a Jewish roommate. That room became "the Jewish room" in that wing. Next year it was assigned to other Jewish students. Now, there were very few black students at Northwestern, and there were [also] designated "black rooms." This was the height of McCarthyism, and so to be involved politically at all was already looked upon askance and to be involved in interracial politics put you into scrutiny. I had gotten a very big scholarship to go to Northwestern and I had not quite realized what a conservative place I had wound up in.

And so I fled to the University of Chicago, which was an atmosphere that was much more welcoming of me and my politics. But I left behind the big scholarship I had. I became more involved politically, although it was still the height of McCarthyism. And during that time and right afterward I began to work for something called *New University Thought*. The *New University Thought* was a kind of chronicle of the developing student movement, affectionately referred to by its initials, the NUT House. I got very involved in SNCC [Student Nonviolent Coordinating Committee].

I did not finish [college] during that time and instead became a full-time activist, went south and worked there for many years.

I know that you're a psychotherapist today. How did you make that transition from the work that you were doing then to what you do now?

Well, in some ways I always was a therapist, so it was finding a role which I was already very well suited to. I mean, I was an activist and I was an organizer, but there were many ways in which, without recognizing it, I was also a healer. And other people told me that in terms of the role that I played in many ways.

How long have you lived in New York City?

I've been here for more than thirty years. I came because I was drafted to come. When I was in Mississippi, I had worked with the lawyers who were doing [voting rights work] for Mississippi, and who then formed, in New York, the Center for Constitutional Rights. I became a coordinator for the Center for Constitutional Rights because I had played a role in Mississippi in coordinating lawyers.

And then it was here that you got your psychoanalytic training?

Right.

And you were living in [Greenwich] Village?

Right. I moved to Battery Park City primarily because my disability was worse. I really needed to use a scooter by that point, but I couldn't because I lived in an inaccessible building that had three steps up. So I moved to Battery Park City because of its accessible terrain [and because] the building was accessible. I had applied for years to accessible buildings that were not hugely expensive and that were subsidized, and had been lucky enough to get this apartment. I had just gotten a scooter not long before 9/11. I live literally in the shadows of the World Trade Center. Had the building not fallen straight down it would have fallen on this building and we would have been crushed. In fact, a good deal of the debris did fall this far and filled up the courtyard and floated through the air and into the windows.

At the time that it was initially hit I was in bed. It was in the morning. I heard the planes roar overhead. It was very low, and it sounded like the loudest sonic boom I've ever heard. And the building literally rocked on its foundation. I had the television on so I could see what initially happened. Like everyone, I thought the first hit was an accident. But I could see the flames pouring out of the top of the World Trade Center from my bedroom window. It never occurred to me to leave my building or to go out into the disaster. The sky was extraordinarily blue but then it became extraordinarily dark. After the second plane hit, I began getting calls from around the country, because people knew how close I lived to the World Trade Center. It still didn't occur to me to get dressed to leave. I just felt I should just stay put. When the sky became filled with the pulverized World Trade Center my associations were almost immediately of Hiroshima. It just looked like snow was falling, like Hiroshima. After all, I had grown up with those kinds of horrors, and those were my wartime associations to what was happening now.

Then, suddenly, they were pounding on our doors saying that we had to evacuate. I was not dressed and it takes me time to move around. Fortunately I had had the scooter all charged up the night before because I was going to the World Trade Center that day to have my hair cut. But I never do anything early in the morning. So I would not have been there at that hour. So as quickly as I could—it was very hard to move quickly—I dressed. Assuming that I'd be back there a little bit later I grabbed only some money, my medication and the clothes that I had on my body. The people in the building kept asking if they could help me, which they really couldn't. They kept the electricity going long enough so that I could get down on the scooter. At first we were just harbored downstairs, as if in a shelter, and then we realized we had to go outside because they were going to shut down the electricity, the water, and everything in the building. We had to evacuate.

When I went outside, I could barely breathe and the air was filled with the debris falling. I'm glad my mind didn't allow me to recognize what I was seeing. I realized only later that what I was seeing falling from the World Trade Center were bodies. But my mind didn't allow me to register the fact that I was seeing bodies. I just thought it was debris. I wasn't close enough to fully see that it was, but close enough that I might have known, and my mind just didn't let me know what I was seeing or the impact of what was happening. I still thought I would be shortly coming home.

There was a volunteer who came out of nowhere who quickly got me. I told him I had to get some sort of mask or something. I couldn't breathe. I'm also a diabetic and I had taken my medication but I couldn't take my medication without eating something. So one of the building handymen ran back into the already evacuated building, came up to my apartment, and found some bananas and water on my counter. He was one of my Good Samaritans that day because he also was the same one who had gotten me out of the elevator in the first place. And then I was met by another volunteer who got me a mask. But I couldn't get out of the area because, by then, the building was surrounded by emergency vehicles and ambulances. The ramps were closed and blocked off so I couldn't leave with my scooter. So he had to go out and get the ambulances to move and he helped me get down to the esplanade. Now, I had never driven in the city in the scooter. I had never crossed even over a street. I had just been in this immediate area. I was a new scooter rider. There was no particular assistance for anybody who was disabled, other than the Good Samaritans who had helped me get out of the building. When I went out onto the esplanade, which was running alongside the West Side Highway, I had a full view of the complete collapse of the World Trade Center. It was hard to comprehend the enormity of what I was seeing right before my eyes. A few of us gathered around a van which had a radio, so we were beginning to hear the news of the plane going into the Pentagon and more of what the damage was here.

Were you with people that you knew?

I was alone with thousands of strangers, and mostly the strangers were fleeing and moving away. I still thought that I was going to be able to come back home. And I didn't know where to go. So I stayed by the highway for hours, and I ran into another person who was diabetic who hadn't taken her medication, and some of the medication was the same as mine. I wound up giving some of my medication to her. She had left in the morning without having taken her medication yet. She had just gone out for a walk.

There were many dramas going on that day of course, but on that esplanade people were fleeing. Some were going toward the disaster and weren't being allowed back in. There were people who were rushing back trying to find their elderly parents left behind in the apartments. There were people who were rushing back from work trying to find their children who they had left in school. There were people going in the other direction, carrying babies and infants in diapers and things. It was all strangely, eerily silent. There was no hysteria. There was a lot of cooperation. Most people's cell phones weren't working. There was one man whose cell phone was working so he was trying to help a number of other people to be in contact with people. People of course were there, looking at the building, having family members who were in the towers, not knowing who had been killed, who hadn't been killed, what had happened.

And I stayed. I began to be confronted with some of the issues very keenly around disability. Not only was I afraid to drive anywhere. I didn't know where to go. And since I had only been out of the area once on my scooter, I went like a homing pigeon to my old apartment in the Village, because I knew if I could find somebody there I could find an accessible bathroom. There were very many rookie cops out because they had been quickly assigned. There was one place where I knew there was an accessible bathroom but they had commandeered the building to become an emergency vehicle place and so they wouldn't let me or anybody else in. So I became preoccupied with very practical things like how was I going to get anywhere? Where was I going to be able to sleep? Where could I go to the bathroom? So I found a working pay phone and I called a friend who had lived in the Village and lived in an accessible building. I wound up sleeping in her apartment for a month. I could not get on and off of her couch, so she and her partner wound up giving me their bedroom. Their bathroom however was a problem for me. I was not able to bathe, not able to get in and out.

When I first arrived there, there were a number of us who were refugees from down here. We were all in a traumatized state. And that's when I had first had the experience of lying quietly in bed. Lying in bed, very quietly, having associations of feeling like I was in a hospital. Part of it, for some time, was the experience of feeling that I had suddenly become paralyzed. It was as if my whole life had become paralyzed, and I could not move. I couldn't go anywhere. And within the first couple of days I had a very uncanny experience, [although] I don't believe in this sort of thing. It was within the first day or two that I was there. Everybody else in the house was already asleep. I was not asleep but I had the experience of my dead father, who had been dead for thirty years, standing in the bedroom saying to me, "I'm so glad I found you." He said, "We knew what happened and I just had to be sure that you were all right." I wasn't asleep. It wasn't a dream; it was just an experience. Whether I believe in it or not, it happened to me. And there he was.

Then I began to have many associations to the past. Not just to the past of about Hiroshima, although we kept hearing about the air quality here. There was no certainty that I was ever going to be able to go back home. And it had been years until I had finally found a place that was accessible. Now it was really questionable as to whether this was going to be habitable and whether I could ever get back home. There was this longing to go back home, which then I realized was the same kind of longing that

I had as a kid, when I was hospitalized with polio and was longing to go home. Because I couldn't bathe and do the ordinary things, and have grab bars where I needed them. And not being able to survive in ways that I was used to by bathing my legs, my legs began to sort of scream with pain. Then they became silent. They were no longer screaming with pain. I thought they had just gotten used to being in pain. Then I realized that my legs were depressed. I began to massage them, and calm them, and tell them I hadn't forgotten them, and I would take care of them.

A lot of my associations were as if my legs had gotten killed in the World Trade Center. Now I'm very glad that I didn't get blown up to bits. I could easily have [been killed] had I been there for my haircut, had I been there closer, had the building, in fact, tipped over. I'm grateful that I didn't get killed. But I'm in mourning for the loss of my own functions. There are lots of us who became, while not literally injured on the spot, increasingly disabled physically, as well as emotionally and financially. I was not able to work. I wound up moving to and sleeping in my office for almost two months, because I couldn't return home because of many logistical nightmares. It was not possible to return to Battery Park City for anyone who was disabled. So there are many hidden and permanent ways that people have been impacted by the World Trade Center. It was extraordinarily frustrating for people who are disabled. Even the agencies were frustrated to realize how hard it was. I couldn't get to the Red Cross centers. FEMA was in great disarray and was initially not equipped to handle people who were disabled. Initially my case was closed because I couldn't comply with requirements to come back to a place which I couldn't get back to because I was disabled. There were many horror stories, much worse than mine, of people being left behind in evacuated buildings. Now because of this disaster and the help of organizations like the Center for Independence for the Disabled, agencies have begun to be aware of how ill-prepared they were to handle the disaster needs of people who are disabled, much less the continued need of many of us who became far more disabled because of this.

Could you tell me about some examples of other people you know who are disabled and their experiences around September 11?

Well, the woman who is now my upstairs neighbor, but lived in a different apartment [building], had emphysema and was on oxygen. You can imagine what the air contamination was like down here for her. Fortunately workmen carried her down the stairs and she was moved immediately into a hospital because she could not breathe down here. It was a long period of time before she could return. They relocated her into an apartment of a woman who lived upstairs from me. She had this apartment because she was disabled. She was relocated into a nursing home because of the stress, and she died. And while it was not regarded as a casualty of the World Trade Center, it certainly was. Her disability was certainly highly exacerbated.

Another man who I knew had a progressive neurological disease. He didn't leave on his scooter. He attempted to walk and really was unable to. So he and his wife returned to the apartment. They were immediately overlooking the World Trade Center. Even though the electricity was off, they stayed in the apartment for some time until they turned on the electricity to allow them to get out. He realized there was no way, physically, he could mount himself onto one of the [rescue] boats that pulled up on the esplanade. Ultimately the police did help him. At that point, I discovered the police don't have any vans with lifts for scooters to be able to transport you.

The [city] transportation [for the disabled], Access-A-Ride, was highly impacted by the disaster. So the disabled and displaced were often stranded. They had left behind their equipment. Access-A-Ride said they weren't an emergency service. People couldn't be transported without their equipment and nobody could get their equipment to them so they were just stuck. There were people who were left who were dependent on having home attendants come and help them dress and help them bathe, or having food delivered to them, and those services were just completely disrupted. We were like a hidden population. The Red Cross said they didn't understand how we lived in this city in the first place. They could not believe the lack of facilities and transportation, much less emergency services for us. They could not find me an accessible place to stay. They would have paid for me to be in a hotel but they couldn't find a hotel in which I could also bathe and get into with my scooter. They were astonished at the lack of coordinated facilities. They kept saying, "Well, move to my town. We have these things." They just couldn't believe how hard, under ordinary, normal circumstances, it was to navigate life here.

By the way, the man who I described who had the neurological disease has also since died. He did have a progressive disease but it was highly accelerated by the stress of this. These aren't even within the statistics of the impact of our disability on the World Trade Center disaster.

Could you describe for me your daily routines when you were living in your office?

It was very hard in my office because I did not realize that my officemate began very early in the morning. I mean, very early, like six thirty in the morning. She saw people before they went to work. So I had to lie in the room very quietly. Again this quiet, still person, as if I'm in the hospital. So I'd pretend not to be there because I couldn't be trampling around in various states of clothes. She didn't want her patients to be aware of the fact that I was also living there. It was very isolating being there. It had been helpful to be with friends—it was difficult to be there. Then the bathing I'd have to do either before or after she left, in the bathroom in between patients, so as not to appear to be living there. I did get a bed. The Red Cross helped me pay for a bed and I did get a bed installed there. Ultimately, through connections with a patient, I got some grab bars installed in the bathroom. But it was very stressful and it no longer felt like my workplace. It felt like either a hospital or jail.

The Red Cross kept visiting me there with great frustration because we could not figure out how I was going to be able to come back home.

The danger was once I got here I wouldn't be able to leave because of it being locked down. This was regarded as a crime scene and we were treated as if we were the criminals. It was very hard to live here. When I got here I was so exhausted that I just slept endlessly, and then when I got here the smells were still very intense, and that's when I still had the strong associations to the crematoriums. It really was like an acrid smell of death, and I thought, "Do I really want to live in a cemetery?"

How has your condition changed since the time prior to 9/11?

Well, I used to be, with difficulty, among the "walking disabled." And I am no longer. Not only do I need to use the scooter outside increasingly, I need to use the scooter all the time indoors. I've always thought of myself as a very resilient person and it's like I ran out of my resilience. As a therapist, I have seen the impact on my patients. But I've also always been the one, despite my disability, who was in more of a helping position in relationship to other people. So it was hard for me to ask for, and get, and utilize the kind of help that I need myself. I am in a dramatically different situation. My life, in many ways, has become much narrower because I can't get around in the ways that I used to. But also, quite honestly, because I'm left with a residual amount of fear that the earth is not steady under my feet.

It [9/11] has accelerated my fears of doing certain things where I know that I feel endangered. For the adventuresome person that I was, I am a more fearful person now, physically. I do feel as if my life has been transformed and as if my legs did die in the World Trade Center. I am in mourning for the lost functions of my own body. And it feels like it was a very significant turning point.

Have you accessed any professional mental health services?

I tried, and the Red Cross would pay for it. But, frankly, it's very hard when you're a very experienced therapist yourself. A few people came that were somewhat intimidated by the fact that I was a more experienced therapist than they were. Also, it's not so easy to get very experienced people to come to your home. While I still have the credentials to be able to get it, and I've been authorized to, I haven't found someone to get here.

But, very quickly, people were resilient in many ways, even in small ways. The people who keep the grounds here are mostly women. They were out here washing every plant, every leaf, tenderly, because everything was covered in the grime of the World Trade Center. And there were small things that would begin to return. If kids could play in the playground there would practically be an announcement in local papers. It was like the slow restoration of life. Of course, the families of those who had been killed were constantly being trooped through here. And people who were visiting. There was a great and constant state of mourning, as well as a constant attempt at revival. And a lot of healing that's necessary, including, as I've said, the healing of the healers. What I mean is—those of us who are healers of other people were also very injured.

8.

Brian Conley

Artist

Interviewed by Melanie Shorin

Brian Conley, an artist who works across media, was formerly based in lower Manhattan. Conley was born in 1951 in Chicago, Illinois, and grew up in Westchester County, New York, and Washington, DC. He earned a BA at State University of New York, Binghamton, and an MFA and a PhD in philosophy at the University of Minnesota. Conley is founding co-editor of Cabinet *magazine, an international art and culture quarterly. He is a professor at the California College of the Arts and lives in San Francisco. On September 11, 2001, Conley was at his home in lower Manhattan.*

FEBRUARY 5, 2002

Before September 11, I lived below TriBeCa [Triangle Below Canal Street], on West Broadway, about two and a half blocks from the World Trade Center. I'd been there for about five or six years, and I had a studio on the same block as well. It was the base of all my activities. It was both home and workplace. I knew lots of people in that neighborhood, both artists and store owners, and some of them became friends.

Your art pre–September 11—did it have a political bent at all?

I've always felt that art making is a public activity. I think that an artist is a spokesperson of a sort. To address personal concerns is only interesting if there's a public dimension to it. Otherwise, it remains locked within subjectivity, and that doesn't interest me. A lot of my recent work has concerned communal acts of violence and socially sanctioned acts of violence.

Art making is so interesting because you're dealing with a physical medium, and you try to invest it with complicated feelings and ideas. There are no rules for how to do it. It's a fascinating process, especially if you've done something like philosophy, which is so language-based. I mean, how do you bring ideas fully formed into a material substance and have it speak with even more clarity than one could speak of things in philosophy? That's why I moved into art. I thought that art could actually be more articulate than philosophical expression.

Before we move to September 11, is there anything that you want to tell me that you think is important to know about you, about New York pre–September 11?

Let me just say one thing briefly about the political concerns. I've had a great deal of trouble with American foreign policy ever since the Vietnam era, and I had a great deal of trouble with the [1990] Gulf War. I see a lot of the most recent U.S. political actions abroad as being about this country's attempt to maintain its corporate interests and to maintain this overabundant lifestyle in America. Because of this, we become involved with corrupt regimes and align ourselves with them. It creates havoc with our own political positions and other alliances. I saw the Gulf War as being part of that. First, we supported Saddam Hussein in his war with Iran because Iran took American hostages earlier. We did this despite the fact that we knew he used chemical weapons against the Kurds. Then we were attacking him to support the Kuwaitis? I don't think so. It really had to do with sustaining our oil interests in the region.

So I think we should move on to September 11. Tell me what you were doing that day.

We were in our place at West Broadway and Murray Street. I was asleep and my girlfriend happened to be up really early that morning. In my sleep I heard the jet coming over our building. The hijackers were actually gunning the engines and the sound was unbelievably strong. It was like being in the center of a tornado or something like that, or like a train engine roaring past. Then it hit the building and there was actually nothing more than a deep dull thud.

With that thud, my girlfriend looked out the window, and then she got me out of bed and said, "You've got to get up. You've got to see this." So I was up within two seconds and I looked out the window. We said, "Okay, we've got to go out on the street and get a better idea of what just happened here." There were all these papers flying everywhere and I could kind of see what happened. But it was just so unbelievable that I really needed to get a very clear idea of what I was looking at.

So we went down on the street. It looked just like a ticker tape parade. There were papers flying everywhere in the most gorgeous sunlight. It was warm, orange, with this really beautiful blue sky. It was the most lush lighting imaginable. Looking straight up the building, we could see the opening that was not perfectly in the shape of a plane, but pretty close. There were lots of people gathering on the street. The street became flooded with people—mothers with their children, and everything.

The event had an amazing, hypnotic effect on people. They were completely captured by the sight of this. People weren't screaming. In fact, there was an incredible silence. People were actually moving toward the building, looking in fascination. We were looking at it in horror. My girlfriend said, "This is a terrorist attack," and I said, "No, no, no, it's got to be an accident." She said, "No, this is a terrorist attack."

While we were on the street in front of our place, talking to some of our artist friends we know, that's when people started jumping out of the Trade Center. The area where the plane had gone in, there was now quite a bit of flame and smoke. Surrounding that opening were people coming out of the windows, hanging out, trying to breathe and figure out how to get out of there. Then slowly, one by one, people started jumping. Then quite a few started jumping, and people started jumping together. We could see it happening. My girlfriend eventually asked me to turn my eyes away. There were children on the street watching this, too, talking to their mothers, asking, "Why are people jumping out of the building? Mommy, look! Someone's jumping out of the building." It was really, really overwhelming.

There were all these people, including other artist friends of ours, pulling out cameras and taking pictures. We said, "This is very serious. I think you should consider getting out of the area." Our thought was that this whole area would be bombed. No one really responded so we started walking up West Broadway and got basically two blocks away. We were by this little elementary school that's across from the Borough of Manhattan Community College. As we're turning the corner, we look up, and then the second plane hit. A gigantic fireball that was just—I don't know how huge it was. It was almost like you couldn't see anything else—it came blasting toward us. It was so huge. I looked at that and had to make this calculation, "How fast is this fireball coming? Is there debris in advance of the fireball? Are there big sheets of metal and glass that are being pushed forward? Do we have to hit the ground?"

At that moment I said, "We just have to get out of here!" We thought that if we go to the East Side, there's City Hall over there and all those federal buildings. Those could be, would be targets. If we move in the middle of Manhattan, going up, say, Church Street, there could be other buildings that would be hit there. The Brooklyn Bridge, filled with fleeing people, would definitely be a target. We thought the safest thing would be to go up the West Side Highway where there are no buildings whatsoever. We started up the West Side Highway on foot, over by the water. There were lots of people going uptown on foot and people going downtown on bicycles. I remember clearly there was a family with little bicycle helmets on, the mother and the father and the children, riding toward the World Trade Center. So there was traffic going in both directions, which was really quite shocking.

Did you feel like you had to warn them or take any people with you?

There were way too many people going in both directions. There was no hope to stop the flow either way. The streets were filled with young business people with their cell phones and radios, and they seemed totally unfazed by the whole thing. Some were laughing. Some were just chatting as if nothing had happened. There were a few that were crying. There were some that were really disturbed but it was a minority at that point.

So we walked up to about the West Village. When we got there we decided we had to sit down. We were really exhausted. We had nothing with us. We just had our T-shirts and wallets and keys. We hadn't eaten at all. We were so disturbed and disoriented that we had to stop. So we found a tiny little café. We ordered food, which my girlfriend couldn't eat. I ate some of it. We were sitting there and the first tower collapses. There was the most amazing sound that came from the people on the street. There was this communal groan, this sigh of disbelief, this gasp of despair. It was almost like you could hear the city as a whole make this incredible sound of grief. At that point, we were so overwhelmed we could barely move. We continued to sit there. And then, trying to regain ourselves, the next tower came down, and the same thing happened. This time the sound was even louder and more visceral. It was like an animal in pain.

At that point, we decided to start moving again and try to get off of Manhattan. We heard that the only way to get off the island was a ferry near the Javits Center on the West Side. There was one ferry to get off the island. So we headed there, only to find an orderly line of about five thousand people, waiting one by one to get on. So we started talking to some of the police around the Javits Center to try to figure out another plan.

At that moment I happened to notice an individual who looked like he was of Arab descent, and he was taking photographs of all the police who were surrounding the Javits Center and all the entrances to the building. I said to myself, "Oh my god, that doesn't look right. He actually went past the police blockade to take photographs of the entrances to the Javits Center at a time like this." So I watched him, and eventually a policeman came up to him and said, "What are you doing? You've got to get on the other side of this barrier." And he said, "Oh, I'm just taking photographs. I'm a Christian. I'm a Christian." He pulls out a cross. Whatever he was doing, I found myself engaging in a form of racial profiling.

We waited on that line for about four and a half hours. When we got on our ferry, it went out into the water. We had a perfect view of the World Trade Center in flames and smoking, and this huge amount of dust and smoke going up in the air toward Brooklyn. For whatever reason, the ferry sat right in the middle of the river for probably forty-five minutes or an hour. We were rocking back and forth with all these people on this boat, watching the towers burn. It was such an overwhelming sight, and we were forced to witness it.

Eventually the boat started moving. We arrived at Hoboken. There were all of these policemen and people in uniforms who met the boat and said, "Anybody who was within ten blocks of the World Trade Center can get off first." We thought, "This is great!" It's a courtesy to people who were close and had to deal with this situation. About a third of the boat got off, including us. They took us and began to direct us into a series of parking garages that have been cordoned off.

We went through this labyrinthine network of parking garages, and then we finally came to a group of at least a thousand people who were being funneled one by one into another area. On the other side of the funneled line are a set of inflated tents with men with fire hoses and maybe a hundred or more people in medical outfits and masks. Everyone was asking, "What is this?" And they say, "Well, you need to be decontaminated." The group responded, "Decontaminated for what?" And they said, "We don't quite know. There was at least asbestos in these buildings, and there might have been biological agents."

We stood for the next hour and a half, waiting on this line. We eventually moved into the area where there were tents with shower systems. Men from the fire department hosed everybody down. They left us completely drenched with water. Then they fed us through this area where there are towels, and medical examiners who ask us if we were all right or if we were feeling sick. Eventually they let us out into the Hoboken terminal. At that point, we went into the terminal like refugees.

We took a train to upstate New York, where we have a small summer house. That was what we were aiming for. We knew we couldn't go back to our place in TriBeCa. That was hopeless. So this was the only other place where we knew we could stay for a while and that wasn't anywhere near New York City. A place to regain our senses and figure out what in God's name we're going to do at this point.

And did you feel the need to contact any relatives to tell them you were okay?

I got to a pay phone earlier in the day to tell my partner in the magazine, to call my mother and say we had survived the attack, and to call my daughter.

We finally arrived upstate at ten at night, thirteen hours from when we began. When we got into the house I called my mother immediately to tell her that we were okay. While I was telling her about what had happened, she kept dismissing everything I was saying. I said, "Hmm, this is very strange." She didn't seem very concerned that we were safe. She eventually says, "Did you hear about Karleton?" I said, "No. What are you talking about?" This whole time, we were worried about getting ourselves out of this situation and thinking about New York City and how we're going to get back to the city. It never occurred to me that there could be someone in my family that would be involved in this. She said that Karleton, my daughter Haven's husband, just happened to be on the first plane. He never really traveled, but in this case he was traveling for business. It turned out he was on [American Airlines] Flight 11, which I think was going to California.

He was living in Boston with Haven, and they had a child there, Jackson. He was working for Hancock Insurance. They were nicely set up in Boston, finally bought a little condominium. He was completely devoted to my daughter and to their family. The job and everything he was doing was all about coming home and spending time with them. He didn't really care about the job that much; it was a means to become a father and to have a family.

So he was on the first plane that went into the World Trade Center, Flight 11. I don't think there was a phone call from the plane, from him, to my daughter, so there's not much information on what happened. There were phone calls, I believe, from several people on the plane at the time and I think there was one by a woman to her husband. She was making the telephone call at the moment the plane was approaching the World Trade Center. She was saying that the plane had been taken over by these hijackers, and they were all being held hostage. From what I recall, it wasn't clear to her that they were going to die. It definitely was not clear that they, the terrorists, were going to take the plane into the World Trade Center. She was recounting, as I remember, that they were flying over New York, and then she was saying they were coming closer and closer to the city. I think she said she could see the World Trade Center, and all of a sudden she says, "Oh, no! Oh, no!" And then they clearly went right into the building. I think the individuals on the plane did not know what was going to take place until the last moment.

When your mother told you, you must have been totally blown away.

Yes. I tried to call Haven, but I couldn't get through. There was no way to talk to her. I sat out there, in the country, in this idyllic place, on the porch looking over rolling hills and a pond, trying to think about what had happened and finally realizing the fact that I was a witness to Karleton's death. When I first saw the opening in the building, in the shape of a plane, that was him being incinerated.

From that point on everything is a blur. I think that we left the next day or in the next couple of days or the next week and drove up to Boston. I saw my daughter at that point. That's the clearest memory. But it gets very confusing. I have to say from about that point on, I have a lot of memory loss. I've been incredibly unfocused and it's very difficult to be organized and do things. It's been really hard. I've forgotten a lot of what happened from then on. I went up to Boston, and there were a lot of Haven's friends there. She has an incredible community, so that's great. And then Karleton's parents were there. That was very difficult with them.

How old was he?

Karleton was thirty. I finally saw Haven, and there really wasn't much talking about anything, because there's nothing to talk about. The event occurred. It was totally irrevocable, and her life is changed permanently. There's just—I mean, it's even hard to think about the loss of Karleton, what that consists of and what that means. So there's nothing to think about. It's so unimaginable.

It turns out that my daughter is also pregnant with her second child. She found out, I think, one day before he took off on this trip. They had one night in which they celebrated the upcoming birth of their second child. The following morning he left and stepped onto that plane. That's part of what's going on now—just trying to make sure that my daughter is healthy psychologically and physically so that she can give birth to this child with no complications.

Do you go there a lot?

I'm trying. It's still hard because I have so many responsibilities in New York, but I'm going up and trying to spend about a third of my time in Boston. Just trying to get her comfortable—well, that's the wrong word, but trying to help her find a way of reconstructing her life. She wasn't working at the time. She was before Jackson. She studied social work and she was working at one of the Harvard hospitals as a counselor for dying cancer patients. She's a hospice counselor. She's the person who helps both the patient and the family come to terms with the death of this person, and what it means and how to go through it, how to think about it. So now she has to take this experience that she's had with so many other people, and now it applies to her. She's actually in a slightly fortunate position, in that colleagues of hers are counseling her on how to get through this.

Her mother was in Boston visiting at the time that all of this happened. Her mother is a nurse, who has worked in cancer wards with dying cancer patients as well. So she stayed up there for four months. She said she lost her job and lost her income.

And your grandchild?

My grandchild, Jackson, he actually seems pretty good. For a long time, I thought that he had actually forgotten his father. Then I think it was several weeks ago, he started talking about his father again, asking, where is he? Why isn't he back? That was really difficult for my daughter, trying to explain to this one-year-old child that his father is dead. How do you do it? But I think, at least for the time being, Jackson is all right and seems to be having the life of a child. Of course, in the future, this is all going to come up in multiple different ways. I hope I can play a role in trying to help him think about this, from all sides of it, from the individual trauma of losing your father to the political dimension of this, which is very complicated. I think it will take someone to talk to him and try to explain in some way, at different periods in his upbringing, how this happened.

Do you feel that for some people who weren't as closely involved, they're sort of feeling that life is going on? Does that bother you?

Well, yes. It's almost as if New York has this incredible rift in it. People below Fourteenth Street—many are still walking around like zombies— and above Fourteenth Street, they're still shopping and carrying on their lives as if nothing had happened. I think there's something wrong with that. I don't understand how people can be so disconnected. So there's that. And then the current political—all the war-making language in American politics and on the part of the American public. That's been very difficult to deal with too.

Where are you living now?

We are living in Williamsburg [Brooklyn]. We tried to get back into our Manhattan place to get some belongings, and the first time we could only get in for less than ten minutes. We needed to have a National Guard soldier with us to go in. We were told it is a crime scene. They combed the entire area, all the rooftops for evidence. There's paper evidence up there. There are parts of the planes on the roofs. There were body parts on the rooftops. The second plane, when it hit, you could see in the video footage. The jet engine blasts right through the World Trade Center: projectiles shooting through. It is a jet engine that went right down West Broadway, past where we had been standing, and ended up in front of a Laundromat that was five hundred feet north of us.

When we finally went into our building, we had to take masks because we'd heard that there was asbestos everywhere. So we wore huge asbestos masks that we bought. We were completely freaked out when we got there. There was no one in the neighborhood at all. It was deserted once we passed the military checkpoint. The World Trade Center was still smoking. There were klieg lights everywhere highlighting the burning/ smoking remains. When we went into our place I saw that I'd left my window open. The cloud that blasted the area after the towers collapsed sent debris inside our place and everything was covered with dust. There were papers from the two floors that were directly hit by the plane. Their papers were on my desk, burned, with family photos and business cards and everything, sitting on my desk. I couldn't believe it.

I went up on the roof. The roofs were completely loaded with dust and it was really deep. God, there were pictures of families that blew off of people's desks and little notes and résumés and all kinds of business stuff. The dust was so deep that after it rained a few times it collected into islands on the roof. I remember that it looked like a desert landscape, but punctuated with photos and business cards from people in the World Trade Center. I remember wondering how it is that this could look like the land where the hijackers came from, what cruel logic could make this possible.

What about your work? Where was it?

We went back and we could take practically nothing because we only had ten minutes in there. The military forced us out. We came back several weeks later and they let us stay an hour. We took a few things, whatever we thought was precious, which wasn't much—photographs and a couple of small things. They eventually let us come in for a longer period. We made an arrangement to spend some time and figure out what we were going to do. There were reports about what was in that dust at the time. They said that there was at least eleven thousand pounds of asbestos that blew down the block. I've done a lot of work with building materials and I know the hazards of asbestos, so I was really anxious about that. After talking to neighbors and going on the EPA site it was clear that there was lead everywhere. You could taste the lead, actually. Every time you pulled off your mask, you could taste this sweet residue on the top of your lip. And then, on the street, the fact that people were saying that the dust consisted of pulverized concrete, asbestos, lead, and also human remains made it really, really painful to be there. I felt I might be breathing in Karleton.

We started worrying about the health problems of being in that area. It became clear that the EPA didn't really know what was in that dust, or did and chose to not inform the public for political reasons. I thought, "I can't risk this. We can't move back here and find out several years from now that there was asbestos, lead, and maybe worse things." I eventually found a neighbor who had his place tested for PCBs [polychlorinated biphenyls], and they were everywhere, even on the ceiling. That's when I said, "Okay, we're going to take the necessary things out of our place and throw everything else out." I had a studio down the block and it was covered in dust as well. I also decided to give that place up.

How much of your work were you able to get out?

Very little. I threw out work that went back at least twenty years. I threw out about 90 percent of it, put it all out on the street. We put all our belongings out on the street too. We took up half of the block and covered it with couches, beds, chairs, clothing, our libraries, photographs, everything. We put it all out on the street. In our new place, we can still occasionally feel our lungs reacting to the dust. We're both totally allergic to it. Every now and then we open up something that has it on it and start coughing all over again.

And your landlords in the original two places—did they try and collect money from you?

Yes, he was a total nightmare. Our landlord—I don't know if he's a major New York landlord, but he's got quite a few buildings—fabulously rich, of course. I tried to sever my leases with him because I didn't want to move back in with all the dust. I didn't want to keep the studio, either, and I couldn't afford it. He kept trying to get as much money out of us as possible throughout this whole thing. I told him that my son-in-law had died and that we'd lost all our belongings. He would convert that conversation instantly to how much I owed him and that he's going to keep all my deposits. He wanted rent for September and October, even though the places were in a cordoned-off police zone. It was illegal for him to ask for rent. I could have taken him to court. I said, "You're boxing me into a horrible corner. Do you want me to take you to court so we can straighten this out?" He says, "If you take me to court, I'm going to sue you for the duration of both of these leases," which comes to around $200,000.

He just continued to threaten me. I was involved in a three- or four-week battle with him on the phone and in person. It was so dispiriting. I didn't have the energy, time, or money to fight him. I tried to negotiate with him but there was a moment where he was equating his financial loss with my loss of my home, studio belongings, and, ultimately, my daughter's husband. It was just too unbearable. I said, "Tell me what you want. Let me out of this nightmare. Whatever it is, just tell me." I walked out the door and then followed through with turning over the Red Cross aid money he asked for, and that was the end of it.

Have you been able to work?

No. I don't know what form it will eventually take, and I feel an obligation to let it sit in the deepest possible place and then see what that results in, whatever it might be. Actually, just up until a few weeks ago, I've spent every minute trying to deal with the emotional and financial fallout from 9/11. It's now almost five months but it's taken that long to deal with aid agencies, to go up to Boston to be with my daughter, to find a new place to live in New York, to get pots and pans and buy some clothes. It's taken the whole time. Finally things are changing and I'm beginning to deal with aspects of my life before this happened.

Over the last year and a half it's been a pretty difficult time dealing with all the consequences of September 11. Trying to find ways of helping my daughter and her kids, and my trying to get situated in the city again. Then, of course, the war in Iraq is hard to absorb—what it means, and imagining the consequences of what this country is doing.

Has 9/11 shown up in your art, in your work?

Since 9/11, my mind has been so scrambled I haven't really been able to make work. I did one project in Turin, Italy, however. The project did reflect September 11 and the death of my daughter's husband. It was a fictional flying vehicle. This flying vehicle has special capacities. It enables passengers and the vehicle to pass through any substance, whatsoever, un-harmed. The name of the vehicle is IVT-1, which stands for the Inter-mixture of Vacuity Transport One. The title is about the way the vehicle works, which comes from the writings of the first-century B.C. Roman poet Lucretius. He is credited as the first person to write descriptions and explanations of the physical universe.

I built it so that it looks like it came up through the floor into the exhibition space and begins to go through the wall. The vehicle stopped right at that point. It arcs from the floor into the corner of the wall. It has a sound track with it as well, which is a mix of insect vocalizations. The piece has an interesting concept but it really looks sort of flat, so I'm not sure how successful it was. But it was a response to thinking about Sep-tember 11. I was trying to think about how I could make something for Karleton to ride in, so that he could have—and all of the other passengers could have—gone right through the World Trade Center building rather than crashed into it.

Tell me about your daughter's life now.

Over the course of the last year and a half she went through a pretty serious depression that no one could snap her out of. She didn't show it that much but she would tell me about it. She had lots of friends around, and there were an incredible number of people who were taking care of her. It lasted for almost a year.

About five months ago she had their second child, Parker. That was amazing in many ways and really painful in others. The psychological pressure of bearing the child of her dead husband was really, really intense. She did get through that pretty well, nevertheless. I was with her the next morning and she seemed great, and really happy to have had the child. I think she was in a dialogue with Karleton in the back of her mind. Now she has two boys and she's doing pretty well. Her mother moved to Boston and has been living there for the last six months. That helped a lot.

Tell me about how often September 11 comes up in your life, internally.

Well, it's certainly in my mind every day. I went to Mexico City last week. That city was so jarring and overwhelming that I actually forgot about all of my concerns here for about five days. Then as the days went by and I was about to come back, I started having nightmares. During the day my conversations with people started turning back toward the war in Iraq, and then toward September 11 too. People are interested in what happened and I found that I can't stop myself from being extremely explicit about it. It all came back and my last night there people left the dinner incredibly depressed.

This war in Iraq though, it's worse than the nightmares—it's just triggered the worst kind of psychological response. All of the warnings about the city, and opening the paper and the full-page spread saying "Chlorine Attack" or "Dirty Bomb" or whatever it is. All the warnings that we've been getting over the last three or four months about imminent attack. With each one of those warnings I feel completely responsive and I feel all the fear that an attack, in fact, will happen again. We prepare for these things to happen—my girlfriend and I do. When Homeland Security is telling everybody to go out and get plastic sheeting and gaffer's tape to make an internal protective chamber, the threat level is red, and food and masks and all that stuff [we do it].

I took the last money I had at the moment and we went upstate in the car to Home Depot and the shopping mall and just filled it with food and water and plastic and all this stuff. And an ax. And this full range of supplies to prepare for this imminent attack. And we felt the anxiety that it really would happen. We actually bought an SUV that had special four-wheel drive so that it could climb over rubble and collapsed buildings. I still have this car.

My nightmare condition, it is triggered so quickly, the nightmare of remembering that day, and then thinking about my daughter, especially. And my girlfriend is even more susceptible than I am. It's been very hard on her, it's really jarred her emotional state. She's trying to complete a doctorate and it's really set her back. We've been spending lots of time just to comfort ourselves and give ourselves some sense of stability. It's completely messed up our efficiency and ability to focus on our work, and come up with creative and thoughtful ideas about what we are doing. I feel that a large part of my mind has been erased, and I don't know when it's going to come back.

It just hasn't been enough time [since 9/11]. I keep having these feelings that everything can evaporate into total chaos, to nothingness. Everything could just disappear. It's like a ghost that lives in your mind that comes to the foreground every now and then. And it's a really destructive thought, because it makes the things that you believe in, that you've worked on, seem not believable or not quite worth the effort because it all might dissolve. So that's been really difficult to shake. I don't know when it's going to go away.

Really the moments that I remember—nothing has been replaced. Nothing has happened to all that material, there's no poetic dimension, it hasn't become symbolic in any way.

9.

Mohammad Bilal-Mirza

Taxi Driver

Interviewed by Gerry Albarelli

Mohammad Bilal-Mirza was born in Pakistan and immigrated to the United States in 1984. He worked in construction and at a carpet factory before becoming a taxi and limousine driver in New York. Bilal-Mirza was forty-one years old in September 2001 and lived in Brooklyn, New York. Bilal-Mirza's uncle Mohammad Rafik Butt died in detention at age fifty-five in the Hudson County Correctional Center on October 23, 2001. ACLU president Nadine Strossen testified about the mysteries surrounding his death before Congressman John Conyers's Forum on National Security and the Constitution in 2002.

NOVEMBER 23, 2001, AND DECEMBER 30, 2002

I was born in Pakistan. I have been living in America since 1984. I'm a U.S. citizen for the last ten years. I was born in Salcutt, Pakistan, the state of Punjab.

What made you come here?

I just look for a better future. I had a dream to come in America and work in this country. I have heard so many times in Pakistan, my colleagues talking about America. My brother came over here for an education and he told me. I see his pictures of the World Trade Center, Statue of Liberty, these places. I have a dream to go to this place and look at that. When I came over here I married an American woman. For seven years, she is my wife. She went three times to Pakistan. And [after] seven years, we had an internal kind of problem, wife and husband, and I divorced her. After that, I decided to stay over here and work very hard in this country. I [am] a limo operator. The limo is my own, and I work there. I am very happy. Sometimes I work a little bit hard for my parents also.

What do you mean you work hard for your parents?

I send them some money over there, you know. My father ran a bar, and about forty years my father has retired, he's not working. Right now, my father is 101 years old and he's in wonderful health.

Your religious upbringing, what was that like?

Sunni Muslim. But I believe in all kinds of religion. All kinds of religion are respectable. In every single religion, people believe in God. There is only a little bit of difference [about] Prophet Muhammad. Muslim people believe in Jesus, too, and Catholic people believe in Muhammad prophet too. There are not big differences, you know. They respect all religions. All religions say that. Muslims respect every single religion. The four books, holy books: Koran, Injil, Bible, Tevrat, the four books are holy and we believe in all books.

Well, tell me where you were on September 11.

I sleeping, actually. I was working at night—driving three days a cab and part-time. My mother is here and I came home late in the morning, and I am sleeping. My wife wake up about ten and hears they have big news about World Trade Center. Somebody blew up the World Trade Center. I woke up right away. All the time I see World Trade Center. I am living on sixth floor. I just open the window and there is white kind of dust in the sky. After an hour, I take my car and go to the downtown area, near Smith Street. I go near by Battery Tunnel, and I can't stay over there even two minutes. There is a smell of burning and I can't breathe, and I close the window. I make a turn to come back home.

Everything is quiet and very sad. These towers, a million times I go and pick up so many people [there]. People talk to me very nicely. People working over there are wonderful. Every time I pick up at the World Trade Center, the people, Japanese, Italians, Irish, they are wonderful, nice people. And I see this blast on to the World Trade Center, I say, "Oh, God. So, how many people inside have died in this tower?" I have a very great sadness. How many innocent people killed?

Two days I sit in front of the television. I not go anywhere. After third day, I take my cab and try to work in Manhattan, voluntarily. I go and take the people to the hospitals and drop them at Staten Island, different locations, no money, no nothing. The Traffic Limousine Commission sent me a letter, volunteer. They take my license; they write down my number as a volunteer for people who come and give the blood to the Red Cross. My whole week I worked voluntarily. I am American citizen and I am proud to be a citizen in the United States.

This is about ten days. I just watch TV, ready to work. I have three boys. They are very little, and one is three years old, one is two, and one is nine months old. Hard for us to live with one month not working. But thank God for America. I always pray for America, you know. I came over here. People give us respect. I make money and I take care of my family.

About three or four times I stop by the hospital and I look at the pictures, who the people [are who] die over there. I cannot sleep. After two hours, I wake up. I feel shock over how many people were killed. Some people, I remember, whom I drop at different locations.

Do you remember some of the people whose pictures you saw that night?

You working about eight, nine years in Manhattan and you [drive] some people three, four times. I recognized two or three people in the hospital pictures and people I delivered to East Side of Manhattan and East End Avenue and York Avenue. I remember one of them, talking to me very nicely.

Tell me then what happened to your relative.

September 13, my other relative tell us—two of my uncles have been living in Queens with their roommates—and they ask me to go over there. They have neighbors who called [the authorities] and say that they are four people, Pakistani, live in this area. And FBI searching the people and looking for a connection with those who were involved this incident. FBI took them and I don't know where he is.

All four of them?

Right. Third day, his roommate call us. He is released, he had a green card, he call us. "Your uncle could be in Jersey City and he is in the jail," he says. [My uncle] had a heart attack in the jail and he died over there.

How old was he?

About fifty-five. He never said he had a heart problem. September 23, 2000, he came [to the United States]. He had a visa for five years and he overstayed about four or five months. My idea is eight or nine million peoples in this country are illegals. But September 11, the INS [Immigration and Naturalization Service] changed their policies for having illegals here, and they try to send them back to their country. Especially the people who are involved with Saudi Arabia and other countries. But I don't understand why the INS took lot of Pakistani people. The Pakistan government helped the United States government [fight] terrorism.

Tell me a little bit about your uncle. What did he do for a living? What was he like?

Four or five months he looked for a job and he didn't find that job. Anywhere he went, they looked for a young man. Finally, before September 11, at last he got a job in a restaurant in Queens as a helper. He was working there a few weeks, and September 13 FBI take him to keep him, I think, for three or four days to ask him questions. They didn't find out anything. He doesn't have any criminal record or anything. They returned him to the INS as illegal. The INS kept him in Jersey at some county [jail], and for one month he [couldn't] call his family. They tried to look for where he was. They couldn't find out which jail he is in, you know.

What did you do to try to find him?

I went to a lawyer and I request a lawyer to [help] him and go [to] the judge. The judge [orders him sent] to Pakistan. His family worried about that. His children worried about that. After [September] 25, I got the call from the Pakistan consulate. A man died in INS custody. His name is Mohammad Rafiq Butt. Then I called back again to the Pakistan consulate, and I speak with a representative over there. He confirmed the guy who died is in INS custody in New Jersey. His name is Mohammad Rafiq Butt. I say, "He's my uncle. Is it possible to look his dead body, to go and make sure he is him?"

I call Hudson County and I ask for the INS people. They gave me a number for the medical examiner. I called the medical examiner. He told me, "Mohammad Rafiq Butt, his dead body is over here, and they sent him to autopsy, and I did an autopsy already."

I ask him, "How is it legal for you to do autopsy, not going to wait for his relatives and other people to give you permission to do autopsy?" They tell me the cause of the death is a heart, his heart is weak. But I have a death certificate. They didn't write anything like that. They said that we have to do more studies to look for a cause of death.

Now, what did your uncle's roommate say about the way that—did he tell you anything about the way that he had been treated or your uncle was being treated?

They said he's okay. The second and third person come out; they say your uncle will be okay. The jail they keep him; they look for clue to [what happened] at the World Trade Center. But he was never involved. He didn't know. I have hope [that they will find] he didn't have any connection. And they definitely let him go. We have hope, you know.

Was he a very religious man? Was he in his appearance in some way Muslim?

No, no, no. Like, I am religious person, but I'm not that kind of fundamentalist, you know. I live in this country. I am like a smart Muslim. Religion is on the side. I respect human beings. My religion does not say that you kill anybody, you know. Muslim religion teaches peace, not killing people. These people [the terrorists] are a fundamentalist people. They have no education.

When the INS confirmed that [my uncle is dead], I ask for his dead body. I give him a shower, myself, me and my brother; the Muslim shower to the dead body in the funeral home. I looked at his body, and there are not any scratches. So many people tell us the INS is hitting people. I didn't find out anything.

So you washed him?

I washed him. Every Muslim person who dies, our religion is we give him, like, a shower and put him in new cotton—a white cloth and wrap him and put him in a box, you know. Then I send him, after two days, to his country.

I found that they put down natural death as the cause. INS didn't give him any pressure, but he was in the jail. I think he was deeply stressed, he didn't see his family for about twenty days; he couldn't call, and always he is thinking deeply in the jail. And possibly [that killed him], you know. This is what the doctor told me, other people told me, and I looked at his body. He has no [bruises], no nothing. He has a very clean body, nothing. So it is possible cause of death is heart attack.

Did you have a second doctor look or do an autopsy?

I suggested that to his family. His wife told me, "You send me the dead body."

I say, "Let me look for other people to talk to. Some legal people told me to keep the dead body for one week over here." And I made arrangements. His family [back home] every single day, every single minute, they cry and want me to send them his dead body. That's why we did not keep the dead body over here.

So you did not do the second autopsy?

No, no, no. If I had seen any [bruises or markings] on the dead body, could be possible I would keep it. But his body showed nothing like this.

But I asked questions of INS people. Do you provide any medical assistance [in jail]? Let us copy his medical record [showing], "Mohammad Rafiq Butt, he felt the pain in the jail, had a heart pain." Did they call any ambulance, anybody come over there to help him? If they help him, and if he has to die, that's okay. Everybody dies one day. But did you try to help the guy or not?

You don't have the medical records?

No. We don't have any medical record. I have only death certificate. The death certificate showed his death as having a heart attack. They just write on it, "We have to do further studies to look for the [cause of] death."

Do you feel that people, Americans, have been restrained in your experience since September 11, or have you felt any change in the way that other Americans treat you as a Pakistani?

No, no. Some people are mad. If anybody killed my family, I would be mad too. If a few peoples talked to me [angrily] I was just quiet. I didn't say anything. You know why? They have a big tragedy. They have pain. Like, two people jumped me on the nineteenth of September. I was walking on the street and two guys come up, and they ask me, "Where are you from?"

I say, "I'm from America."

He told me, "No, you tell me where you from!" He used bad words and he asked me, "Which country are you from? Where were you born?"

I said, "I'm from Pakistan."

He told me, "You are a terrorist."

I said, "My friend, I am not terrorist. I live in this country long time. I am American, and one day your father came from another country too. Go and ask your parents and grandparents. Everybody came to this country an immigrant, and I love this country. My kids were born over here. Now they are by birth American citizens. You talk to me the wrong way. I love this country the same as you do. I have sad feel same like you." They turn around to the car and go away.

How many times do you think people have asked you that question in the cab?

A million times. I pick up thirty people every day, and fifteen people ask me, "Where are you from?"

I said, "From Pakistan."

[One old man] yelled bad words. He said, "You are terrorist. You fucking Muslim. You this and that. You go back." Why did he say that?

When he opened the door I said, "God bless you. Thank you very much!"

He feel shame. He came back to me. He said, "I'm sorry, Gentleman." This is my way to beat him. If I use the same words, what's the difference between me and him? He is living over here in a very educated country. Civilized people live over here. I came from backward country, you know. I learn many things over here. This is the sea. When you swim in the sea, you learn many things.

10.

Yamira A. Munar

Office Assistant

Interviewed by Amy Starecheski

Yamira Munar was born in Brooklyn, New York, in 1978. She graduated from high school in 1996. Shortly after graduating, Munar began to work at Fidelity Investments, a firm two blocks from the World Trade Center. On the morning of September 11, she was rushing to run an errand before work. She was walking on Liberty Street, crossing south of the World Trade Center towers, when she heard the explosion.

FEBRUARY 1, 2002

I looked up and I saw red and orange fire and debris mixed in with the fire, very high up in the sky. I knew that there was something wrong with the World Trade. I thought that there was a bomb. I'm in the middle of the street, diagonally across the street from the World Trade. This is the first plane. I'm walking in a crowd and all of us just looked up. Finally, they start running. But imagine people running with nowhere to hide. They're running and nobody's screaming. Imagine that. That's the most frightening thing, at least to me, because that's to show how much of a shock you're in, when you're running, to not even know where you're going to run to, and nobody screaming.

So I started to run. Now me, I'm wearing those clogs, it's like a closed toe but open back. As I'm running, I fell. I guess I had twisted my left ankle. I tried to get back up because I knew the debris was falling now. Then that's when you heard people screaming. The debris began to fall on top of me. I was scared for my life. I'm like, okay, all these years I've heard of what death is. Nobody really knows what death is because they hear interviews here and there about what death is. You read in the Bible what death is—death is a deep sleep. You're not conscious. But I wasn't ready to die. That's what was scaring me. So as the debris is falling on top of me, I just covered my head, because I guess that was the first instinct. And I just kept on screaming, "God, you know my heart. God, you know my heart." Growing up in a Christian home, I knew that was the first name I had to call upon, the creator of the universe.

So I kept on saying, "Lord, you know my heart. You know my soul, Lord. If I die, please let me see your face." I kept on screaming. I was crying at this point, hysterical. And yes, the debris was landing on me. Big chunks of metal. I don't know if it was from the plane or the building itself, but I remember stuff falling on my back, like my rib cage area, my head. Some stuff fell on my arm. It pretty much fell all over my body. But one piece of metal I remember falling on me was right here on my thigh, and I still have a little shadow of the bruise there. It's amazing, after how many months now? Five months? But this big chunk of metal just landed on me. I can't remember the pain, because I didn't feel any physical pain. I think I was going through more of an emotional pain. I think that was far greater than the physical pain to me.

As the metal landed on top of me, I just pushed it off. It must have been the adrenaline or something, because that metal was huge. As I pushed it off of me, that's when I got up. I left my purse. I said, "I'm not even running back for my purse." And I had a lot of stuff in that purse too. So I began to run. As I'm running, I hear a lady in back of me screaming, "Somebody help me!" She's screaming at the top of her lungs, "Somebody help me!" I turned around, I believe I did see her, but I just turned away so fast and kept on running. It didn't register until later on that day that a lady was screaming for help and I did not run back. That's where the guilt came into me. I felt very guilty. I felt if this lady is dead it's because of me, because I couldn't help her.

But getting back to when I got up, I saw a *City Post* truck. I ran inside the truck for shelter. I saw people running everywhere. There were flames of fire, pieces of paper, flames of fire falling from the sky. So I'm still crying at this point, and I saw four ladies, and I guess they saw me run for shelter in the truck so they ran inside the truck too. We're huddled up against each other, holding arms and hands. We were praying to God, "God, please do something." And I kept on screaming. All of us kept on screaming, "God, remember our souls. God, remember our souls." I guess because I started it off they kept on saying it as well.

As we were praying, there was metal landing on top of the truck. I saw flames on the floor too. I'm screaming now, "We have to get out the truck. The truck can blow." So I ran inside Deutsche Bank, because that's where the *City Post* truck was. I ran inside.

I was already bleeding at this point but I really didn't feel any physical pain, other than my left ankle. I went to the courtesy phones. There were people already making phone calls, because at that point I couldn't use my cell phone. I called my mom but I got the voice mail. I let her know on the voice mail that the building was on fire, and that I'm here at Deutsche Bank. Then there was an announcement on the loudspeaker. There was a lady's voice saying, "Everybody has to evacuate the north end." She must have said it about four times with urgency in her voice. Once again, that freaked me out.

So my ankle was really hurting at this point. We had to walk up the escalator and as I got to the top I saw a security guard. She said, "You have to go to the ninth floor to triage so you can get cleaned up." Because I had blood all over me. I had blood from my head. My wrist was bleeding. She saw I was limping. She saw my knees were bleeding and she saw I was distraught. So she said, "You have to go to the ninth floor and get cleaned up." And hearing those saving words, hearing the word "help," I said, "Okay. I'm actually going to get help." And as I'm at the elevator banks, something told me, "Yamira, do not go up to the ninth floor." It wasn't audible but I felt it in my heart. And I kept on hearing that voice, "Do not go up to the ninth floor." So I went back downstairs and that's when I was able to call my mom. I said, "Mom, the World Trade Center is on fire." I was not calm when I spoke to my mom. She was trying to be very calm herself. She was trying to kind of soothe me but it didn't work. She's getting upset. Now, she's like, "Jammy, just get out of there. Just get out of there. Run for your life." And as she said that, I heard another explosion. I saw more people, running inside Deutsche Bank, screaming.

As I heard the other explosion, I said, "Mom, I have to go." As I ran outside, I saw people crying there. I saw a lot of people crying. I'm like, "Death. This is death right here." I started crying, and as I'm crying, I saw some stuff. I wasn't sure what it was, but then it dawned on me, this is people falling out of the window. And I saw some guy smoking a cigarette right where I was at. I said, "Excuse me, sir."

He's like, "Yes."

"Are those people?" I started stuttering and everything. "Are those people falling out of the window?"

"Yes. They're jumping. They're not falling out; they're jumping." And when he said that, that's when I broke. I'm seeing these people jump. Now I myself, I've been to the Twin Towers before, and I've looked down. I can't even imagine jumping from that height. So I just started crying, and I just ran from Liberty Street all the way to Bowling Green. It looks like I got the last number four train out to Flatbush, because after that everyone had to walk over the bridge.

I thank God I was not there to see the buildings fall. But that was also a devastating sight. The first thing I did when I came home, I put on the

TV. Then my mother called. We just cried on the phone. That's when it dawned on me, "Yes, God delivered me from death that day because I must have a purpose somewhere." It's a good thing to believe in God. It's really sad to say this, but in my life there's been many times where I've actually put God on the back burner. For instance, my boyfriend—I believe I put him before God. We broke up now and thank God we did. But when you look at things like [the attacks] and you see that you put God on the back burner, and then you see what he's done for you, it revolutionizes everything.

That day on 9/11, I believe that he saved me for a purpose. What that purpose is I have no idea but I know that he had his hand in it. Not to say that those that perished on 9/11 were evildoers and wicked people that did not believe in God. I'm sure there were a lot of people that believed in him that perished that day. But it's changed everything, and changed my outlook on everything. It changed my life because I came very close to death. I was scared to die, but then again I wasn't. It's really hard to explain, because I wasn't ready to die, because I don't know what to expect, but in a way I was ready to die because I know who I believed in. Know what I mean?

How could something like this happen? In a way it doesn't make sense, but everyone has to come up with some explanation to make it make sense for themselves.

You know what? To me it doesn't make sense. But then again it does make sense, because knowing what I know, and I guess reading the Bible, getting my knowledge from that—we're in end times. And nobody could deny that. They think that that's bad? There's a lot worse to come. You know, there's a lot worse to come. I mean, watching the news before you came here to interview me—I'm watching CNN and they have a new tape out from Osama bin Laden. He's talking about how "the terror's going to begin in America. If they kill our children, we will kill their children. If it is according to God's Will." Can you believe he is using the Lord's name in all of this terror? So, I mean, this is definitely the beginning of the end. Has to be. America is being humbled in the dust. That's what I see it to be.

I'm not righteous or whatever, but I am just really looking forward to Jesus Christ coming. That's what I'm really looking forward to at this point. Because there's nothing else to look forward to here on this Earth, because it's a wicked world that we live in. Satan is just out on a rampage, trying to stump everybody's spiritual growth just so he could bring them down with him. But if anyone hears this interview, I have to say, "You guys just stay strong. Lot of hard times are coming, but you have to say that with Christ you can endure those times." You can't endure by your-self, because you'll go crazy. You'll go really crazy. But, yes, those times are coming.

How has it changed your life, having the knowledge that this is the beginning of the end?

I guess it took a few months for me to realize it, but even though we live in the wicked world, I have to say this event has caused me to actually ap-preciate life all the more. It is because I'm able to fix things in my life that need fixing. I'm able to tell my parents and my family and friends I love them. There's not one day that I go without telling my family and friends that I love them. My friends think I'm going crazy. Like if I tell my friend Robert, "I love you," he'll look at me like, "You're a psycho." [Laughs] Like, "What is wrong with you? You haven't said that before." But you know what? It's important to tell people that you love them, because what if that day never comes where you had the opportunity to say it but you never do?

You're going to be going to veterinary school in Tennessee in May. When did you make that decision?

It's not really veterinary school. It's a four-year college. But I'm say-ing I want to do veterinary science because I love animals. I'm actually rethinking that too. I'm thinking about majoring in theology, which I love. Not because of 9/11—I guess it plays a part. Like, last year they had a program at Southern [Adventist] University. It's called Smart Start. I took a theology course there called Life and Teachings of Jesus Christ and I really found a deep interest in that.

How else has your life changed since September 11?

It's going to really sound weird right now, but I have to say I'm a happier person. It sounds weird because of the events of 9/11. But before 9/11 I was very depressed. I could not find my purpose in life. Going to the same old nine-to-five job, feeling unappreciated, not going to school yet, not having a degree at my age. But now I look at it like there's a reason for everything, and you can't rush it. A lot of people rushed to work that day and didn't make it back out. So I guess sometimes it pays to be late.

Do you feel differently about New York now? I mean this is your home. You lived your whole life here.

Yes. Even though I was born and raised here and I have a lot of friends here, I have no desire whatsoever to be here in New York anymore. When I leave, I will miss my family and my friends. I feel New York is like another Babylon right now, and I feel it has nothing to offer me. I have nothing to offer it. And it's time for me to go.

I feel everything is changing very drastically. It's important that we take heed and understand what's happening in our world so that we [may] be prepared for more things to come. Not so much bad, but all for the good. We have to prepare ourselves, daily, and we have to know that the battle is not ours but it's the Lord's. This is what we have to constantly remember, because it is truth.

11.

Debbie [Dhaba] Almontaser

Conflict Mediator, Educator

Interviewed by Gerry Albarelli

Debbie Almontaser was born in Yemen in the 1960s and moved to the United States when she was three. Her family settled in Buffalo, New York, where her father worked as a steelworker for Ford Motor Company. Almontaser is the oldest of eight siblings. She grew up in a Muslim family and learned Arabic as a young girl. She became a public school teacher and a specialist in literacy training. She was the founding principal of the Khalil Gibran International Academy and a co-founder of Brooklyn Bridges, the September 11 Curriculum Project, and We Are All Brooklyn. She is also a board member of the Dialogue Project, Brooklyn Borough President's New Diversity Task Force, Women in Islam, Muslim Consultative Network, and Saba: The Association of Yemeni Americans. In September 2001, Almontaser began teaching at Public School 261 in Brooklyn.

NOVEMBER 13, 2002, AND JUNE 24, 2005

So September 11 I was teaching fifth grade. It was actually the third day of school. It was this beautiful, sunny, blue-sky day. I remember looking up in the sky that day and saying, "God, what a beautiful day it is." That day, for some reason, [the students] were really wonderful. I finished reading [to them] and then I asked the kids to take out their independent reading books and read individually. As they were doing so, I got a knock on the door and it was a PTA parent who came over. She said, "I need to speak to you outside the classroom." It was very odd, because I didn't expect a parent to come up, and it wasn't one of the kids' parents. She said, "I just want to let you know that one of the World Trade Centers, one of the towers has just been hit by a plane. We have reason to believe it was an accident, but you just might start hearing sirens and what have you. Try not to let the kids go out to the bathroom. We really don't want kids to start panicking."

I was in shock. I went back into the room. I pulled myself together, continued with my day. About a half hour later, maybe even a little longer, the same parent came back again, and she said to me, "I just want you to know that the second tower was hit." And I was in total disbelief, like, "This can't be happening." She said, "We don't think it's an accident. There is an attack, and we don't know anything but we're waiting for the district to let us know what's happening, what we're going to do. Just keep the kids doing what they're doing. Don't let anybody out of the room."

At that moment, when she told me, my heart dropped. Even when I heard about the first one, I was like, "Oh God, please don't let this be a terrorist attack." And I don't know what was making me think along those lines. But then when she told me of the second one I had my suspicions, as everybody else did, that this was a terrorist attack, and I was very shook up. I don't know where and how I got the courage to keep calm and cool, and to keep going with my day. I was scared. I was also thinking about my family because my husband works in the city. My older son works in the city, and then my younger son goes to school in the city.

So, about ten thirty, the first parent from my class came and picked up her daughter. And she was in a panic, you know. She looked really hysterical. She wasn't crying or screaming but I calmed her down. I said, "I know what happened. I really need you to calm down. I don't want your daughter or the kids to see you in such a state. I don't want them to panic. I'm sure their families are going to come pick them up, but I don't want the kids to be afraid." Her daughter questioned. She's like, "Why are you picking me up?" And the parent couldn't really answer.

I said, "Your mom said you have an appointment that you have to go to. She forgot to tell you." And so she made her exit quietly. And then the second parent, and the third parent, and the fourth parent, and the fifth parent—the same scenario. And then the kids started to get suspicious.

Eventually, one of the kids asked to go to the bathroom. It was about eleven o'clock and I knew that this kid had to go. So he went to the bathroom and he saw the towers and the smoke. And he came back and what was really interesting about Steven was that he didn't scream to the kids about what he saw. He came over to me and whispered, "I just saw the Twin Towers aren't there anymore. I see a whole bunch of smoke outside, and everybody in the hall is running. What are we going to do?"

I said to him, "You're safe here and you don't have anything to worry about until your parents come. I really don't want you mentioning to the other kids what happened because I don't want them to get scared and start crying and screaming. What if someone wants to leave and they run out of the school and they end up being in more danger?" He was great about it. He didn't say anything to anybody.

Eventually, half of my class was gone, and the kids were like, "Debbie, why is half of the class gone and why do we keep hearing the PA system calling people to leave? And we're hearing sirens outside. Did something happen?" At that point I couldn't keep it from them. I asked all of them to go to the carpet. We formed a circle and I explained to them what had happened and how I found out, and the importance of not panicking, and remaining in our classroom was the safest thing for us to do, and just to understand that something has happened but we have to stick together as a class, as a school, as a community, to overcome this. The kids had so many questions, like, "Who did this? How did this happen? Why the Twin Towers?" I didn't know what to say to them. I was grappling with those questions myself at that moment.

So twelve o'clock came and it was time to go to lunch. The first thing I did was run into the office to call home. Of course, every phone in that office was off the hook. One of the secretaries said, "Your husband called and he left a message to tell you that they're okay." One of the Arabic parents came in, hysterical, crying. I walked her into the principal's office. I calmed her down, gave her water. Finally, she was able to tell me what happened. As she was walking toward the school, there were a group of parents who were out there talking about what had happened, and as she was approaching them, this tall man yelled out, "This is all happening because of you and where you come from," in a really loud and nasty voice. And she had no idea how to react to this, what to say, what to do. She was terrified to leave the building. She came to pick up her three kids, and she's like, "If I'm leaving alone, it's one thing. But if I'm leaving with three kids, I can't afford for anything to happen to my kids. Because if this man, who's a parent here, is reacting like this to me, how will strangers, complete strangers, who don't know me, how are they going to react to me and my kids?" So I didn't let her leave. Nobody knew what to do. I started calling people who lived in the community and said, "Please, I need somebody to come take this woman home. She's afraid to leave." So she finally got a ride.

After lunch I went down and I picked up my kids. They all lined up, and as we were walking, one of the kids said, "Debbie, Debbie, we know who did it. We know who did it."

I just turned around and looked at him, and I said, "Who?"

And he said, "It's those dumb Arabs. It's those dumb Arab terrorists who did this to us."

I said, "Really. How do you know it was Arabs?"

He said, "Because everybody's talking about it at lunch. Everybody's talking about it and that's what they were saying."

So we got into the classroom. I told them that we needed to have a really serious talk. We went to the carpet area. We sat in a circle and I said, "I was in the main office. I did not hear any of this news that you heard, that it was Arabs. Nobody knows exactly what happened but they do know it's not an accident. Now, who are the perpetrators? We really don't know yet."

The kids started saying, "Well, it's got to be those Arabs, because they always do this to us." And so we got into a conversation of how sometimes it's not good to speculate when you don't have enough information.

I said to them, "I know, guys, that we've only been in school for three days. But I could have sworn that at one point or another when we were sharing about ourselves that I had told you guys that I'm Arabic."

And the kids looked at me. [Laughs] And I remember Michael's jaw dropping, and he's like, "Debbie, I'm so sorry. But you wouldn't do that kind of stuff."

I said, "But do you think all other Arabs would do that kind of stuff?"

And they all looked at each other, and they're like, "Well, no. I don't think that everybody would do it."

I said, "Well, then I think we need to really talk about how would we phrase something when we want to say something. We don't generalize, where we don't make a whole society or a whole nationality pay for the price of a few people who'd done something really horrible."

One of the kids said, "Well, right now we really have no information whatsoever who did this. We do know that this was a terrorist act. We don't know the nationality. For all we know it could be somebody from Oklahoma, you know, just like the Oklahoma bombing. So I think we shouldn't put any nationality or any cultural ethnic background to this, and just leave it at that."

[*When it was time for Almontaser to go home, her husband and the school principal warned her not to travel alone. Rose, a teacher who lived nearby, gave her a ride.*]

We started driving the car, and ten minutes into the drive we had to stop for a traffic light. People were crossing and there was this man who looked into the car and saw me sitting there. That day I was wearing a baby-blue *hijab*. While we were waiting for the light, he was talking to other people standing there and pointing into the car at me. Just rambling on and on [saying] all these horrible things. I was just terrified. I said, "Rose, that man looks like he's going to come over to the car. What is he saying?"

She said, "Remain calm. The light is going to turn and we're going to move." Just sitting there, waiting for that light to turn, felt like an eternity. Luckily, the light turned and we drove off. Eventually I got to my house.

When I was sitting in the car, I was thinking about what was going to be the next measure for us as a country. I realized that the National Guard was going to be called in. They're going to need all these rescue folks. I was so terrified that I was going to get home and not find my son there. But I was like, "No, it's too soon. Why would they call him? And anyway, they'd probably call people who are much more experienced." So I remember getting to the door, opening it, and calling everybody by name. My daughter came down; my husband came down. My younger son had come home, and they were all three in front of me. I was like, "Where's Yusef?" Nobody said anything. They just kept quiet. My son and my daughter just walked back up into their rooms, and my husband said, "This morning he was pacing back and forth, watching TV. He was also calling his unit but he couldn't get through. Finally, he just couldn't take it anymore. He packed up all his stuff, put on his army suit, and he left."

I couldn't believe what my ears were hearing. I'm like, "What do you mean he left?"

He said, "He went to his unit."

I just remember collapsing onto my knees and he started comforting me. He was like, "Shortly after he left the call did come in, and I told them he was already on his way before them calling him." I remember that night just going upstairs. I made my prayers. I wouldn't even think about dinner. I don't even think I ate that day. We [turned on] the TV and were just glued to it. Then about five or six, the president of the school board called to speak to me. He was basically asking me, the following day, to come to meet with him and the superintendent and other people from the district, to strategize what they needed to do, being that the district had a large Arab and Muslim community. As he was explaining this to me, the superintendent just grabbed the phone and said, "I need you here, and I need you here tomorrow. We have no one else to turn to. You understand the community. You're highly respected in the community and we need to know how we can make everybody feel safe."

So I said, "Well, right now I'm trying to figure out how I can feel safe because when I came home this is what happened."

She said, "Don't worry. We'll arrange for a parking spot for you right next to the entrance. Come with your husband or whoever you want, but we really need your input."

So with that, and then just knowing that my son had left—we didn't hear from him that night; we didn't hear from him the following morning—it was very emotional for us. At that point I was crying at the drop of a hat.

We went that morning. The Department of Education declared that day as a day of no school. One of the things I had mentioned to her was that it was important that representatives from the Arab, Muslim, and South Asian communities in those schools go to the office and be there as a resource, as a friendly face, to translate or do whatever was possible for the families. The other thing was making the letter that she had written to the whole district community, to have it translated. So I ended up getting it translated in Punjabi, Urdu, Arabic, and then we had to do it into all the other languages so that way we could make everybody feel a part of it. One of the things that we ended up having [the volunteers] do was helping call the families, because most of the kids did not come to the school. They were terrified of leaving their homes. It was very difficult to get families to come out and bring their kids.

[*Almontaser's own daughter and son were afraid to go back to school. The girl went to an Islamic school. The seventeen-year-old boy went to an alternative school in Manhattan.*]

Let's just say that he did not want to go back into the city ever again, after September 11. The following week came and he kept saying, "I'm not ready to go. I'm not ready to go." With him at that age it was very hard for him to say, "I'm scared. I'm afraid. I don't want to go to the city." He just kept giving us excuses. Eventually, Thanksgiving came. He was still home. I was in constant contact with the school and the guidance counselor was like, "You can't force him. But we think he needs to go to counseling." It was very hard to try to get him to go to counseling. After Thanksgiving I said to him, "You have to make a choice. You have to tell me why you don't want to go to school. There has to be something."

He broke down and cried to me. He said, "I'm afraid. I do not want to go to school in the city. It's too far out. I don't want to be on the train. If something else happens, I'm far away from home. I don't want to ever be put in that situation again." He was in his senior year of high school, as well. I tried to get him into another program. Couldn't get him into anything because it was his last year. They had these continuing education programs for high school students but all of them were in the city. Finally, I was chatting with a friend of mine who does continuing education for adults and I was telling her the whole story. She said to me, "There is this Catholic Services Program in Sunset Park that does continuing education for high school students, for people who drop out of school. Give them a call and see." So I called and they told me that the semester had already started. I didn't give up. I went over there and I spoke to a sister [running the program]. She didn't want to see me in the beginning, but I was very persistent. I said, "Please, tell [the sister] that my son's story is extraordinary and that she really needs to give me the opportunity."

So I shared with her the whole entire situation of what happened and she just turned around and looked at me.

She said, "I can't turn you down. I can't make you leave here without saying yes. Your son's story is extraordinary and if we can help him get his life back together, we'll take him in, even though we started already."

So we got him into the program. It was career training, preparing him to take his high school equivalency test, training him in a profession that he would be interested in, and also career counseling and self-improvement and self-esteem building. So he was going to the program at eight thirty on the dot. He couldn't be late. You had to wear a suit. You couldn't go in jeans. So this program changed his whole personality, as well as his appearance. Like he had a whole new look on life, which was wonderful.

What is he doing now?

He finished the program, graduated, took his GED, did extremely well, and he was placed at a stock brokerage company. And you're not going to believe where it is—in Manhattan. And when he came home, he told us he went for the interview and he got the job. We were in total shock that he was actually going to go into the city to work.

[Almontaser described the experience her oldest son had as a National Guard soldier at Ground Zero.]

There were days he would call and he wouldn't find us home, because he had no sense of timing. He didn't know what time of day it was. He would call and we were at work. And it was really painful because, when it rained, I used to have all these scary thoughts in my head of mudslides and all the worst things that could happen, knowing that people had gotten hurt when it did rain, people slipping and what have you. It just terrified me. My son was experiencing such a tragic, firsthand experience—finding dead bodies and body parts and all that. [To cope with that] I threw myself into trying to figure out what I could do to make sure the community is safe and that the community's voice was being heard. With the Arab-American Family Support Center, I was going to churches and synagogues and different community centers, talking about Islam and Arabs and the issues. Every place I went I was getting phone numbers of people who would be interested in escorting families and doing shopping, and just helping in any way, shape, or form they can. Just throwing myself in the work helped me deal with the fact that my son is out there, and he's doing what he needs to do, but I need something to put all that energy into.

In the months to come, the detentions started to happen. People were being rounded up and detained. Many families did not know where their sons or their husbands were. They were afraid to call the police and report their husband or son missing, because they were, as well, undocumented, and were afraid there might be repercussions. We started to organize. We were doing "Know Your Rights" forums. We were doing workshops on how, if you're stopped, what do you say? If somebody comes knocking on your door, don't let them in. If they're the FBI or the police, you ask for a police warrant. The simple, small, basic things. It was quite challenging and daunting because the communities were so diverse, and the languages were so different. And trying to find people to work with to get these services out was very difficult to do.

We organized weekly demonstrations at the detention center in Brooklyn, in the Sunset Park area. We were out there every Saturday afternoon, just demanding, "Give us the names and give us the charges. Why are these people being held?" It was amazing. Every month we marched through a different neighborhood. One time we did it through Park Slope, another time from Bay Ridge, just to educate the public, educate the communities that had this detention center. What was startling was that many people had no idea there was a detention center [near where they lived]. They thought it was just storage but were totally shocked.

In the midst of all this, my son remained at Ground Zero for six months. I remember speaking to him just before Thanksgiving. He was like, "I want to come home, but I don't know if I could come home."

"Well, why don't you ask?"

And he said, "I don't want to ask because if they need me, I really want to be here." It was not a Thanksgiving for us that was merry, because he was away. It was difficult on the entire family. I remember that weekend just being so overly exhausted from everything that was happening—working as a classroom teacher from eight to three and then doing community work from four to eleven at night. None of us were in any festive mood to have a luxurious dinner. I remember my son calling on Thanksgiving Day. "You're not going to believe it. I actually could come home for dinner."

So my husband comes to tell me that he was going to come home for dinner. I said, "We didn't even buy a turkey! What are we going to feed this kid when he gets here?"

So he went to a local Muslim butcher and they were selling fresh-slaughtered turkeys. He brought it home; he cleaned it; we stuffed it and did everything we needed to. And that turkey was a miracle turkey because it cooked so quickly, as big as it was. And it was the most delicious turkey we'd had in a great while. My son came home. He had dinner with us. It was just so great to see him. That was actually the first time we had seen him since he had left on September 11. I could not believe my eyes. This was not the son that I had seen the day before he left. He looked like he had aged fifteen or twenty years. I was in total shock to see how he had become really withered out from lack of sleep, from the lack of food. He looked skinny; he looked tired. But it was so great looking at him eat. It was a pleasure to watch him eat and really get full.

My son came home at the end of February of 2002. It was extremely difficult for him to fall back into his routines of going to school, and going back to work. It took a great deal of time for him to be able to sleep a full night. He used to wake up with nightmares of finding body parts—just horrible things that it took him a long time to share with us. Eventually, he was able to get back into his routine. He was able to talk to us about a lot of things. The thing that was the most painful to hear was his justification of why we went into Afghanistan, and the importance of going after anybody who is suspected and the importance of racially profiling people [laughs], and making sure this country was safe at all measures. As some-one who was seeing the devastation of how people were being singled out and targeted when they were innocent, it was so difficult to hear my son talking in this way. When the discussions about going into Iraq started to happen, he was in total support of us going to war with Iraq and had a firm belief that there was a connection to 9/11 with Iraq. Trying to have conversations with him was extremely difficult. We couldn't talk politics at the table. It was just really scary to have one of your children have such different views than you. My son firmly believed, when the president said, "We are going to surgically remove Saddam Hussein." He actually sat at the dinner table, justifying, and telling us of the equipment they have to make this a "surgical removal."

After we had gone into Iraq and he saw the devastation of the bombs, I could see in his face that he was really devastated to see those. It took just months later for him to finally say, "I can't believe that my country is doing this." He started going to the library. He started taking out really interesting books on American history and foreign policy. One day, he started talking about how disappointed he was. That he was living this dream of being a part of a country that has such high stature in the world yet has caused so much devastation across the world for a long time. So him coming out of that trance, or that illusion, was just amazing and uplifting. I remember when they had the March 20 [2005] antiwar dem-onstration here in New York City, he made sure that he rallied many of his friends. He brought home signs and asked family members to join him.

12.

Jaron Lanier

Author, Computer Scientist, Composer, Visual Artist

Interviewed by Karen Frenkel

Jaron Lanier is a renowned author, computer scientist, composer, and visual artist. He is a pioneer in the field of virtual reality. In 2010, Time named him one of the 100 most influential people in the world. He has been a visiting scholar and scientist at the University of Southern California, Berkeley, Microsoft, and Columbia University. In his book You Are Not a Gadget: A Manifesto, *Lanier is critical of Internet technologies that value information over individuals and lead to a dehumanized culture. Lanier was born in 1960 in New York City and raised in New Mexico.*

FEBRUARY 26, 2002

I'm a computer scientist and I'm also a composer and I'm also a pundit or a critic, social commentator, particularly on matters related to how technology and culture interact, and I'm best known for that old stuff with virtual reality these days. I wonder if in forty or fifty years if anybody remembers me it will be for that or other stuff. I'm sort of an eccentric character, and I live in a loft in TriBeCa on Duane Street with a whole, whole lot of musical instruments and odd computer equipment.

Do you want to just say a few sentences about your pioneering work in virtual reality?

The notion of it was to try to use technological means to open up new channels of communication between people that might be less reliant on verbal strategies and more reliant on the creation of things that are experienced directly: a notion of sort of waking-state intentional shared dreams; that was my original youthful intention. Then, of course, it's become useful in industrial technology. But as a popular metaphor it's frequently used in a somewhat less positive and faithful way, and instead is used to either refer cynically to false experiences or perhaps to assertive juvenile extreme video game experience. So I have no idea of what the future of the term will be.

And you are a musician.

Right. I am a composer and musician, and I work with a range of different musical forms, from the Western classical orchestra to improvisatory work on instruments from many cultures and varying historical periods. I have at least a thousand instruments here in the loft at TriBeCa of different sorts.

Okay. Now let's talk about what happened to you on September 11, 2001.

That was a highly unpleasant day. I had come back the day before from travels in Thailand and France. So just immediately previously I had given a concert in Paris with a flute player named Robert Dick, who's a wonderful avant-garde flute player. Then just before that I'd been in northwest Thailand in the area of Chiang Mai, both giving some lectures and doing some research on musical instruments in the region. I also performed saxophone with a trained elephant orchestra and various other adventures. So I'd just come back.

I remember that morning going out and seeing that my favorite corner deli had closed while I was away, which was disappointing. The neighborhood had been in a state of rapid change. It had been in a process of shifting from a neighborhood of artists who'd occupied unwanted industrial spaces, such as the Civil War–era shoe factory that was turned into the building where my loft is, where you are now, and had been occupied by a new class of young wealthy couples that were drawn by the proximity to Wall Street. Typically either one or both of the parents in these couples worked on Wall Street in investments or finance of some sort. A lot of them were associated with the dot-com boom, which was a sort of tulip craze for Internet stocks that perhaps will still be remembered for the folly it was in forty or fifty years. So this caused all the prices to rise, and therefore for a lot of the original artists in the neighborhood to leave. And it created this sort of ironic effect of capitalism, in which increased wealth decreases diversity, instead of increases it.

The story was, I'd had coffee at an outdoor café on West Broadway, an alternate one, since my favorite one had been closed by the rising costs. And I was walking toward my door when the first plane came in. My first thought was, since there was a lot of construction going on in the neighborhood to create these massive penthouses and things, I thought perhaps it was the sound of a crane or some sort of machinery on a roof falling over or something like that, although it seemed far too loud. It was a very curious sound, a sound I hadn't heard before.

I looked toward the intersection and people were staring toward the World Trade Center. I was initially afraid to turn around and look. I asked somebody, "What's going on?" And this neighbor of mine, a medical researcher, had a sort of odd—almost like an amused—emotion. I'm sure it was just due to the shock of the moment rather than any genuine sense of amusement. But he said, "You won't believe it. A plane crashed into the World Trade Center."

I think the initial assumption was that it was a mistake, some sort of awful accident. But there's a sort of New Yorker spirit of, "Well, things are all screwed up anyway, and people screw up and we all make it through." So that in itself was something that could be well integrated with the sensibility that's required to make it through any day in a city this large that was built centuries ago to be much smaller and where things often don't really work quite right anyway. So the sensibility initially applied, and people were staring at it.

I saw a friend of mine, who's an actress, in the street staring at it, and I went up to her. And I turned around and finally looked at it, and it was the strangest thing. The first thing was that it was obviously a large plane, but I had assumed it would be like a little, a tiny plane, the sort of plane that an amateur pilot would have piloted, maybe with a couple of seats, and had just made an error. You know, there was once a plane that hit the Empire State Building. So I figured it was just another small plane. And then, of course, it was surprising that it had gone through the building.

There was an enormous span of air filled with fluttering office papers that evoked little tourist mementos that are on sale called snow globes. You can pick it up and shake it and it seems to be snowing. There was that sort of sense of this massive amount of billowing paper, which was settling very slowly, so it appeared to be suspended like the flakes are suspended in water in those toys.

The impact appeared to have generated a hole that simply went through the building. There was apparently debris falling out the other side. So the impression one had was of the sort of thing one sees with cartoon animals that run through a door and leave a hole in the door that's the shape of the animal that ran through it. There was this sort of hole right through the building.

So I was starting to calculate in my mind, you know, this was a big plane. I started asking people, "What kind of plane was it?" And somebody said, "Well, it was just a silver plane. It didn't look like it had a logo."

I was thinking, well, it had to have been a big plane. And I thought maybe it was an American Airlines plane, because they look sort of silvery and it's hard to see the logo from a distance. Then I started to think there will have to be a structural failure, because there's a lot of this building missing, and I started to wonder to myself, what sort of structural failure will there be? The initial impact was at an angle, and it seemed to me possible that the top could start sliding off. Perhaps there could be an implosion. But somehow I put that out of my mind, because—I don't know. I suppose it's just not something that I wanted to believe.

So I saw a friend, an actress, who was there on the corner, and she was looking at it and crying. I went up to her and held her and I wanted to help her find her husband. So I called him on the cell phone, and at this point the cell phones were still working. Of course, the cell phone transponders for our neighborhood were on the towers, so they would soon cease to work. But her husband was at the next corner. So I walked her over there to get them together. He was looking at the impact and he said, "There are people jumping," and she was very, very upset, as was everyone.

I looked at it and I simply could not see the people jumping. This is interesting, because I have excellent eyesight, and we were quite close, and obviously the information of the people jumping, as I saw later in videotapes, was present. It hit my retina. But somehow my brain filtered it or wasn't able to receive it, so I didn't perceive that, and I'm grateful for that. Of course, we had made a point to be far enough away that we wouldn't have seen them land or see what was going on immediately on the ground by that time, so I didn't directly perceive that.

I was looking away toward the north for a moment when the second plane came in. At that point, I tried to think about what I should do, and I had a few thoughts. One thought was to try to get out of the city quickly and take my friends and whomever else I could find and pile the people in my car. I have a car in the neighborhood, and I thought, "We'll just leave." But then I thought a million other people will have that idea and we'll be in this huge traffic jam. And that traffic jam might have us on a bridge or in a tunnel or something, which perhaps is not the safest place to be if there's a coordinated large-scale attack going on. So I decided against that.

Then I thought, "Perhaps I should start running toward the north," away from the financial district, if the financial district was the target. But then I thought, well, a million people also have that idea, and once again one would just be clogged. So then I thought about what the possibilities were, and it seemed to me that it was unlikely that the events at the towers would have an immediate impact on my apartment, which was five blocks away. My reasoning for that was that I had actually taken the precaution of measuring what would happen if they fell from the base when I moved in. It's an awful thing to say, but I moved in something like '94. There had been an earlier attack on the World Trade Center, and I had thought to myself that the towers might be attacked again. I'd actually read an engineering paper about the towers and what it would take to topple them. I had thought about a scenario of a very large bomb toward the base of the towers, and the possibility that they might fall to the side, and had concluded that I was just outside of the zone of having to be concerned about that. Although I thought it would be more likely they'd fall in a different direction if that happened. So it's a grotesque thing to say, but I had actually thought about it a little bit.

So I decided that what I would do was simply go back up to my house and stay inside and see what happened. I figured, I'm in a low building and if there were going to be other attack sites in Manhattan, all the other places I could think of would perhaps be more likely to threaten me if I was in motion than if I just stayed put. Such as the Empire State Building. I tried to run through my mind what other things they would want to attack. It seemed to me that they were playing for a home audience and would probably attack things that would make good television and would have been familiar already to their audience. So the Statue of Liberty was more likely than something in Midtown.

So I was inside when the towers fell, and there was an earthquake associated with them that reminded me of being in modest quakes in California. After the towers fell, the dust cloud was truly extraordinary.

Right out these windows it was absolutely opaque. It was as if somebody had put black velvet against the glass. So once again, I thought, "Well, I'll simply stay inside. I'm breathing air here that's reasonably insulated from the outside. I'll simply wait this out. I still think this is safer."

Then I don't know how much time passed, it's not clear to me, but at a certain point I heard a bullhorn on the street. By now the air had cleared substantially. My particular neighborhood was somewhat fortunate in that the wind was blowing toward the east and so the dust cloud was moved away from my neighborhood. The voice on the bullhorn said, "If there is anyone still in these buildings, you must evacuate immediately. These buildings could be demolished at any moment." So I said, "Okay. I think that means I should evacuate." I was aware that there was a woman in the next building who had broken her leg and was having difficulty getting out. So I went down to the front door, and there were some police who just grabbed me immediately and said, "Get on this bus. You're getting out of here." I told them there was a woman in the next door and they said, "Okay. Thanks." And I was just on this bus with a bunch of people. A very sort of surreal moment, because here we are on this bus and there's a bus driver who's just a typical New York City bus driver, and we all just head out. We weren't talking much. The street was covered in an awful-smelling yellow dust, inches thick. So there was this sense of being on a combination of a lunar surface and a horrible mass grave site. But as soon as we turned the corner, there was much less of it. A couple blocks up the dust was mostly not visible.

We were in this bus and the bus driver said he could not make any stops. He didn't know where he was going. He was simply going north in Manhattan. Of course, nobody really quite knew what was going on, although it seemed to me that the police were quite well organized from the start. That impressed me a great deal and was very comforting. I felt that they seemed to know what they were doing. I think it subsequently was shown that they did.

The bus just moved north. Then a police officer got on—I suppose we were on Central Park West somewhere—and he stopped the bus and said,

"Okay, out." It was just a corner. There wasn't any particular place. So I got out and I started thinking in my mind, "Who is around here?" I tried calling some hotels to see if I could get a room and all the switchboards were busy. I walked to a hotel and it was completely full. I presumed that every hotel would be full with people like me. So then I started to think about friends in the neighborhood, and I thought of a friend who lived nearby, a block from Central Park West. So I went and just knocked on his door and ended up sleeping on his floor that night, in his living room, because he didn't have anything else.

The next morning I got up early and there was this sort of foul-smelling haze as far north as the Upper West Side. I realized it was certainly not possible for me to go home. And I couldn't just sleep on the floor. What I should really do is just get off of Manhattan. The news was that the bridges and tunnels were closed, but that there might be trains running. So I went to Penn Station the next morning and waited for a train to leave. I got on a train, the first train that was heading out of town. It was heading east to Long Island and I stayed on it. My cell phone started working and I was able to call people. I then entered this very surreal week, because I found a friend who has a Hamptons beach place. I just ended up staying out there for a couple of weeks until we were allowed back in. This area— at least this sort of beach strip of the Hamptons—is a retreat for the very rich. It's a very narcissistic, immature place.

When I came back to New York, it turns out there was some damage to the roof of the apartment building. Some debris hit our roof and did not cause extensive damage but caused a leak. The rain came through the building and caused water damage. I lost a lot of instruments. I also lost the original concept drawings for virtual reality, which I had up on the wall, framed. They were soaked, and by the time I got back they were completely molded. A lot of my documents related to my career are kept at the Stanford Library.

During that time it was very hard to get in and out of the neighborhood. I had to go through three different checkpoints where I was questioned and had to show documentation in order to get in or out of my house. I don't remember exactly when we were allowed back in. I think it was approximately two weeks. For a significant period of time my street was the frontier zone. All of the crowds of people who wanted to see the site could get no further than my block. And so walking out the door was very uncomfortable because there were sidewalk vendors and hucksters of all sorts. There was sometimes a bit of a carnival atmosphere. There were very moving scenes of relatives putting up those little posters hoping that someone who was missing might actually have just been walking around dazed or there might be some other explanation for their vanishing.

There were [also] provocateurs. I remember, for instance, an incident of a family who very aggressively dressed to appear both Muslim and Arab, wandering around looking at the site and cheering in an apparent attempt to create some sort of incident. There were no takers, nobody would respond to them and they seemed disappointed in that. There were people trying to sell rickshaw rides, since they could get them past the cordon. There were people selling photographs. There were people recruiting for all sorts of religions. Right outside my door there was some sort of fundamentalist Christian organization. All of that moved south eventually, closer to the site. But there were all sorts of Christians, particularly, and then some Jews and even some Muslims. People approached me and would say, "Have you prayed today? This happened because people weren't praying enough," that sort of thing.

The most unsettling experience of being here was the stories of people who'd apparently known about the attack in advance. I believe that either most or all of them were false. However, some of them are hard to put out of my mind. That bothered me a very great deal. A friend of mine, who at that time was running a hospital, one of his surgeons had been intercepted by a neighbor. This neighbor was Arab. I don't remember from what country. It happened that the surgeon had business in the World Trade Center the morning of the attack. This neighbor prevented him from going, tackled him essentially, and said, "No, let's go to the beach with our families." And then blocked his car and said, "Listen, it's such a beautiful day, let's do something else." The surgeon found this completely bizarre. But the neighbor just wouldn't let him go and made him very late. Then after the attack, the neighbor suddenly vanished. Completely packed up the family and their essential goods and just disappeared with no notice or anything. So that's disturbing.

How would you say your relationships have been affected by this experience?

Well, in varying ways. I entered into a new relationship shortly after the attack, and it's been hard. For one thing, it's just been hard to be fully relaxed and calm in recent months. But there's also something of a barrier between people who were close to the attack and people who weren't. I think people who were a bit more distant from it, even just farther away in Manhattan, have a very, very different sense of it. I mean, the further away you get the more absurd and perhaps cynical the view of the attack becomes.

In France, for instance, there are many people who, in private, state with the fashionable paranoia of the left, "It must have been the Americans attacking themselves to achieve some sort of goal." I also heard people in California saying, "Well, we're sorry that you had this experience, but on the other hand, it was all those financial bastards in the World Trade Center." I felt that that was so wrong since I do live in the neighborhood, and I know people who worked in the World Trade Center. I know people who were killed in it. Nobody who was very close to me, but people I knew.

Can we talk about the lecture that you gave at Carnegie Mellon for a moment? Because it was so close to September 11.

I talked about various things. I presented a history of how violence and technology were related. I suggested that in human prehistory, our ability to do harm to one another was similar to the ability of assorted other animals to do harm to one another. One person could harm another, but if there were a few people together it would be hard for one person to do them much harm. With the advent of the technologies of metalworking and basic vehicles and better control of fire, it became possible for people to have increased power, both to defend themselves or to do violence, if they worked together in large groups.

So as you have swords and shields, the ancient Greeks discovered that it was possible to march together in a formation with all the shields connected together to simulate what we would do today with a tank, to make an impregnable conveyance that could do great damage. This led to a period of great empires that leveraged the use of technologies to do large-scale violence, but still required large numbers of people. This was the age of armies and empires that lasted from ancient times until quite recently.

In the twentieth century there was a turnaround because of weapons of mass destruction. With the atomic bomb, it became possible to do so much destruction that there was really no defense against it. So we entered a period of Cold War and détente and mutually assured destruction. The idea of the massive army was made somewhat obsolete. That was the latter half of the twentieth century. These weapons of mass destruction still required huge infrastructures, so they were still only useable by empires.

It seems to me that we're entering a phase now which is entirely different, in which the access to information, the variety of materials, and the cost of the materials have all conspired to create the potential for small numbers of people to do great damage to large numbers of people. And that has never been true before.

I don't pretend at this point to have a set of conclusions I am willing to advocate, but I can just share some of my thoughts about it. One alternative that comes to mind is a sort of benevolent police state, in which you have a state authority with enormously expanded observation powers in order to prevent small numbers of people from damaging large. The classic problem is that [approach] only works if one can really trust that apparatus. History has taught us that inscrutable characters are drawn to such points of power. So that perhaps is not a good solution.

I've become increasingly interested in the notion of omni-transparency, where not only would the government be able to see what everybody's doing, but everybody would be able to see what everybody's doing, including the government. The historical precedent for this is perhaps in the Netherlands, where a maniac could harm a dike and kill many people. Everyone had to cooperate carefully to maintain the dikes and maintain mutual safety. Essentially the system of dikes created an early simulation of what it would be like to have weapons of mass destruction around. So Dutch society is, on the one hand, unusually tolerant, open-minded. On the other hand, it has a strong work ethic. It is efficiency oriented, unlike some societies. But beyond those things it's quite transparent. It's a society in which it is expected that one will leave one's curtains open.

Recently, in Amsterdam, particularly, there hasn't been enough transparency, because terrorist groups have been working there. But the principle is an interesting one—a society in which secrets are simply not kept. The argument for such a society is that that's the only way to have enough eyes to really see problems before they become bad. There's no way a government apparatus can be large enough to spy on everyone effectively, to protect us. But if we're all spying on each other, it works. Furthermore, if we're all spying on each other, it's not really spying anymore. And none of our secrets are really all that special anyway. Maybe secrets aren't worth having. I don't think such a society would become inhumane at all. I think it actually could be significantly humane. After all, the secrets that we worry about are, for the most part, really not any big deal; they're just human things. So perhaps a radical level of openness would be one solution. And in that society of radical openness, I don't think the attack we saw could have happened. It just would have unraveled. There would have been somebody who would have seen it. Our society right now is based on a coupling of extraordinary openness and extraordinary privacy, which is what I've been raised to expect and I enjoy it. But I think I could imagine a different society that I could adapt to.

I also thought a lot about the psychology of the attackers. At the time I gave the talk there was less information than there is now about them, but there was already a little bit [of] information. It was striking that these attackers had a very different profile from what might have been expected. They were not Palestinians or Bosnians or Chechnyans or anyone who had seen their houses destroyed, or their families. Rather, they all came from upper-middle-class, well-educated, well-to-do families. They all had had experience in the West and, in many cases, advanced degrees, technical degrees. They were all closer to the profile of a Patty Hearst than some sort of Palestinian suicide bomber or something. They were disaffected, upper-middle-class educated kids. They were more like the Baader-Meinhof [Gang or the Red Army] Faction, say, than Tamil Tigers. I was struck that a number of them had gone to engineering school.

I had a few thoughts about that. One is that we are making an awful mistake in the way we conceive of and teach technology as a sort of a dry and nonhuman discipline. It's not just technology. Another one of the major terrorists, the fellow who just murdered an American reporter in Pakistan, went to the London School of Economics. Many of our disciplines are taught with a degree of abstraction that can allow one to get an advanced degree without ever having really interacted with anyone else in our culture. So if you look at the history of science and technology, these things did not come about out of the ether. They came about because of generations of rather eccentric and likable characters who were curious about the world. There was a kind of a curiosity and a desire to engage the world, and a desire to improve the world that drove the majority of people who have contributed to increased understandings in science and technology. If all you're taught is the results of that process, if all you do is learn some formulas and some techniques, and take some tests to prove that you've done so, but you're not exposed to this very positive and human and endearing culture that generated all of those results, can that really be said to be an education? We're teaching these subjects divorced from the humanity that led to the creation of all this subject matter, and that disturbs me.

It also seems that the nature of the attacks indicate[s] that they bear a lot in common with other terrorists attacks that we've seen recently from people with extremist ideals. There are plenty to compare them to. There's the sarin gas cult in Tokyo. There's the Peoples Temple suicides. There's the Heaven's Gate suicides. There is the David Koresh suicide, plus attack.

There is the Unabomber. There's the Oklahoma City bombing. So we've had a rash of events that are not all extremely similar, but all have some characteristics in common. They all involve people who commit violence on the way to suicide. They all involve people who, I think, really want to be on television. They are people who are striving for some sense of significance, who want to believe that they matter. If you look at the rhetoric of all the groups I just mentioned, as well as Al-Qaeda, they all share an infantile sensibility that "I'm the one that matters. Pay attention to me."

In the videotape that was discovered after the attack, of Osama bin Laden bragging about it in his fantasy world, it was interesting that he said people were having visions of planes flying into buildings. But then he said, "People have been calling from all over who are now interested in Islam." He got a lot of attention; it was sort of a publicity thing.

I think there is a twentieth-century disease of a large population exposed to all this one-way media and culture, where they're on the receiving end of all this broadcast stuff, TV particularly, but also other media. It must make them feel very small. I think people have always had a problem with feeling small. Certainly, there have always been paupers and kings. But it must be quite harsh and severe now compared to the past, because there's this palpable possibility that if one just does certain things, like mass murder, that one can be in front of the cameras instead of just receiving. Ultimately, a lot of terrorism is really just an infantile mind saying, "Look at me," and nothing more than that. It's just this desperate need for acknowledgment, attention, and an existential feeling of significance.

MARCH 18, 2003

[*By the time of this second interview, Jaron Lanier had moved to California.*]

As far as the decision to move, there were a number of reasons for that. One is the obvious one. I just really wanted to get away from living next to the site. I was very tired of being at the World Trade Center site every day, once I had been allowed back into my home after the attack. And, by the way, I don't like calling the event a tragedy. I think there would be something wrong in calling a massacre we were responsible for a tragedy, as if it were a passing thing. I wouldn't want to call it a lie or a tragedy. I would want to call it an act of murder. That's how it should be referred to. I mean, there has to be some acknowledgment [that we] are going to take responsibility for our own actions or hold others responsible for theirs. But I reject that word. An earthquake, or something, would have been a tragedy. Anyway, I just got sick of seeing it every day.

Another factor was a practical matter: I had a very large instrument collection in my apartment, a lot of which was damaged by the attack. I had sufficiently cleared out to make it feasible that things could be fixed, and the effort of moving everything was so great that it opened up in my mind the notion of leaving the city altogether and just moving to another location. I thought the beautiful adobe atmosphere of California would be kind of a relief.

I was initially determined not to move out of the neighborhood during the recovery period, because I felt that I was able to contribute something to the neighborhood at that time. In many cases, that contribution was specific. In the immediate months after, it was helping rescue workers or whoever was around there. Often it was helping visiting families of victims. But then the neighborhood changed very much as the recovery period started to come to a close.

And I have to say there were a couple of things that happened that made me uncomfortable staying. There was this sort of mini-competitiveness to being part of the artistic response to it. For instance, there was an organization called Creative Time that was asked to put together a little music festival for the reopening of offices in the vicinity of the site, and they invited me to be one of the composers for it. But then when I got involved in it, I realized that it was this very political sort of thing with various composers trying to be on the "in," and a lot of pushing with who would get the press and everything. I decided to withdraw from it because I didn't feel it was appropriate. I was unhappy about that. And there were some other instances of a similar character. I started to feel the art scene in the post-attack environment wasn't one that I really felt as much a part of, or that I really wanted to be in. I didn't like the feeling of the response.

Then another issue was wild real estate speculation. I had a situation with my living space where I had a shared interest with another person, and there was a lot of pressure to sell it or to rent it for very high amounts of money. Suddenly the real estate values went up. So a lot of money was flowing into real estate, even though I was just living next to a horrible mass grave. Who would want to live there? This run up in real estate value just put a lot of pressure on people to leave the neighborhood, which was an irony.

There's a sense in which it's probably healthy that people come in [to the neighborhood] who weren't part of the attack experience, and it probably will revive it. I also have to say I'm very unhappy with the reconstruction plans that have been selected. I wouldn't want to live there. I don't want to live next to a big version of the Holocaust museum. As with my rejection of the term "tragedy" to describe what was an intentional massacre, if it was something we had committed, and was sort of our fault, and we had regrets about it, as in the case of the Vietnam War, I think this notion of "the pit," as we have in the Vietnam War Memorial, would make sense.

This interview is taking place the day after President George W. Bush spoke about going to war with Iraq, and told Saddam Hussein that he had forty-eight hours to leave his country. I wonder if you would like to comment about how that feels to you in the context of what you experienced during 9/11, and in this past year and several months.

I have mixed feelings about it. Right now it's extremely unfashionable to be hawkish. I know socially almost no one would support the president right now. And yet I have to say that I don't think the position is irrational.

I think there is a case for going to war now, as awful as it sounds on the face of it. The case is simply that we've entered into a situation which I think is different from any in the past, in which small groups of people can do great damage, a level of damage, previously associated only with a giant army invading. But even worse, those small groups of people can do that damage with anonymity. So the logic of deterrence can't be used as it was during the Cold War. We need to come up with a different idea of how to have world peace. If you no longer have deterrence, and if the barrier to entering war is lower, that's a very different set of circumstances from any that we've ever had before. I think that the idea of having to keep the peace, and the circumstances, will evolve. My personal belief is that the ultimate way to do it is a way that I think a sort of liberal-minded people would like a lot, which is a society of extreme transparency in which there are fewer secrets and everything is sort of exposed.

Probably the Bush administration doctrines of unilateral preemptions is in many ways the least destructive of the options I can imagine, because I think this is a case where waiting would make things worse. So I'm at odds with just about everyone I know on this. The metaphor that I've been thinking of is, if you have to have surgery it really matters whether the surgeon is good or not. If you have a poor surgeon that you don't believe in you might want to put off the surgery until you have one that you do like. I'm sort of concerned we have a poor surgeon here, in that I think the Bush administration has been really terribly reckless in economic policy, and with diplomatic policy, and the social policy and so the foundational level of managing the thing that you're defending seems to be so out of whack.

I'm very angry at the American left, and the protest movement, and I can't support it even though my background and inclination is along those lines. When I was a kid I got arrested for liberal causes. But I'm furious at the American left for splitting the vote for Ralph Nader. I guess the American left is very immature and would prefer to be able to whine and complain about Bush than to actually take responsibility of being part of a winning coalition, and that's really disheartening to me.

We talked [before] about what effect 9/11 had had on your relationships. I wonder if you would like to talk about how you are relating to people who weren't [near the Twin Towers] while you were.

Well, I've chosen to immerse myself in an environment surrounded by people who weren't there, and I've done that in part because I want to get out of the framework of the post-attack, the feeling of it. I wanted to think about other things. I do think it's been helping me. It definitely makes me different from people around me. Perhaps if I hadn't been there that day I would be less willing to think favorably of Bush's idea of war right now, for instance.

I think the whole world should be able to live a dreamy extension of childhood, of the sort that people live in Berkeley, and that's the way reality should be for everyone. [Laughs] And I don't see anything wrong with it. But I do think it creates a sense of difference. It's definitely made me feel more connected to past generations. I think my family has survived concentration camps, or pogroms or whatever, and what I've gone through wasn't nearly as bad as what they'd gone through by any stretch of the imagination, but I have a little more of a sense of what it's like to be a refugee and to experience real uncertainty and real fear.

13.

Jay Swithers

Captain, Emergency Medical Service

Interviewed by Gerry Albarelli

Jay Swithers was born in Brooklyn, New York, on September 11, 1961. His father worked in Pan American Airlines' cargo department; his mother was a homemaker. The family lived in a small apartment in Bay Ridge, Brooklyn. Swithers is an Emergency Medical Service captain and an official in the Bureau of Health Services of the New York City Fire Department. He also volunteers at a medical center and an ambulance company in Bay Ridge. Swithers is married and has four children. On September 11, 2001, Captain Swithers was a member of the New York City urban search and rescue team, and was one of the first emergency medical technicians to arrive at Ground Zero.

DECEMBER 15 AND 17, 2001

For the last two and a half years I've been working at headquarters. They needed somebody with a little bit of knowledge in workers' compensation.

They needed an administrator, liaison for the agency, to work with the insurance company. It's a horrible job, deciding who would get benefits and who would not get benefits, and what injury is legitimate, questioning injuries and having to go to workers' compensation hearings, and pretty much a very difficult job. But two and a half years later, back in August, I was promoted to captain.

September 11 happened to be my fortieth birthday. I got to work about seven thirty, which is pretty normal. My department pager went off, identifying that an airplane had hit Tower One, the North Tower. I am on the urban search and rescue team. This team was created ten years ago following disasters happening in the United States where they didn't have resources. At headquarters I have a fairly large locker in which I kept my bunker [firefighter] gear, which is unusual for the EMS person to have. But having been on this team of approximately sixteen guys at this point, I had bunker gear. I had boots. I had my own harness. I have a unique helmet and some other equipment as well. I have cargo-type pants that have pockets and also boots. I put on my boots and told Mary Ann Pisatola, my employee, that I was going to the World Trade Center. I assumed that this was an accident, that it wasn't a terrorist attack. Then somebody said another plane had just hit the building. I didn't know what to think.

People were scurrying around the building looking for transportation. I ran out of the building. I ran to the Brooklyn Bridge, where I was met by a female police officer at the footpath, and she told me to stop. Other people were yelling, "Go! Go! You've got to get there! You've got to get there!"

She told me to stop, and I said, "What are you talking about?" There's a lot of traffic coming off the bridge, a lot of people coming off the bridge. She said, "Not that I'm telling you to stop, but why would you run over the bridge when you could get a ride?"

I said, "A ride from who?"

She said, "Just stand out in those three lanes of traffic and somebody will pick you up."

Within a few moments, not anything more than thirty seconds, came a black Crown Victoria, very shiny, with a light on the dashboard and lights on the grille, and the headlights flicking back and forth, with the sirens screaming, and the person driving that car was a male. He was in a suit. I don't know what agency he came from. The car came to a screaming halt right in front of me. He opened up the door and he says, "Get in." And I jumped in with my equipment.

He said, "You going to the World Trade Center?"

I said, "Yes."

And he took off over the Brooklyn Bridge. Although all the lanes were open, I never drove so quick over the Brooklyn Bridge. I don't know how fast we were going; it could have been a hundred miles an hour. I was actually amazed at how fast we're moving with the sirens on. Then, going down, there were people that were standing in the lanes of traffic, trying to get a better view, trying to climb up on the side rails. As he was approaching that he was yelling, "Get down! Get down off the side rails! Get down off the bridge! Everybody get out of Manhattan!" He was yelling that on his PA. As we came down off the bridge onto Chambers Street, there were crowds of people, and he was just yelling on his PA, "I got a paramedic! Get out of the way!"

My thought at the time was, "This guy's a little bit eccentric," overexcited, yelling on his PA about the one paramedic that he had on board the car. He continued this all the way down, dropped me off at Church Street.

He says, "Is this good enough? Can I leave you here?"

I said, "I guess so. I appreciate you bringing me this far."

I jumped out of the car with my equipment, and there were crowds of people just running away from the World Trade Center. Meanwhile you could hear sirens from ambulances, police cars, fire trucks, from every agency, just all over the place, in all different directions. A few moments I walked south, and I met up with a police officer. I asked him, "Do you know where the fire department command post is?"

He didn't know. He says, "Just keep walking. You'll find people."

I got to the corner of Fulton Street and Church Street, and I noticed a lot of people that I knew. They had set up a triage area, which seemed to be working pretty well. We were standing right in front of the Millennium

Hilton Hotel, which is a thin black building that faces the World Trade Center. A lot of the patients that were coming out of the plaza were running right to this area, and immediately the EMS crews on the scene were giving them triage tags.

Those are tags that we use to identify who should go first. They start out with a green, which are people who are walking wounded, who could basically stay. Then it goes to yellow, which are people that basically will need an ambulance, but they're not serious at the time. The next one is immediate. Immediate is a red code. We use those for people that need immediate ambulance transportation, that their injuries are life-threatening. Then a black tag, which means that the person is dead. They're not going to be moved from the scene.

In New York City we have what's called a preplan for just about every disaster that can be planned. And believe me, this disaster, we did it before. The preplan actually says that we would set up triage inside the lobby of the World Trade Center. But they had moved the triage point from right outside the lobby, to the curb, to right across the street at this point. Nobody in any of their minds thought that the buildings would fall.

On the ground, there were more than enough patients to be seen. They were just running hysterically over to where we were. One woman that I remember, dressed in a red dress, who became very popular in magazines and newspaper shots, she was covered from head to toe in blood. I remember other patients that were brought over that were burned severely to the face, where their skin on their face, on one side of their face, was actually peeling off, and the patient was conscious, with debris all over him.

Ambulances were showing up. A lot of patients were hysterical, crying. The Millennium Hotel staff became very helpful. They were bringing out their nicely padded chairs from the lobby, their beautiful chairs that they had brought out to sit patients down. While we were coordinating, trying to get vehicles in to transport these patients, everything was pretty much going very well.

I remember one of our medical directors who was on the scene. He walked over to me. He had a radio clip that was attached to his shoulder.

He tapped me on the shoulder and said, "The Pentagon was just hit." It was at that point the reality hit me that this is definitely a terrorist attack, and you didn't know what was going to happen next.

It was only maybe moments later, where a woman, a heavyset black woman, was brought over to me. She was nicely dressed. She was hysterical, crying. I put her into the chair. I took out a stethoscope that I had, and I listened to her lung sounds. While she was hyperventilating, I told her, "I'm going to put you on some oxygen, and I might even give you a treatment, but you need to calm down."

It was at that moment you could hear an explosion, really a loud explosion. I had no clue what it was. My first feeling was that it was probably another plane hitting a building, as this seems to be a series of events. Somebody yelled "Run!" at that point. I turned to look, to see what was going on. For the most part all the patients started getting up and running, some with their tags hanging off their necks. The EMS people, the police officers that were there, all started running. There were news cameras; they all started running.

I didn't think at all that anything was happening other than another plane was hitting the building. My first concern was that the patient that I was treating would get up and run. And she had no problem getting up and running; that chair was vacant. When I looked up, I could see the debris coming off the building. It was constant and I just started to run. And when I got around the side [of the hotel], they had a truck sitting at the loading dock. The last thing I remember being able to see as we were just engulfed in debris, flying debris, was that truck.

I aimed just to make it right underneath the truck, and I landed on my belly with my hands down. I pushed down the visor on my helmet and I remember crawling up to the bays of the hotel, underneath the truck. The force was unbelievable. It was almost like you were in the middle of a major storm, and it was just constantly a wind blowing.

The ground was shaking and you could hear crashing noises. You could actually hear the I beams falling off this building. It was unbelievable. The sound was atrocious. At that point I realized my major problem was that I couldn't breathe. I cupped my hands, I put them over my face, and I was just trying to take in breaths of air. Breathing was as difficult as taking your head and putting it into sand.

And every time you went to take a breath, you just felt the dirt coming into your mouth, coming into your nostrils, and going down into your airway. You wanted to cough, but you couldn't get air to cough. For those few moments, the sky became black. Not gray, not brown, but black, where you couldn't see anything. And all that could be heard was large pieces of metal dropping, and roaring.

For a few moments I believed that I was going to die. Different things were flashing through my mind. It was as bizarre as, "Should I have stayed in the office? I should have never left the office." I also realized again that it was my fortieth birthday. Being my fortieth birthday, I didn't know if I wanted to die on my fortieth birthday. I actually, like in my mind, I envisioned [my wife's] response to my death. My son, being three, probably wouldn't understand. But how hard it would be for him to cope without his father. And my other son, being one and a half, probably would never even know I had existed. His memory, that bothered me for those couple of moments.

I envisioned my daughter actually holding my helmet at a funeral. Just as you've seen in so many pictures, a firefighter's death, the helmet would be the only thing, my family just lined up, and my wife hysterical. I just pictured that. And then, being the workers' compensation coordinator for the city, thinking, "I don't have enough death insurance. My wife isn't going to get enough money." Then I realized at that point that they won't be able to make it without me.

I think that's what really pulled me through as far as believing that I had to live, because it's so easy just to give up. For a few moments I just prayed that one of the I beams, rather than suffocating, would just come down and hit me. Then it went from that thought, "Just don't let me suffocate. Let me die," to "Please, let me live. Let me survive what's going on."

I had no clue beyond my farthest dreams that the building was falling down just around the corner. It was beyond my farthest dreams. I actually thought of the potential of dangerous gases, or maybe perhaps another airplane just crashing right around the corner. What could be so loud as what had happened?

Once it all stopped, for a few moments I didn't know if I was there alive, because it was still very, very black. There was no sound. So I wasn't sure if I was deaf, if I was blind. In a few moments, and it couldn't have even been thirty seconds of just being there in the peacefulness, I started to hear. I could hear the fire department alarms. Firefighters, they have an alarm that they have on them so if they stop moving for a long period of time these alarms will go off. But they could also set them when they're in trouble. At that point I still had my hands in front of my face and [was] still just trying to breathe. I felt somebody grab my helmet. I could hear him yell, "There's a firefighter here. He'll get us out."

I realized there was somebody else with me now, and I could hear another voice. They said, "What do we do? What do we do?"

I said, "We need to know how many people are here. So everybody just count. Count out loud so we know how many people are here."

So one guy said, "Okay. One." And then another person said, "Two." Another person said, "Three." And I could hear the people counting I believe all the way up to nine. I said, "Wow, there are a lot of people here." I said, "I need to know one thing. Am I blind? Or is it black?"

And somebody said, "It's black. It's black."

You could hear the people vomiting and coughing and crying. It was only maybe thirty more seconds that, having been in the blackness, you could see an orange glow in the sky. That gave us the opportunity to see that we weren't trapped, that it was just a very high amount of debris and dirt around the vehicle. For the most part, a lot of it was like sand. We were able to just push the sand or the debris—very loose debris, lots of papers—push that out and everybody climbed out. Once they got out, they asked me, "What do we do?"

I said, "Listen. I don't have any equipment. I don't have any radio. I don't know what happened. Go northeast. Just go north." And I kept on saying, "You just got to get out of here."

I started to stagger around and I could see the building behind me engulfed in flames, just burning out of control. I continued to walk. And there were people getting out from underneath cars. They had injuries, a lot worse than what I saw earlier. When I got to the corner, heading eastbound, I met up with Lieutenant Bruce Medjuck, who also works an inside duty job. He was still wearing his white shirt, his administrative uniform. He asked me if I was okay and I said, "I'm not sure." I said, "What happened?"

He said, "I don't know."

I said, "Well, let's regroup. We need to regroup." And he agreed. He had a radio and he was on the radio, and there were no other EMS people to be found at that point. There were a lot of people just wandering like the *Night of the Living Dead*, just coming out from nowhere, coughing, and hacking, people carrying people. There was a bank on the corner with an ATM [lobby]. We started to put people into the ATM [lobby]. One man showed up with a wheelbarrow with an unconscious person in a suit in the wheelbarrow, like it was taken off the construction site. This is right on Broadway and Fulton. This is right there on the street.

I remember somebody telling me, "Come down into the subway." There were a whole bunch of people in the fetal position, or just on their knees crying. They looked at me and they said, "What do we do?" And I didn't know what to tell them. I said, "This seems to be a safe area." It wasn't as bad air down there as it was up above. "Stay here. Just stay here. You'll be safe here." I ran up to the top of the stairs. At that point a clean ambulance, one of our fire department ambulances, rolled into the site. The two EMTs jump out of the ambulance and we proceed to open up the back doors. People just ran toward the ambulance. We tried to coordinate to get the most serious people onto the ambulance, onto the stretcher. Even the man with the wheelbarrow came running over. We were able to take the man out of the wheelbarrow and throw him into the ambulance.

One thing I was very happy to see was that the woman I had been treating for asthma comes wandering out of wherever, a store or crevice, wherever she was. She's still hysterical. At that point the ambulance was full. An EMT is yelling, "We're full. Too many. Too many."

And I said, "This lady's getting on." I couldn't lift the lady. I was weakened already and she was very, very heavy. I told this woman, "You're going to have to help me. I can't get you up on your own." She just sort of climbed in on one knee and brought up the other knee. Her feet were hanging out, and everybody on the inside was yelling, "No more. We can't fit. We can't fit any more."

And I said, "Well, this one's getting on."

And I pushed the door, and then I pushed her leg, and she just sort of flopped onto the floor of the ambulance. I just closed that door and I ran up to the front and I said, "Get out of here. Go. Get out of here."

Later on, I didn't realize the amount of time . . . I was just sort of standing in the middle of Broadway all by myself. I heard rumbling, similar to the rumbling that we just heard maybe twenty minutes ago. I said, "That's the same thing."

People started, once again, running eastward. I forget the name of the street, but I started running east on that street. I turned to look, and I saw the black billowing coming after me. It was gaining on me. You have to realize at this point the North Tower, Tower One, has to be maybe two blocks away. I knew that cloud was moving fast enough to knock anybody down. I got only a third of the way down the block, I'm guessing, and there were these bay doors to the building on my right-hand side. The bay doors were down about halfway, and there were people, citizens, waving to anybody who was running, "Come in here. Come in here."

When I ran in there, a bunch of men were standing there in suits. These were all civilians. They were saying, "Let's pull down the door. Let's pull down the door." The sound became louder and louder. We started to pull down the door and people were still sliding underneath the door, until the blast came right up to the door. The door rumbled and the next thing I knew we were all down on our knees.

Once I was able to get up, everybody who was in the back of the bays of this loading dock had run into a door, into a hallway of the building. It looked to be a drugstore, like a CVS or Duane Reade. People ran straight for the bottled water. They were pouring it over their heads. They were pouring it into their eyes. They were drinking it. A security guard came running over, saying, "Stop. You can't do that. You can't do that." A cop ran over and grabbed the security guard, pulled out his gun, and said, "They're doing it. You understand what's going on here?"

And at that point the security guard said, "You're welcome to the water. Just take as much water as you need."

It was pitch black, once again. Some of the debris was billowing in. There was no longer a blast, but it was just the amount of dirt in the air. You could see it coming in through bits and pieces of the glass, of the store. A police officer stood at the door and held his gun and said, "Nobody's leaving. Nobody's leaving."

It was at that point that I looked down at my cell phone. I picked up my cell phone and I called my wife. I was able to get through, maybe one or two tries. My wife was hysterical, crying. The first thing I told her was I was all right. I said, "What happened?"

And she said, "They're gone."

And I said, "What's gone? Are the children gone?"

And she said, "No. They're gone. They're gone."

I said, "What's gone? What could be gone?"

And she said, "The towers. The towers are gone."

I said, "They can't be gone. They were just there. The towers are a block away from me."

She says, "No. They're gone." She says, "Where are you?"

I said, "I'm in a building. I'm in a store. I've got to work. I'm okay."

She said, "All right. Just be safe."

The police officer said, "Nobody leaves here." The people started to panic, saying, "We need to leave. We need to get out." And the police officer said, "Nobody's leaving here. This is a safe place. Look at it out there. It's pitch black."

So somebody screamed. A lot of people were under the impression that a bomb or something had knocked the buildings down. That's what I had believed, that there were bombs set after the planes had hit, a secondary device to take the buildings down. I could never imagine the plane taking the building down. Why didn't it fall to begin with? Nobody thought the fuel from the plane would cause major fires, which would melt down the building structure.

Somebody yelled, "There's a bomb in this building." They ran to the police officer, almost knocked him down, ran out of the building. When I got out to the street the air was not breathable. But you could breathe it with something over your face. Coming from the south were [groups] of people from the downtown Wall Street area, covering their faces with rags, walking toward the Brooklyn Bridge. A lot of them were just grabbing us and asking questions like, "How do I get out of here? Are the trains running? Are the buses running?" And we couldn't even give them answers.

[I] walked all the way down to the ferry terminal, where there were a lot of doctors, a lot of nurses, a lot of EMS people collecting. They're putting out cots. Equipment was coming in, truckloads of equipment [were] coming in, but no patients. Looking down, you could see a sea of ambulances lining up along the street that goes along the Battery Park.

When the ferry showed up, looking down at where the ferry allows the cars to come out, it looked like thousands of firefighters. As many firefighters that could fit on the ferry were coming from the Staten Island Ferry. They marched off, uptown, like in twos or fours, almost as if they were [an] army, carrying equipment. They walked up in their bunker gear and there was a crowd of people that applauded the firefighters as they were coming off the ferry. An unbelievable amount of firefighters, and the people were applauding.

[*Captain Swithers made his way back toward Ground Zero.*]

I walked all the way up Broadway. I got down to Chambers Street and West Street, and that's where our mobile emergency response vehicle was. They're treating a lot of people there, and I met up with the USAR guys. The first urban search and rescue medic that I see there was Captain Jimmy Booth, who was pretty much organizing the group there. He says, "You look horrible. You better clean yourself up. We have a lot of work to do." I went back to an area where there was a big barrel of water and I proceeded to take my shirt off, clean my hair out, comb my hair, clean my face up. I felt like a new person. I walked back and he said, "Good. Much better. Much better."

At that point they told us that our equipment, the cache, was coming on the flatbed trucks, and that we should go up Chambers Street. A lot of equipment, two tractor trailers worth of equipment. These are gigantic circus tents, refrigerators, pallets of food, medical supplies, stretchers, meals ready to eat, everything—enough to keep a team at a location for eight days on its own.

We were very anxious to get our equipment together to go in, but they said, "Nobody's going in until Building Seven collapses. That's the rule." Building Seven . . . it looked like a fifty-story building that was maybe three blocks away from us. And around four o'clock you heard the rumble. The same type of rumble, and the crunching, and I looked at everybody standing next to me, firefighters, police officers, and I said, "Run!" And we started to run north. You could hear it falling, and one of the police officer lieutenants, who is one of the team managers, yells, "Stop! Stop, you pussies! You don't run unless I say so. Don't you just run away." And as we turned around and looked, you could see that the building sort of fell, and the billowing out didn't go as far as we, you know, as I would anticipate.

One of the guys said to me, "What made you say 'run'? What made you say 'run'?"

I looked at him and I said, "Once you have two 110-story buildings fall on you in one day, you sort of become a specialist in this area and you run when anything is falling until you know that it's safe." And he looked at me and he sort of like snickered, as if [to say], "I guess I would take your advice and run."

Then we returned to our equipment and we pulled out our boxes, our medical vests, and we started to fill them up. At that point Captain Jimmy Booth decided that we're going to have an entry team go in for a few moments. Then another team would go in for a few hours and come out. I was told that I was going in at 7:00 A.M. I said, "Wow, that's pretty late, but all right. I'm a little bit tired. I could sit back and help set up here, and relax."

I called my wife and told her, "I'm not going in until 7:00 A.M. so I'll call you later on tonight." It was at that point one of the members wasn't there to go in. I volunteered to take his place. I geared up, and we were brought by [Chevy] Suburban right into the site. It looked like hell. Worse than what you can imagine out of any movie. Flames were burning left and right. Pieces of debris were just sort of hanging off of adjacent buildings. You could see clearly the I beams stuck into buildings across the street. Glass was out from all the windows. Cars were crushed. You could see ambulances that were mangled, twisted, with the doors left open. I was convinced, we were all convinced, that there had to be people alive in that area.

It was such a scary sight. We were scared to be there and we sat down to huddle. Anthony DiGennaro points to the ground, in a puddle, where people have been walking back and forth. We all turn to look. It was a hand, a female hand from the wrist down, with a diamond engagement ring on the finger. The nails were well groomed with nail polish on them. The hand wasn't dirty at all. It was just a hand. And we looked down, saying, "Oh my God, there's a hand." In shock. There's a hand, where people are stepping on it. Somebody ran over with a bag and picked it up and bagged it and tagged it and carried it away, and at that point I said to myself, "Well, you guys could sit here all night long, but I need to get out there. I'll get out there and do what I have to do."

I realized the most helpful people were the people that had search dogs. We were in there only three hours after they started searching. Anything that was on the top layer was obviously already pulled out. I wandered around with a search dog [team], and the dog happened to find one body after another. In fact, they were torsos with the head, with no arms, or maybe legs without the torso, or just a leg or an arm.

I remember firefighters identifying one body. It was a man, fully intact, however his intestines were hanging out. We looked at him and they said, "It's one of our brothers. Look at the pants. It's one of the brothers. That looks like bunker gear." And I remember jumping down there and starting to dig with my gloved hands and his arm was stuck underneath an I beam. They were using airbags and devices to pick up the I beam to get the arm out. And we dug him out a little bit more and we realized the pants were from Gap. It was a sigh of relief for the firefighters. At least it's not one of the brothers. We rolled this body into a body bag.

Then I remember there was a major goal to try to find living people, not so much to take out dead people. So they started to go for the I beams. You could almost step from one I beam to the next, as this structure of the World Trade Center was like maybe eighteen inches of window and an I beam, eighteen inches of window, I beam. You could sort of step over from one piece to the next piece. There were guys out there with torches. It was dark, and you could see these acetylene torches burning with sparks flying as they're cutting the I beams. Looking just a little bit further, you could see red flames, coming up from just anywhere, with smoke billowing out.

I remember working and uncovering one body, more like parts, one body after another, up until the point where David Russell had tapped me on the shoulder and said, "When do you want to leave?"

And I said, "Didn't we just get here?"

He says, "It's three o'clock in the morning. When do you want to get out of here?"

I said, "Three o'clock in the morning. We're only supposed to be here until like midnight, one o'clock." And I remember saying, "Okay, we'll leave." And we walked back [to our staging area]. I had a little bit of water. I sat down on these boxes that we carry our equipment in. I just lay down and the next thing I knew I was cold, and it was sunlight. I realized that I had fallen asleep, and now it was daylight.

Somebody said, "It's your turn. It's your turn."

I didn't know what was going on, but I was like, "You're right. It's my turn. It's 7:00 A.M."

So I put on my equipment again, having [had nothing but] water, marched out there. And it was a little bit more organized down there, within just a couple of hours. They said, "You're matched up with this rescue team." I remember introducing myself to the fire chief that was there, and he was like, "Good. You'll be standing by for us. We're doing a lot of work and we're removing a lot of debris. We're finding a lot of bodies."

Somebody had called for me to come up higher [on the I beams]. I got to the highest point, which must have been maybe eight stories high, but this metal was very, very hot. If you looked straight into the metal, you saw a female body laying right on top of the structure, just laying right on top of the structure. You could actually see a rebar; it went right through her. She was just lying sprawled out, obviously dead.

At the time I was very nervous and I was too scared to jump over to the other side, to where she was, in fear that I would fall, or in fear that the piece of metal that I would come in contact with would burn me. I was very impressed to see an ironworker—they were fantastic, unbelievable— just wearing a T-shirt and a yellow helmet, jump from one I beam to the other. This ironworker actually climbed up there and said, "What do we need to do?"

I remember the firefighters bringing up a saw and saying, "We need to cut the I beam." They cut the I beam from underneath her and she started to fall. And the ironworker actually held her from falling in between all the other I beams to a place where we wouldn't have been able to get her. He was holding her, and I remembered a face of disgust, like, "Oh, this is so gross."

I remember him looking at me and saying, "You guys do this all the time, don't you?"

And I was thinking to myself, "Yes, right. We don't do this all the time." You know, I've seen some bad things but this is far beyond what we would normally do. I sort of nodded my head and they brought up a body bag. They rolled her into a body bag and a bunch of firefighters and a bunch of rescue workers, NYPD guys, daisy-chained the bag down to a lower level.

I remember regrouping with the team. Somebody said, "We have a live one. We have a live one." Carl and I, we both had our equipment. We started to run over the structures, a wave of structures, and it was pretty unique because at certain points where one section would connect with the next section, there's maybe a three- or four-foot jump. All the firefighters and all the rescue workers that were down there created a daisy chain, just pulling our arms, making sure we made it from the next step to the next step. As we looked forward, we could see a major part of building number one, maybe fifteen stories high, with a daisy chain of men all up to that point. Then a ladder going up a bit, with people climbing on debris to get up to the rest of it, and then a rope going from one tower of debris to another. They're like, "We're going to bring this person down."

And then came down a [rescue] stretcher, but because of the positioning of the I beams it was easier for them to hand the stretcher to the next person and to the next person. We had radioed to the paramedics at the end that there was a body coming down. We weren't even sure if that was a live person or a dead person. We were able to look at her. She was intact. Her clothes were totally off of her, and I remember her eyes being closed. Her forehead was swollen and I remember seeing just a little bit of pink in her mouth, which was a good thing.

When it got to the end, they started to lift the patient out of the stretcher; she started to move. These two paramedics treated that female, and they said within minutes she started to talk. She told them all she remembered was that she was working on the thirty-third floor of Tower One of the World Trade Center. That was the last person that we pulled out alive.

She was just lying on top of what was a stairwell. She was not crushed. It was a miracle. She was unconscious and somebody found her and they actually thought she was dead. Next to her was a dead body, which was removed just moments later on that daisy chain.

I realized at that point that it was very late in the afternoon, that we were there just about the whole day. My relief finally came. And it was a two-block walk [to the staging site], and I was very tired for that two blocks. Five people walked up to me saying, "Call your wife." And I realized that I'd told my wife I was going to call her the night before, around ten o'clock. My cell phone was dead, but luckily enough I was able to borrow a phone from somebody. Actually my phone wasn't completely dead. I remember seeing that I had messages, and listening to the messages saying, "Hon, I hope that you're okay," to "Hon, I'm starting to worry. I'm really starting to worry. Would you please give me a call? If you're alive, please call me. I'm going to call your work now." And then my work, at my office, saying, "Jay, I hope that you're alive. We're praying for you."

And I finally had the opportunity to call, and you could tell there was a sigh of relief, saying, "Where were you?"

I had to apologize, and I had to explain really quick what had happened, that [my relief] disappeared and I had to go out there. We were out there and I fell asleep and the next thing I knew somebody was patting me on the shoulder saying, "Go back out there."

I apologized to my wife. She's like, "You are taking care of yourself?"

And I said, "Yes, I am." That was that day. That night I was able to get that whole night's sleep, a good eight hours, and I was fresh the next day.

[*Captain Swithers was assigned to the day shift. He continued working at Ground Zero.*]

I remember pulling up to my driveway [one evening], and my house didn't have an American flag. I said to myself, "Oh, this is so bad. This is really bad." My wife still had [the] flag out from the summer, with flowers on it. I pulled into the driveway and my kids met me at the door, and they were carrying little American flags. They were marching in a parade sort of deal.

My wife said, "I didn't tell them to do this. They did this on their own."

I gave them all a kiss, and my wife said, "How are you doing?"

I said, "Okay. I have to go back there tomorrow. I need to get some sleep."

She said, "You know, these neighbors, these freaking neighbors, they have no respect. They have a problem that there's no American flag out on the building, outside on the house. I've been nothing but glued to the television ever since." Then she told me that she had a big argument with her father, who lives two doors down. He was talking about the fact that we don't have an American flag out, and she told him where to go, and then she said something about, "My in-laws are concentrating on the wrong people. They're worried about firefighters from other families, saying that they got out safe, and meanwhile you were in the collapse—don't they understand?"

I was like, "Please, just don't fight with them. You might need them. You might need them. I don't know what's going to happen next, but you might need them."

[*The next morning Swithers was back in the disaster zone.*]

I was matched up with some rescue workers. They were real tunneling guys. I remember going with them, and at this point Makita, Milwaukee, all these companies that make power tools were just handing them out from stands, saying, "You need these tools? You need batteries? We'll give you the stuff." Everybody had a power tool. Power tools to the left, power tools to the right. We're going down, tunneling into these parking garages. It was almost a goal for the fire rescue guys to get further than anybody else has gone before, to the point where I wasn't able to go, because there was only so much room. But I stayed behind with the radio, for support. I was actually treating [them]; numerous guys were getting little abrasions and lacerations and whatnot. I remember a firefighter came to me, this big guy said to me, "Do me a favor. Shove this in your bag." And he gave me a sign that said, "Basement Level Three." He says, "They said that nobody's been there, but I've been there."

I looked at him and I said, "I could do that."

He shoved the sign into my bag, and at the end of the day he pulled it out, and said, "Thanks a lot." That proved that he was someplace where nobody has gone before.

That day it rained. It was a very discouraging day because they managed to lift one of the fire ladder trucks off the bridge going across West Street. When they lifted out that fire ladder truck, like a little Tonka toy, they found fifteen bodies of firefighters that were just sprawled out underneath it, just laying there looking for cover, just like I did from the beginning. I was thinking, "Well, you picked the right vehicle to hide under." Unfortunately, there's nothing that could keep you safe from a whole building falling on top of you. At that point I was thinking about my life, hiding underneath a smaller truck on the east side of this debris. I was at that point really glad that I was alive.

The next day was another rainy day and I got matched up with a bunch of firefighters. Going down into the subway, we wound up in an underground mall which was half-collapsed. All the windows were smashed. The ceiling fixtures were all down. But you could walk around, climbing over this stuff. At one point one of the firefighters needed something to drink and he walked into a store. He opened up where the soda was and left money on the counter for a drink, a Gatorade or something. I think he was just trying to be amusing. But I could appreciate the honesty that was so much there.

There was everything—jewelry stores, watches still on display, and clothes. We continued on, and we were going into a clothes store, and it was collapsed. I remember crawling up with my flashlight and looking down at a mannequin, saying, "I think I found somebody." And then looking down further and saying, "Oh, it's only a mannequin. I feel like such an idiot. I feel like such an idiot."

The guy's like, "Don't worry. Don't worry about it."

So we're at the mall level and this is something I will never forget. They said, "Why don't you stay here at the top stairs?" I sat down and turned off my flashlight. They said, "We're going to go down looking for Vinny." You could hear them yelling, "Vinny, Vinny, Vinny, Vinny,"

getting lower and lower and lower. While I was sitting there, I saw flashlights coming down the mall—two guys with flashlights. I saw two guys
and I said, "Vinny, is that you?"

They're like, "No, it's not Vinny." And these two guys walked up.
They're wearing the yellow helmets. They're wearing yellow raincoats.
They had a clipboard and keys and boots on.

They're like, "Are you looking for somebody?"

I said, "Yes, we're looking for a firefighter. He's just got misplaced."

They said, "Oh, it sounds serious."

And I said, "No, no. They'll find him. They'll find him." And I sat
there and these guys wandered around as if they're taking a survey, looking
at things. The next day I saw one of those firefighters [I'd been working
with]. He came up to me laughing, and saying, "Remember those guys
that were wandering around? Ten minutes after you left, sheriff cars pulled
up, and they ran down into the mall and pulled up those guys. They were
looters. They had watches and all different things. They were down there
posed as rescue workers but they were looters."

And I said, "Wow. You had me." I remember sitting there and thinking that they were officials, and I felt pretty comfortable that they were
around. I said, for the most part, I don't know how much money I had in
my wallet, but they could have just hit me over the head and just left me
there to die. Nobody would have known the difference.

On certain occasions I really was looking forward to going home. We
did twelve hours on, twelve hours off. The team would have to meet at the
Bureau of Training in Queens, get a vehicle, and relieve the team on-site.
So the day wasn't actually a twelve-hour day. It was really a fourteen-hour
day with the transportation back and forth.

I remember saying, "Let's just take the Brooklyn Bridge home. That's
clear, and we'll take the highway. That'll be clear, and go home." The
members on the team, the guys that were with me on that shift, would
say, "You know what, can we please just go up Hero Row? Can we please
just go up Hero Row?"

I kind of liked Hero Row but I was a little bit tired. In any event, I thought it was healthy, because you would be able to get into our vehicle and roll down all the windows. For the most part I always was in the back. We would drive up West Street where there would be hundreds, if not thousands, of people applauding, applauding. Every vehicle that was going up there would be driving maybe twenty miles an hour, purposely, just to absorb that appreciation from New York City.

If you stopped at a light, people would be handing us water, or cookies. These weren't just like Oreo cookies; these were things that people made, little goodie bags and stuff. It was a really good feeling. The vehicle said "New York City Fire Department," and the people would be clapping. "Firefighters! Firemen! New York City Fire Department! Fire Department!" And the guys would give that little bit of hero wave out the window. I remember that. That was a good thing, to make people feel good, because it was so depressing at that point. I sort of was a little bit depressed to say, "We're really not giving these people anything. We're really not finding anything. Other than going into this pile, and this mess every day, and risking your life looking. It would be nice if we could just come up with some more live people."

It was unbelievable thinking about going through that street. People were holding big signs, applauding. There were people that were willing to give out hugs, you know, young girls that were purposely making themselves look really, really pretty and throwing kisses. It was a little bit longer of a ride home, maybe took an extra half hour, which was a lot of time. I was very anxious to get home to see my kids.

I remember one of the nights where I was pulling into my driveway and my neighbors had come. To begin with, one of the earlier nights my wife didn't have a flag out. I said to my wife, "You've got to talk to the neighbors. You can't just leave them in the dark [about] what's going on." So I dragged my wife out and I said, "My wife has been glued to the television as I've been out doing urban search and rescue. I was in the collapse."

My neighbors were actually very apologetic at that point, and said, "I'm sorry. We really should have been there for you."

I said, "Well, that's why we don't have a flag out, but as soon as we can get a flag up, you'll see a flag up. My wife wasn't even able to purchase a flag because they weren't available."

The neighbors were really upset about the flag?

Oh, very upset. Very upset. It was a major issue. There was a house across the street that is probably not owner-occupied. It's rented. And on the window he put up a big sign, the tenant, "Flag to come." Sort of like a message, "Don't give me a hard time. I'm still searching for my flag."

Then one night when I pulled in front of my house to open up the gate to drive my car into the driveway, our neighbors had come over, and they were like, "Oh, we really are concerned about you. Thank you for doing such a great job. What is it like down there?" And I explained exactly what it was like.

Here we are in December, and my mortgage broker had sent cards, knowing I work for the fire department. There were maybe eight cards, like from kids, and they had their addresses on the cards. I purposely made a form letter, and sent it back, acknowledging the cards. And I made sure they were distributed through several firehouses with some of the other cards that came in. Just yesterday my wife opened up the mail, and there was this big gigantic envelope filled with Christmas cards, made by small kids from California, like thirty or forty of them. Those cards were all over the place down at Ground Zero. They're pinned, glued, or stuck to every wall, where you could stop anywhere and read cards from small children from all over the world. And the fire department, all over the walls. I didn't get to see the commissioner's office, but they described it as like being Santa Claus's mail. Like *Miracle on 34th Street*, they said, the bags of mail would come in.

Sometimes the days were very eventful, and sometimes they weren't very eventful. But we didn't find any living people. Pretty much the people that we did find, for the most part, they weren't all together, they weren't all intact.

Did you find any children?

Amazingly, I didn't see any children. There was not one child. There were people that said they saw children's toys. However, I didn't see any children. On the scene there were an incredible amount of shoes. As people are in an explosion, one of the first things that happens, like when somebody's hit by a car, their shoes come flying off. There was an incredible amount of shoes on the scene.

As the days went on, a combination of that ability to almost do anything, that you're invincible, along with the depression, the fatigue, you sort of start to lose your footing. Your boots become a little bit heavier. Some days it rained and you were miserable. Some points of the day it was hot, and some points of the evening it would get cold. You lose focus. You start to get exposed more to the outside world, the emotions of what people are thinking on the outside. It's very hard to stay focused for a long, long period of time.

How they set up the urban search and rescue teams, they don't want any teams to stay on any site for more than eight days. In fact, even though it's at a tremendous cost, at the World Trade Center, FEMA sent in teams, and on the eighth day they would pull teams out and another team would be coming in from another state. As a rule of thumb, they find that people work better only staying eight days.

When it became the eleventh day, a decision was made to downsize the medical component to the rescue team, because we were strictly rescue, not so much recovery, and it was less likely that you would be able to find a living person. And the first ones they asked to return to their regular duties were the officers with other responsibilities, [and] I was one of those people.

NOVEMBER 7, 2002

[*Captain Swithers returned to his job in the fire department's Bureau of Health. Workers' compensation claims increased dramatically in the wake of September*

11, including complaints about respiratory problems from breathing in dust and fumes. Swithers says the main aftereffect for him was nightmares.]

I'm being pelted by pieces of debris. And I'm having to make a decision whether to run, to duck. Or what would it be like to be somebody else? Or what would it be like to be dead? You know the scenario of looking down at everybody and not being able to change anything, sort of like the movie *Ghost*. In the beginning it would [recur] very often. From the beginning, you could dream that dream over and over again, maybe three times a week, which is extraordinary. So that has tapered down to maybe once every two weeks, I have to say.

And do you wake up from it?

I've woken up from it. Sometimes waking up from it is good because that really gets me excited that I got some sleep. As far as the World Trade Center, you kind of hope that you could wake up from it. This is a good thing that you're crawling out of bed and waking up in the morning. Or looking at your clock to say, "Oh good, I have another three hours to sleep."

Has it affected your relationship with your wife?

I think there's been some of it that has affected it. However, we're pretty strong people. My wife complains every once in a while: "I have to deal with you. You don't sleep and you keep me up all night long." You know, "And you don't talk." I don't talk to her. That drives her crazy, I guess. But I shelter her from all the other issues.

This has been a year of funerals. So tell me about some of them.

I didn't have as many to go through because I've been very busy. But I've been to more than what I ever can imagine—twelve. A year before it was really unique for somebody to have died in the line of service. That would be something the mayor would not miss. Where it seems as if we're doing the same thing over and over and over and over again. In a lot of these cases, especially the firefighters, they pushed themselves to go from one funeral to the next, maybe three in one day. In most cases, not even able to get the opportunity to go into the church, standing in line outside saluting as the casket went by. To me, that was very draining. I wish that I don't have to do any more of that. However, I'm sure as DNA tests continue, and they continue to figure out body parts or bone fragments of missing people through these tests, there'll be another funeral that I'll say, "I remember him. I know him. Let me look at my calendar. I'll be there."

JUNE 24, 2005

Were you wearing a mask on that first day? Were you wearing a breathing mask?

I wasn't wearing a respirator. I was wearing a helmet with a visor. Some form of a respirator was handed out, probably the next day. We were actually given better respirators on day three, and a lot of that stuff was donated.

And so do you have health concerns?

I have health concerns. To be honest with you, I really believe that while we've seen a lot of people get sick within the last couple years, from what we call black lung, or World Trade Center lung, or hyperactive lung disease, my biggest fear is that, perhaps in ten or fifteen years, the bad diseases will manifest. I know that I'm a little bit more winded than I was before the World Trade Center. During one [examination], it was figured that I had a piece of metal in my lung. I had an MRI done, and they had told me, "Well, it's really not an issue right now. It's not something you should be worried about." However, they're not actually sure if it's a piece of metal or not.

How about the psychological impact of the events? How have you carried that? Over the years, have you personally sought counseling?

Well, the city and fire department have provided numerous forms of counseling, if you're interested. Myself, I'm shy of counseling. For myself, being involved in this interview project, being able to talk to people, feeling that I'm making a difference, it's counseling for myself. I really don't think talking to a counselor, from my point of view, would be very helpful. I think this type of interaction—being able to talk to people and express my feelings otherwise has been very helpful.

What's really strange is that in our community, my partners who work as paramedics, we really don't talk about things among each other. I know that because, during other oral history interviews, I overheard some of the answers and I was absolutely amazed at how my partner had such interaction at the World Trade Center site, in the things that he did. My other friend, best friend—my best man—actually drove a vehicle into the tunnel, turned it around, and carried people who were running out of the Brooklyn Battery Tunnel. These are things we don't discuss among each other. We kind of just have those stories inside.

Why do you suppose that's the case?

To be honest with you, I don't know. Perhaps we really don't want to talk about our stories. Perhaps we don't want to feel that we are the heroes, that this is what we do. It just seems to be normal.

14.

Inder Jit Singh

Dentist, Anatomy Professor, Author

Interviewed by Amy Starecheski

Inder Jit Singh is a dentist and a professor of anatomy at New York University. He was born in 1937 in Gujranwala, India, and moved to the United States as a teenager. He earned a PhD from the University of Oregon Medical School and his DDS from Columbia University. He is the author of two books of essays on Sikh faith and culture, Sikhs and Sikhism: A View with a Bias *and* The Sikh Way: A Pilgrim's Progress. *Singh is also a public speaker on the Sikh faith and its traditions. On September 11, 2001, Singh was in his office at New York University when he witnessed the smoke rising from the towers.*

JANUARY 20, 2002

I was born in a town called Gujranwala, which is now in Pakistan. And you know that there was no Pakistan in 1947, and I'm a bit older than that, so I was born in Gujranwala when it was India. Pakistan was formed in 1947 and we migrated from there to what is now India. Good historians tell you that over eight million people migrated from one part to the other. The issues of refugees at that time was greater than in Europe after the Second World War. Likes of which nobody has ever seen. I've seen trainloads of people being killed, and I was seven years old at the time, or eight years old. And I've seen houses burning at night. And we escaped courtesy of the Muslim driver who used to take us to school every day. Otherwise, I wouldn't have made it, you know? [Laughs] We escaped with basically the clothes we had on our backs. So there are experiences of that kind. They're a part of my memory which will stay.

America is a very open country, you know. There are problems here, yes. There are issues that I disagree [with], that I've always disagreed [with], I suppose. Issues of racial discrimination, Vietnam, and so on. I lived through those periods here. But there's more opportunity in this country than anywhere else in the world. This is a more open society than any other society that I know, or ever thought of. So there are the pleasures of being here, which should be taken into account when I say critical things about the country. The opportunity that the country gave me, and simple ordinary Americans gave me. But of course, when I came here, I was perhaps one of two or three Sikhs in New York in 1960. Perhaps there are about three hundred thousand Sikhs or so in America [now]. There's always in this country an undercurrent of resentment against new immigrants. The Irish rioted in the streets of New York because they thought they were being discriminated [against]. So did the Italians. We have not done that, but the undercurrent of resentment is always there, because discrimination is always there to some degree. And I suppose one should not be surprised by that. That's perfectly normal. Perfectly natural.

But what happened after 9/11 I found a little disturbing, and surprising, and I'll tell you why. As a turban-wearing guy, I can understand why many Americans would look at a turban and say, "Ah, there goes another guy who looks like Osama bin Laden." But most people don't know the difference, just like most Indians don't know the variety of 250 kinds of

Christians that exist here. And I'm not even a Muslim. But you know, even if I were, the issue is not that. I mean, an American living here peacefully as an American deserves to be accepted as such, even if he is Osama bin Laden's brother. If he's not responsible for what his brother is doing—that's perfectly all right. No need to discriminate, no need to harass him.

Sikhs have been harassed [since 9/11]. You know, one was even killed in Arizona. One Sikh was killed, another couple have been attacked, and we are not Muslims. So there have been cases of mistaken identity. And that bothered me. I got calls from the press in India, for example, who said to us, "Are you rethinking your strategy of wearing a turban and long hair?" And they were rather gleeful about it. And I had to say to them that whatever America's problems may be, to me they are temporary, and they pale in comparison to what you people did in 1984, and I feel safer here, even the way it is. I feel much safer here than I would in India.

In India, in three days of 1984, when Prime Minister Indira Gandhi was assassinated, for three full days it was open season on all Sikhs. And across the country, mobs of non-Sikhs, mostly Hindus, mostly led by leaders of the ruling political party, went about hounding Sikhs, killing them, murdering, raping, burning. They had lists of Sikh homes and businesses and truckloads of people and weapons. And this was in India! You must realize that in India, trucks are not easy to get. Weapons are all licensed and registered. To have kerosene to burn, you got to stand in line. It's rationed. These people had all these supplies, they came in truckloads, they looked at an address, they had a list, they burnt the houses, and they were Sikh houses. And for three days it happened, and the government did nothing. Police arrested nobody. The government now admits that over 2,700 people were killed in the capital city of Delhi alone. And how many people were arrested? Zilch. Absolutely zero.

So things of that nature happened there. Here, one lone man was killed in Arizona, and the attorney general made a note of that publicly, the FBI director [Robert] Mueller made a note of it publicly. Even the White House made a note of it, though the White House, at that time, could not tell the difference between a Sikh and a Muslim. That tells you the level of ignorance under which we operate here. But still, they recognize that what happened is gruesome, not right. It's outside the law, and not right. And they did act on it. The man was arrested, has been arrested. Interestingly, there was a debate on the Internet in the Sikh channels on what should this man get. Should he get the death penalty or not? And the opinions of most young Sikhs was, No. They could not quite get to the point of forgiving him, but the death penalty we didn't want. There's no point in that. There's no education in that.

What I was going to tell you [is that] most of us did get a lot of remarks on the streets here and there. And stares. People looked at us with the glare of strangers. And the look of a stranger is very different from that of a friend. But the Sikhs did have a couple of blood drives here in New York to commemorate the victims of the World Trade Center disaster. They did have a couple of candlelight vigils, one in Central Park for the same purpose. The good thing that happened from it, the Sikh community which was living in isolation now tried to build bridges with the communities around, which we should have done and which we should do. Partially, we were remiss. We did not try to build bridges with the host community. But they were remiss too. The American custom, or the American tradition, is that when I move to a new neighborhood, neighbors come with a welcome wagon to meet me, welcome me. I don't know them, they don't know me, but they come to welcome me to the new community. So we did not build bridges. But you didn't bring the welcome wagon either. [Laughs]

I'm going to be talking at a Unitarian [Universalist] church introducing Sikhism a week from today. And then a week from that, February 2, I will be doing this lecture on Sikhism at the public library in Flushing [Queens]. And they have a series now, like public lectures the kind you see in Europe—there's the lecture on Islam, Hinduism, Buddhism, and so on, and now the Sikhs, I will do that. And I'm glad of that. So some good has come out of this, you know? A lot of good has come out of the tragedy and the mess.

So were you forced to move [from Pakistan], or did you decide to move?

Yes, one of the fundamental premises of forming Pakistan was the fact that the leadership in India, which was fighting for independence of the country, was somewhat Hindu dominated. Pakistan was formed as an Islamic country, a Muslim country. Strictly. And in a Muslim country, any non-Muslim was not really welcome. There are very few Hindus or Sikhs left in Pakistan. That's what religion can do at its worst, you know? A fanatical attitude that says, "The only way is my way, anything else is wrong." And to me that is not the American way. And to me that is the problem with the people that attacked the World Trade Center, the fanatical attitude that says, "We are the only true path and anything else is an infidel and therefore their dying doesn't count." And that's not right, that's just not right. And I think that's what happened here. But that's not the way of Islam, that's not the way of Sikhism, that's not the way of Christianity.

So when a security man tells me that he wants to remove my turban, I don't accept that. That is not right, that is not consistent with the spirit of this country. I mean, you don't ask somebody else to remove her—to drop his pants, or something of this kind. If your [metal detector] goes off around my turban, then you have the right to take me to a private room and suggest that you want to look under it because security concerns so dictate. But that should apply just as well to my shoes. If your beeper goes off, please, I'll take my shoes off too. No problem. Or my pants off too, for that matter. But if the beeper doesn't go off, why should you do this? Just because I look like somebody who may have come from somewhere else. That's got nothing to do with anything. Everybody here has come from somewhere else. Everybody. Even George W. Bush [laughs], you know?

How did you practice your religion being the only Sikh around?

I don't need other people around to practice it. The religion is ultimately a very personal matter. It's your relationship to what's within you. There is no god sitting up there; it is not a three-decker universe. No heaven or hell out there—it's the heaven or hell that you create here.

What do you think are the characteristics of American Sikhism?

Sikhism is very modern, to my mind, a very modern religion. Very egalitarian. It treats—it teaches—not always practices, but teaches—that men and women are to be treated equally. There's nothing in the temple that I can do that you cannot. And there's nothing that I cannot do that must be done by a priest or a minister. So it's a very modern religion. It has no caste system. It tells you: there's one God, and all his children, and God can be discovered through his creations. So the principles are simple.

Where were you on the day of September 11 and how did you hear about it?

In my office. And from a window we could see the World Trade Center. And we looked out the window and I saw the smoke rising out of it. Then the trains stopped of course. The Long Island trains [to my home] were not running in the afternoon. And a colleague of mine who lives in Merrick drives to work so I took a ride with him. But otherwise it would have been a disaster. Thursday I went [by train]. And I saw some hostile stares. You could see that they were not happy to see me there. Their attitude was, "Why the hell is this guy there?" You know? "Should we tie him down? Is he going to bomb the train or what?" But of course many had seen me every day. Because you usually ride the same train and a lot of the same faces see you.

So you noticed an immediate change in how people reacted to you.

Walking around the streets, one had to be a little afraid. One had to be a little careful. I know a kid—a Sikh kid—who was chased by people. You know, and he had to run away from them. *Newsweek* published a picture of a Sikh physician, a doctor. As a matter of fact, I know him. He was one of the first physicians giving help at Ground Zero. And while he was coming home, he was harassed and attacked. And that, to me, is very strange behavior. I had not experienced that in this country. I know it happened in India; I've seen it in 1947. I've seen killing of people there. But I thought Americans were a little bit above that. I know that Americans interned a lot of Japanese during World War II and I think that was dumb. It was contrary to what you call "American values." And that's the American religion, really, [it] is the American values.

In fact, the early proposals of the security act—the homeland security policy—that Bush and the attorney general [John Ashcroft] tried to suggest and push, I thought it very bad. You know? Anybody, any immigrant that you think is not the right color skin, you're going to arrest him and put him in jail. Don't have to tell him why he's arrested, don't have to show him any evidence, don't have to give him any legal safeguards—that's certainly not the American way. And we have to recognize that the country is made up of immigrants. You can't just base this on what your looks or accent might be from, your religion might be. That doesn't make any sense. So I think the country was caught in a bind. That was the first time that such a major attack on the mainland had occurred. And they had to do something. Bush was a new untested president. He had to do something to show that he was a leader. And so they made policies, or recommended policies that were absolutely foolish. The only saving grace is that they have not really put them into large-scale practice. But all that does, that kind of policy, it really fosters war hysteria. It makes citizens behave in manners not right. I think if people here sometimes discriminate or harass people or kill people, partially it is because politicians have made dumb comments.

As it became clear that after the eleventh that Sikhs were going to be targeted by ignorant people as Osama bin Laden's followers, did you change your behavior at all?

To some degree, yes, I became careful. I put a flag on my car and a flag on my lapel. If that reassures the people out there. I usually wear a black turban or a blue turban—maybe blue to work—conservative colors. A couple of days I wore a maroon color. Why? Perhaps, because these idiots out there on the street will not associate maroon with—you know— Osama bin Laden does not wear maroon. I didn't walk around alone at night. People have been chased by hoodlums. We invited politicians to come to our places of worship. I met the mayor—the mayor's office and the team there several times. And in groups—

Mayor [Rudolph W.] Giuliani?

Yes, and the Manhattan borough president, Virginia Fields, too. And sometimes we met with Muslim groups; sometimes we met alone with the politicians. Our people went to see Bush as well. Met him for an hour. The president. We've been distributing flyers to people, telling them about Sikhs and Sikhism. The idea is to inform people and perhaps an informed people will be better. But you know, when the economy is bad, people always resent immigrants. Because the first thought is that the immigrants are here and they are taking my job and if they were not here, I would be making more money. That's not always true, but this is natural.

Besides the fear of harassment and the outreach that you've described in the Sikh community, have you noticed any other changes in the community since the eleventh?

The first couple of days that I went to town, I saw not many Sikhs with turbans on their heads. Some of them cut their hair. Some of them got those polo caps, you know, the baseball caps, and that's what they wore. Many of the taxi drivers, that's what they wore. Many of the Sikh taxi drivers put together a group to give free taxi service from Ground Zero to hospitals, to doctors and to patients and to people that were found. And that went on for a number of days.

September 11 is now four months ago. Have you noticed a change in people's reactions to you from the eleventh to now?

Oh yes, yes, yes. When we started working with the television people—from Geraldo Rivera, to NBC's Town Hall meetings, to CNN and others—they highlighted Sikhs. They interviewed quite a few. And once they started doing that, I thought the attitudes changed. On the trains and others. Things have now changed pretty well to normal. Initially, even the White House was confused that the Sikhs were Muslims. The statements that the attorney general made and some of the statements that President Bush made reflected the confusion in words. I do realize that Bush makes a statement that's probably handed to him. He probably doesn't know anything about it. You can't expect him to. But things have changed. They have known the difference and they have learned some. I said, there's a lot of positive, good things that have come out of it.

It has been four months. And what I see now, though, is people who stole from the stores in Ground Zero—you know, expensive watches and things. And the misuse of funds by those who collected charity money. And some of that sickens me. I didn't really expect that in America. I thought that here, people have plenty. Even those who have nothing have plenty, really. And this kind of behavior they shouldn't have done. But then I look at Enron and that kind of behavior—they shouldn't have done [that] either. [Laughs] You know, what can I say? I mean, to collect in the name of a disaster, the World Trade Center, and then to misuse those funds, or embezzle those funds—that, I think, is unforgivable. Whereas in India, everything is crooked from the bottom to the top. From the prime minister or president down to the local policeman or the garbage collector. They're all crooked. They all take money. And this is not the case here. For the ordinary man, life is fairly honest, fairly straight, fairly law-abiding, and there's no problem. And I think there my confidence is a little shattered. I expect George Bush to buy the election—that's okay, if he can. [Laughs] You know, he did it. But I don't expect the charity man to do this. Not in this country.

Over the course of your life I see two times when your hometown has been disrupted by extremely violent events. Partition, in the town where you were born, and now in your second hometown, New York, September 11. Do you relate those two events at all?

When I look back, they're very different. You know, [partition] was a very traumatic event of really untold proportions. It never registered on me then; I was much too young. I realized later there were eight million people running across the borders and starving, literally, no infrastructure to feed them or take care of them. That was a very different level. Here, a few thousand people [died], but there is an infrastructure to the country and the rest of the country was at peace, and it was a progressive, prosperous country. It was more a blow to our own sense of pride, sense of self. Ego, perhaps. How dare those idiots with nothing come and attack our most prestigious institutions? Our financial institutions and our mightiest institutions like the Pentagon. How could they do that and get away with it? Can't allow it. [Laughs] You know? So that's a very different thing altogether. They are very different things.

Has September 11 affected your relationship with your family, your friends, co-workers at all?

My colleagues know that I am not a Muslim and I think they are understanding of it. My students sent e-mails. So in some ways the relationship is better. Some of them even know the harassment problems that occur. And a lot of our colleagues are knowledgeable enough. My concern is not them. My concern is, you know, the guy I meet who delivers my newspaper. The cabdriver who'll drive me out there. What do they think? Many of them don't know much better. They are uninformed. And I suppose the relationship there is affected to the extent that I would not wander out alone in areas where I might encounter some of them. You know? [Once], at this time of evening in Manhattan, I might walk from NYU to Penn Station. Not now. Now, I take a cab. Is that really because people have changed, or is it because I have changed? Their fault or mine? I don't know. But I'm not about to find out. You know?

Have you heard personal stories from people in your community about being harassed? Do you find it to be pretty common? Or is it isolated instances?

Not anymore. The first month or two, yes, it was a story a day. You know, cabdrivers being chased by others. Their property, their shops, being broken into. Threatened. One kid was chased by a gang of kids and he jumped over a turnstile and ran into a subway. He figured, well, if I get arrested, so be it. That's better. You know? And I know him. He works on Wall Street. In fact, his job was in the World Trade Center. He was about fifteen, twenty minutes late to work that day. His train was late, and he was walking, and he saw it. And when he was [going home] he was chased that day.

Has there ever been a time in your life when you've stopped wearing a turban or contemplated stopping?

Oh, I did! For one year. A long time ago, in the sixties. For one year, and three months, I did not. [Laughs] I was still going through a stage where I was still thinking about myself. In a sense—what am I? Should I do this or keep it or not?

But since the eleventh you've never considered . . .

No. No, no, no. Since the eleventh, I was one of few people walking around with a turban. And I said that I'm going to do that. And if I get killed in the process, so be it. I'll be careful. But that's the way I'm going. That's the way I am.

Are you surprised in any way by the turn that events have taken, by the things that have happened over the last year?

No, I think that if we can somehow contain Iraq without war and establish very clearly that some behavior will not be tolerated and war will result, and then contain it, I would think that, to me, is preferable. The country, I suppose, supports the president, particularly in times of war. I recognize that from the fact that the *New York Times*, I think this morning, reported that over 70 percent of the people think that some of the hijackers who attacked the World Trade Center were Iraqi. They're so poorly informed.

In other words, the lines have been so beautifully blurred by the administration's war hysteria—no, war efforts—that people do not even know where the facts are. What are we going to war for, and who are we fighting, for what reason? It's one thing to fight people who attacked us. It's another thing to try to contain Iraq. It's the third matter altogether to fight for a regime change and to impose our will on what the geopolitics of that area ought to be, and I'm not sure that we have the right or the authority to do so.

But I suppose in politics, moral authority comes after the fact. If you win the war, then you have the authority. If you lose it, you never had it. Let's put it this way. The battle for Iraq we will win. The war for that area, I don't know.

You mentioned last time that you thought that the changes in America were basically temporary and that America remained a country where people would be judged on the work that they did and who they were, rather than their ethnic background or religion or whatever.

Ultimately, yes. America remains a very open country. The fact that I'm here talking to you and saying these things in the middle of an imminent war, that can only happen in America. I could not do that in India. I think if I did that in India, I'd probably disappear very rapidly.

15.

Talat Hamdani

Public School Teacher

Interviewed by Gerry Albarelli

Talat Hamdani was born in 1954 in Karachi, Pakistan. Hamdani, her husband, and her infant son, Salman, immigrated to the United States in 1979. She worked the night shift at a drug company for several years until her husband, Saleem, found another job. Hamdani was trained as a teacher. On September 11, 2001, she was teaching at Flushing High School in the early morning program. Her son Mohammed Salman Hamdani was an accomplished student working as a research technician at the Howard Hughes Medical Institute of Rockefeller University near Sixty-third Street. Salman Hamdani earned a BA in chemistry from Queens College. He was a paramedic and a former New York City police cadet. His dream was to become a doctor.

I'll ask you to start by saying your name, and to tell me where and when you were born, and a little bit about yourself, your early life.

When you say early life, what do you mean? Before coming to America?

Yes.

Okay. My name is Talat Hamdani, and I'm a native of Pakistan. I was born in Karachi into a family of eight children. My father was an educator, so was my mom. They gave us a wonderful education. I have four siblings who are medical doctors, three sisters and a brother who passed away in '81. And three brothers are engineers—a civil engineer, a nautical engineer, and a computer engineer. Of the eight siblings, I'm the only one who took after my father's profession. I was a teacher back home in Pakistan. It's a very different country—it was much better than what it is right now, you know. It was much more open and more liberal. It was not so religious at that time. There were regular mosques. There were no madrassas [Muslim religious schools] at that time. I went to a parochial school. It was normal to be in a parochial school and be taught by nuns. I remember praying "Oh Lord, I pray thee," whatever, in the morning prayers.

When I was growing up, the lower-middle-class [women] would wear the veil, but the majority—nobody would wear veils or the wraparound, or whatever. I used to play in the streets with boys and girls. I would whistle, and my father would say, "No whistling, you're a girl." I would ride a bicycle. I was forbidden to ride a bicycle, eventually, because I was a girl. I used to play in the streets with boys. I was forbidden to do that. I would wear shorts. I was forbidden to do that. Everything was [forbidden] because I was a girl. So finally, one day, my father started teaching my brother to drive, who was two years younger than me. I went up to his face and I said, "How come you're teaching him driving, and not me?"

He said, "Well, you're a girl."

I said, "So what? Is it a crime to be a girl? I am driving."

He said, "Oh, no, I can't teach you."

I said, "You think I don't know driving? Come sit with me in the car." We had a Datsun stick shift, and in the afternoon, when my parents used to sleep, I used to push the car out the gate and drive it back into the garage. That's how I taught myself driving. I sat my dad in the car and I took him on the wildest ride of his life. We went through the ditches and over the roundabout and then he says, "Okay, okay. I'll teach you. I'll teach you." And that's how I got my permission. I guess because I grew up with two younger brothers, so I was like a tomboy. But I fought for everything. I had to fight for my man, my husband.

In what sense?

So when I became friendly with my husband, he used to be a neighbor. My father knew his parents. But he did not come from an educated family. So they resented that, and they were not rich, ever. They were not even middle class. When I met my Saleem I was fourteen and he was eighteen. He used to come home every evening at a quarter to seven with his jacket on his shoulder, right shoulder. So after a couple of our first meetings I said, "Where do you come from every evening?"

He said, "Well, I work."

I said, "Why are you not in school? You should be in school, at least in your college, first year."

He said, "No, I'm working." And then he gave me a story that "I was caught cheating three years ago so I was disbarred. But next year I can go back, so I'll go back to college." And that year, that poor man took his GED and he went to college for me, and he got his bachelor's.

Tell me about the decision to come here, to the United States.

My sister was already here. In 1962, one of my aunts came here. She got married to her husband in '62. America is like a dreamland. It is the place to be. A big career is being an American doctor or lawyer. On that side of the world, America is *the* place to be, because you can be who you want to be. If you have the ambition. And my husband always wanted to come to America. So on December 28, 1977, I had Salman, my first son. At that time my husband was working as a manager for Three Star Battery, which is equivalent to Duracell over here. It was a nice position, a nice job. Then one day in May my brother comes home, my youngest brother, who happens to live in America. He said, "The visas are opening up." But he said, "I can't go because I can't leave my mom. She's a widow. So let's send Saleem." Saleem was looking at us, and then I remember that night we all sat up—Saleem, my mom, my brother, and myself. Should we send him or not? Should he apply for the visa or not? Because he was well set [in Pakistan]. But he always wanted to come to America.

He came in July 1978, and he found a job, eventually, at Blood Brothers, in Mamaroneck. A wreckage place—what do you call that? A junkyard. He worked and then he sent tickets for me and my son.

What were your first impressions?

First impressions. I was very happy. I was very happy I came here. He had already found an apartment in Greenpoint, Brooklyn. So we came to our apartment. There was nothing in it except the wooden floors. Our friend had a car, so we went to Coney Island and we purchased all furniture from there: a bed, a couch, and some old, rotten carpet that you could clean. Then we bought some utensils.

Did you continue to work?

I was a housewife, basically, for a couple of years. Then he got his own business. He bought a business in Greenpoint in '85. I worked with him over there for like ten years, until I got my teaching license, in '92. Then I began public [school] teaching.

Okay. So tell me now about September 11 and take me through the day.

It was a beautiful day. It was a Tuesday. Salman was a paramedic but took a second job at the Howard Hughes Medical Institute during July 2001 at Rockefeller University, to make extra money. So I left at seven twenty with Zeshan, my youngest one, and dropped him off at Queensboro Community College. Salman was still sleeping and my husband was sleeping. I was in the classroom from 8:00 A.M. to 10:20 [A.M.]. So when I came out, I saw some teachers huddled in the hallway. I could sense something was wrong. So I stepped up to them and I started listening to the conversation. They said, "The Twin Towers are burning, and one has fallen down."

I said, "Oh, they must be crazy. They must be misinformed." So I went to the Teachers Center, I dialed my home number, and my husband picked up, and he was crying. He said, "You know, the second tower is just coming down, and Salman is there."

I said, "Salman doesn't work there."

"No, he's in Manhattan."

I said, "Manhattan is a big place. It's not like a one-mile radius, or a five-mile radius. It's a big place. He's on Sixty-third Street, and this is downtown. He's in Manhattan but he's not there." I remember I was crying too. Then I said to myself, "Why am I crying?" I don't know. We both were talking when the second building came down. And that's where they found his remains.

Anyway, I said, "Oh, he'll be fine. I'll just contact—." Because his brother and his brother's wife also worked in Midtown Manhattan. They worked on Thirty-fourth Street. So Saleem said okay. Then we would call Salman's cell and he wouldn't answer his cell. The lines were also broken and everything. His brother responded, and his sister-in-law called, "We are fine." I just [kept] calling his cell and no one called back. There was a call given out for teachers to volunteer to stay behind with the children, so the parents can come and pick, so I volunteered.

So I came home like four thirty and that's when his brother called. He said Salman never showed up [at work] that day. Okay, for him not to show up at the job is a lot. And the type of person he was—he was very kind and compassionate. He was a different soul. Very different. So I said, "Don't worry. Definitely, he's gone down [to Ground Zero] to help." Because if he was driving, and there was a disabled car or someone in trouble, he would stop the car to help them. That's him, you know? He would bring home sick pigeons and nourish them back to health and everything. So he was that kind of a person. Then he didn't come home that night. So I called my son in Binghamton, and I said, "Bhaijaan, Salman didn't come home today."

He said, "That's okay, Mama. He must be helping down there. Don't worry. He'll come home tomorrow."

So Wednesday, my mother came home. "What's happening? Salman has not come home?"

I said, "No, he has not come home." Next day, in the morning, we got up. I wasn't crying but my husband was crying. They were very close, father and son, really close, really close. He was really proud of him. So we went to Salman's office [the] next day.

The security guard says, "Okay. Who is your son? We'll see who it is." They were closed that day. Nobody was in the building. The offices were closed.

And I said, "We need his cell phone." Because he told me he'd forgotten his cell phone there. So finally they went and got his cell phone for us. And the security guard said something which, later, made sense to me.

He said, "Oh, I know people in the FBI. I'm going to give them his name and maybe they can help you find him very easily."

I said, "Fine."

From there we went down to St. Vincent's Hospital. First we stood on a very long line, then we looked at the records, the dead list, and then we looked at the injured list, and he was on neither list. Then we came home very tired. The third day we went back again. The same thing, sifting through the records, no name, neither in the injured nor in the dead.

Then we made a flyer with his name and we went down there again. I think it was the second day. No, it was probably the third day. I don't even remember now. There were many people being interviewed, and I had his picture, holding it up, [asking] if anyone had seen him down there. This was near the Armory, to give our DNA, you know? Then there was somebody from television who asked us, "Why are you here?"

I said, "I'm looking for my son." My brother had made that flyer, and it said, "Sal Hamdani." The picture came on CNN. They covered me across the world because I had family in the Middle East, in Europe, in Pakistan, in Australia. After a few days, we went down to Manhattan, to the World Trade Center site. It was really bad, the stink was bad, burning your lungs. We showed the flyer to firemen and everyone. No one saw him at all. We just prayed and prayed and prayed. Then I wrote a letter to President [George W.] Bush on October 2 because someone told me that many Middle Eastern–looking people had been detained.

"So maybe your son was picked up," someone said.

I said, "Hopefully." So I wrote a letter to President Bush, registered and certified, return receipt, and I mailed copies of it to ex-president [William J.] Clinton and [Senator Charles "Chuck"] Schumer, I think. I don't know who else. Mayor [Rudolph W.] Giuliani, Governor [George E.] Pataki, and Hillary [R.] Clinton. Nobody responded. Then in October I said, "Let's go to Mecca. Let's go to Mecca. Maybe we'll get an answer from there, whether he's alive or dead." At that point we really didn't know what to believe. And they were saying to call up the mortuary, because they had bodies over there, to come down and identify your loved ones, if he or she is there. So I had courage that day. It was a Saturday. I picked up the phone and I called a number that we had. Or maybe I dialed one of the digits off, I don't know, but the [voice on the other end] said, "Why are you calling here?"

I said, "I'm looking for my son."

"Who is he?"

"Mohammed Salman Hamdani," I answered.

So he says, "Why do you call here? Who gave you this number?"

I said, "This is the number that was given to me by the Armory, for further investigation."

He says, "Well, that number is different. Call over there but wait. Hold the line. I will look into your son's case." Then he asked me, "What was he wearing? What did he do? How did he look?" All those questions. What time he went there.

I said, "Where are you going to go now?" Then, that guy, he blocked my cell phone. He kept calling me back, again and again. So my hope was that he was talking to my son, whom he has detained. Then someone called me that night, again, with the same questions, the same exact questions, from 11:00 P.M. to 1:00 A.M. The next day, two cops came to my house from the Criminal Investigation Bureau, a lady and a man. They said Howard Hughes [Medical Institute, HHMI] had sent home a box of all his stuff that was there: his computer, speakers, his prayer rug, whatever he had, a radio or something. They put them in a box and they had brought it home to us, and they told us, "He has an insurance policy. You should file a claim for it but you need a death certificate."

I said, "No, I don't want to file a claim. I don't think he's dead. I strongly believe he's detained."

So President Bush did not return any phone call or message back, nor any other politician to whom I had mailed [the letter]. So we decided to go to Mecca. The day we are leaving a police officer called. He said, "I want his computer. I want to check his computer."

I said, "Why would I give you my computer? You want to check on me. You come here and check."

"No, we want to check it at—."

I said, "No. It's my only computer."

"Why won't you give it to us?"

I said, "I use it. My boys use it."

"What was his password?" he asked.

I said, "You're American. You think he would give me his password?" I just lost [my temper] that day. I said, "I'm not going to talk to you until and unless you tell me where my son is. If you're holding him, give me my son back."

Then they didn't call back after that.

A *New York Post* guy comes [to our house]. Then a *Daily News* guy came in, and then a *Newsday* guy came in. So I said, "What has brought all of you back to my house a month later?" They said, "A flyer is circulating the NYPD [New York Police Department] precincts with Salman's picture, asking anyone who knows him to step forward." I later got the flyer. It was Salman's picture. Written in bold letters: WANTED, and giving his physical details. So I told them we were going to Mecca. So we left the eleventh of October and on October 12 the newspapers came out, the *New York Times* came out, *Daily News* and *Newsday*, a very positive, compassionate statement, "The family who hopes their son's alive has gone to Mecca to pray." But the *New York Post* gave his graduation picture, high school, with the heading, "Missing or Hiding?" And saying his picture is circulating NYPD precincts looking for him. The *Post* went on to insinuate that he was seen by the Midtown Tunnel at 11:00 A.M. and that he had [an] NYPD ID and could cross security. There was a very discriminated, prejudiced article about him.

But we were in Mecca at that time so we couldn't defend ourselves. My sister told me that [New York congressman Gary] Ackerman's office called. She said, "They have some news about your son."

I said, "When I get back, I'll call you." We came back after twelve days or something. I called their office and Congressman Ackerman spoke with me. He investigated. So many things were against Salman, poor kid. He was a Muslim, number one. He had a light beard. Because he was lazy in shaving, you know. He had kinky hair. He had a Koran on him. We all read the Koran in English. He had an ID, what do you call it? EMT [Emergency Medical Technician]. He was a certified EMT. So everything went against him, you know. Ackerman investigated everything and he said, "He could be with the INS [Immigration and Naturalization Services]."

I said, "Well, he's a citizen."

He said, "Well, the dividing line is whether you're born here, on U.S. soil, or not." So one thing that happened was I got to know Mr. Ackerman very well, through that experience. Then, in January, President Bush's secretary replied, "Thank you for your letter. We're forwarding it to the FBI." Five days later, the FBI replied, "We only investigate criminals." So that's not a denial! So the hope was still there that he was alive and detained. Then, on March 14, or something like that, the Voice of America called me. They interviewed me, and I said, "They have people detained. If you want to do anything, if you want me to work for it, if you want to get involved, I want to get involved in getting those people liberated."

Then I asked him, "When will you air this?" He said, "It will be aired March 21, starting from midnight." So it was about to start airing, my interview, revealing the detention of all those people. The two police officers came to my home at 11:30 P.M. After this tragedy happened, my husband didn't sleep in the bed. He was sleeping in the living room [hoping] that the door was going to open and Salman was going to walk in soon. So on March 20, 2002, at 11:30 P.M., they came in and said, "This is the number of the medical examiner's office. Call them. Your son has been found dead."

And my husband, heartbroken, he just sat down on the floor and started to cry. And he says, "Call now, call now." I said [to the police], "Do me a favor. Just leave us, please."

So they left, and I said, "You know, I don't really want to do anything. Let's go to sleep. Nothing is going to change, except more aggravation and hassle for the whole family." So we went to sleep. The next day I called my family and we all went down to the medical examiner's office. He had a big file and he was trying to convince us that this was where [Salman] was found, by the Custom House—the tower that collapsed second but was hit first.

I said, "Prove it to me, that he's my son."

So this is his file and he drew it toward him and he said, "Okay, Mrs. Hamdani, go get yourself a lawyer."

I don't know why he became so defensive. I said, "Just prove it to me, that he's my son. That he's who you're saying he is."

He said, "Through DNA, we have identified."

I said, "What did you find? What if I want to have my own test conducted? To verify that, indeed, these are his remains? Why did it take you so long to confirm them? When did you find his remains?"

He said, "They found his remains in the third week of October. The twenty-third or twenty-sixth of October." We came back from Mecca on October 26. Those dates coincide.

So I said, "It took you five months for DNA? To verify somebody?"

"Oh, no," he said. "There were, like, thirty-four pieces. We had to verify all these pieces with your DNA, then with your husband's DNA and with all the thirty-four parts found."

Bull crap. I'm not stupid.

He said, "You have two options. If you want to have someone conduct a test to verify that these are the remains of your son, they will have to come here and do the test in our presence." Now who is going to defy the federal government? Nobody. [He said,] "Or, you take the death certificate and his remains and do whatever you want to do." Same thing. They wanted him declared dead.

So we had no option. We decided to pick him up. We had a funeral for him April 5. My family had to come from Pakistan and Dubai and England. We had it in the mosque where he used to go to pray for his Friday prayers, the Ninety-sixth Street mosque. And the NYPD gave him a very good, honorable send-off, with the bagpipes and the American flag and all the NYPD cadets came. Commissioner [Raymond W.] Kelly came, [Mayor] Bloomberg came, and Congressman Ackerman came. So Salman got his dignity and his respect.

Salman was very humble and very loving. He would never allow me to celebrate anything for him. So no birthday parties for him. No high school graduation. Even when he finished his bachelor's [degree], he said, "No party. I'll tell you when to celebrate." Two years before, one of my nephews had died. He was with the New York Police Department. So when Salman saw the funeral that he had gotten from the NYPD he said, "Mama, this is honor. This is how I want to go." And that's how he went.

16.

Salmaan Jaffery

Banker

Interviewed by Gerry Albarelli

Salmaan Jaffery was born in Karachi, Pakistan, in 1971. He is the son of Zaheer Jaffery. As a boy in Pakistan he witnessed the Afghan refugee crisis that resulted from the 1979 Soviet Union invasion of Afghanistan. Jaffery learned English and Urdu growing up and was raised in a Muslim household. His family immigrated to the United States in 1987 when Jaffery was a teenager. He received a BA in International Relations from Colgate University and an MBA from Cornell University. After graduating in 2001, Jaffery received a temporary assignment at the investment bank Merrill Lynch, which was located in the World Financial Center. His father also worked at the World Trade Center in the North Tower. On September 11, Salmaan Jaffery took the subway to work.

DECEMBER 3, 2001

Here's what's interesting. I would always position myself on the platform for the 1/9 [train] in the forward-most cab because the staircase at the 1/9, [at] the World Trade, was right there. So it just saved time. I tried doing it this time but at Seventh Avenue there was a huge line of people on the platform. The train was running late, so I couldn't actually make it to that super spot in the first cab. I was in the second or third cab. I get to the World Trade. Because of my positioning, rather than being the first person up the stairs, into the shopping area, I was in this long line on the platform underneath the World Trade Center. It's progressing nicely for about fifteen seconds. Then all of a sudden there's a stampede, people running down saying, "Someone's been shot!" Probably because I haven't had my first cup of coffee or because I couldn't care less, I'm skeptical. So I just stood my ground and a few of us braved it and said, "Look, how bad can it be?" We walked up and into what would be the shopping area and it's eerie. There's no one there and there's a very strong, acrid smell. I look left, and there's this guy being carried by two men. He had blood on his foot or something like that, and he seemed a little bit in shock. So that didn't disturb me. I [said], "Huh." Then this gentleman walked by, I said, "What happened?"

He was like, "Some plane hit the North Tower, I think."

At the time, I thought it was a Cessna. Because the week before, some idiot had gotten himself stuck on the Statue of Liberty. I recall some paraglider. So I said, "Okay, some weekend warrior has probably gone off-track." So I proceeded along the exact same path I take every day calmly. I made a left up one more flight of escalators. And up those escalators, I would have been in World Trade Six or Seven, one of those shorter buildings right in front of the North Tower.

I get out of the escalator and now I'm on ground level. I'm not outside yet but the building I'm in is glass, so I can see outside pieces of the [North Tower] falling. There's paper everywhere and chunks of the building, like, pieces of metal. I realized that this was really serious. So despite that, I go through the revolving door and now I'm outdoors. I'm in the open but, the reality is, I'm covered by the overhang of the building. But I can smell everything. It's powerful. I make a right toward Vesey [Street], and all of a sudden this thing in the corner of my eye slams to the ground, maybe thirty feet away from me, and it's a body. I knew it was a body immediately because it had the form, it had the head, the arms, but it was burnt. It was a loud thump. This woman, who was evacuating with me, she said, "What's that?"

I said, "Nothing. Don't worry about it." Half a second later I turned my head. I had seen enough. Meanwhile, the moment I got outside I started calling my father and that's when the panic started to hit me. I knew he was in the North Tower and I knew he was high up. But I didn't know what floor he was on. So I walked down Vesey and I redial, redial, redial, nothing. Looking up in absolute horror. But very calm.

Then very quickly, after maybe four or five or six or seven calls, and looking at how black the smoke was [coming out of the North Tower], and how raging the inferno was, I suddenly realized, "You know what? My father is probably gone. He's probably dead by now." I looked up and it wasn't like a hysterical, "Oh, my God, he's gone." I knew he was up there and I see that fire. He has a bad leg, and people are waving their flags from there and people started jumping. There's no way he can escape this.

I walk to the edge of Church and Vesey and everybody else is looking up at people jumping. That was really horrifying—even more than the body. Because the body just sort of happened. I didn't sit there and stare at it. If I had stared at it I probably would have been more moved. The body was more like sort of a piece of flesh. The people [jumping] were actually kicking, and you could see them. Their arms were waving as they were falling. Then there was the collective angst—the collective angst when you're with people. Because they were saying, "Oh, my God." People were crying. So it magnified the grief because you felt people feeling pain.

So I'm just standing there, looking up directly at the North Tower when suddenly the South Tower explodes and this plume of orange fire comes racing toward us. It's very vivid in my mind because I was staring at the towers. I remember it was very loud. Then an instant later, my reaction was, "Wow, this building is going to fall." People suddenly started to stampede because the pieces of the building started falling. Some of the pieces fell as far as where we were, Church Street. Some people panicked. That's when I first got really afraid because people were stepping over each other. I mean, there was a baby carriage that was pushed over. So I decided to just be calm and I pulled into a building for about ten seconds, and the wave of people sort of subsided. Then I'm basically weeping profusely because I'm convinced, without a shadow of doubt, that my father's dead. So I need to find someone that I know. I walked toward William Street, where my father-in-law works. I went all the way up to his building. I couldn't find him. I look like a derelict because I'm walking around and my eyes—I'm tearing—I'm sniffing and tearing. I couldn't find this guy.

Then I just kept going east. I went to this bar at Fulton [Street] and, mind you, I'm phoning constantly. Nothing was working. I'm at the bar with coffee, smoking a cigarette, drinking coffee and weeping. I couldn't get through to anybody. And all of a sudden you hear the news that the Pentagon's been attacked. I couldn't believe it.

[*Jaffery heads north to his cousin's apartment on Twenty-third Street.*]

[During] that walk I was preparing myself for all the conversations that I would have to have later on that day. First and foremost with my mother. I was reviewing in my mind how I would break the news to her, how she would react to my father's passing. I had done scenarios in my mind of how our lives would change with his demise, what I would need to do. I thought about my baby brother, who [was] fifteen, and what I would have to do to help him through this. All those conversations I was going through in my mind. [That was] in addition to just the pain of my own loss. I'm very close to my father. My father is my best friend.

So at three o'clock—I'm watching CNN [at my cousin's house]—and there's this young guy being interviewed by someone on the top of some building, and he says, "I work for the Port Authority and I was on the sixty-fifth floor." By this time I had spoken to my brother and he said, "Yes, [our dad] was in the sixties somewhere." So this guy was standing there and he was alive and well. He said, "Yes, as far as I know, all of our colleagues got out." That was the first ray of hope.

Shortly after, we get a phone call from home. It turns out that my mom had received a phone call from a complete stranger saying that a Mr. Jaffery has said that he's fine. Of course, then life became—I mean, it was a whole new day.

So when did you see him?

Oddly enough, I didn't see him for another two weeks. Once he got home to West Windsor [New Jersey], I spoke to him, and that was sufficient. But I did not go home for about sixteen or seventeen days afterward because I would have just burst out crying, or I would have been very emotional. That's exactly why I didn't go.

How has your life changed, if it has changed, since September 11?

It's changed significantly. First and foremost, I lost my job. I mean, my job went away because the Winter Garden and the annex building were damaged. My job moved to New Jersey and then they don't have the budget [to keep me].

Emotionally, I think everyone around us, we were all affected, and we all talked about it for a good two months afterward. The first five, six days was literally nonstop CNN watching, around the clock, this obsession with why, what, where information. Not much reflection, not much digestion of the information, but just information. The Sunday following [9/11] was the first time it really hit me, and a sense of despair just came over me.

But then something else happened afterward which was even more disturbing. Because even beyond the day-to-day sorrow and the death and

the trauma, things that affect who you as a person [become] very powerful. So this whole question about who is responsible [had a big impact].
What does it mean to be a Muslim? What does it mean to be a Pakistani
Muslim? What does it mean to be an American Muslim? Why are Muslims doing this? Are Muslims doing this? The terrorists were Muslim. I
happen to be someone who was very soul-searching to begin with. I also
know a lot about our history and I'm a keen, keen follower of foreign
policy in the Middle East. I've been active, I've written, I've read. So this
was a very, very big question for me, and it's continued from that day until
today.

The first couple of weeks I did not leave my neighborhood. I was
afraid. I wasn't afraid I'd be attacked. I was afraid I'd face someone who
was belligerent, who I could not counter because it was such a moment
of national grief. When people are upset you can't say things to un-upset
them. So I kept a very low profile. Plus, there were killings in Texas and
Phoenix. A Sikh guy got killed in Phoenix. A Pakistani was killed in Hous-
ton. A couple of friends got harassed. For the month and a half afterward,
I shaved every day. I hate shaving and I do have a pretty thick beard, [but]
I took no chances. I'm even ashamed to admit this—no, actually, I'm not
ashamed. I dressed as "Yankee" as I could. I didn't wear [my] black leather
jacket or black jeans or black shoes. I wore shorts, my vest, my baseball
cap, because I just didn't want to stand out.

I had been reading very vigorously before 9/11, by the way. It's so
weird because I had been reading books about Islam. I was pissed off at
us. Muslims have lost a PR battle. We have given in to fundamentalism.
We don't look at all the great sort of nonpracticing things in our religion.
Unfortunately, we have become a religion that people associate with violence, and it's not.

DECEMBER 4, 2002

When we spoke last December, I was looking for work because my full-
time job offer was rescinded a week before I graduated from business

school the prior May of 2001. So in December I actually found contract-based work at Merrill Lynch in equity research—spent about five months there until May, using it as a platform for a full-time job search and landed a great job here with American Express [AMEX]. In August, AMEX moved back to lower Manhattan, 40 Wall Street, and the rest of the organization moved to the AMEX Tower, which is a big structure right across from what used to be the World Trade Center.

Is there a way in which you are haunted by what happened?

Yes. Well, I want to be very clear on this. For a long time, me and about ten million other people were haunted by the images. But the images fade when you don't watch them on TV. So then we were haunted by the absence of the buildings. But that, too, in time fades, because the absence becomes part of the skyline also. Then you're haunted by feelings, right? Remorse, sadness, whatever, and those fade also with time, because you heal. But I will tell you that being so close [to Ground Zero] in some ways is good, because it always reminds me of that day. When I drive by the pit, or when I walk from here to AMEX for a meeting, I always have to go around the World Trade Center. So if I'm talking to someone I just stop talking. I sort of absorb the moment.

The buildings that are all around [Ground Zero], I wonder, are they still coated somewhere by ashes from the buildings [that fell] that weren't washed away? And if so, does that mean that there's a piece of someone, somewhere around? People have thought this place is a graveyard and I wonder if the collective dust of three thousand people went up in the air and dissipated over this entire sixteen-acre area, and then over into Jersey and into Long Island? Part of me thinks that, in some ways, everything is dusted with people's souls. The fact is that you have very fine dust everywhere, and I'm wondering, could it be that I'm breathing in a minute particle of someone as we speak?

We can talk more about 9/11 if you want, but I actually want to take the conversation in another direction.

Let's go.

I want to tell you about why it's important to me now. Personally, I still have not felt any [backlash against Muslims]. But I'll tell you something. For the first time in the sixteen years that I've been in the U.S., I have thought very seriously about moving to the UK [United Kingdom] for a couple of years. The change in attitudes [in the United States] about Islam, people from the Middle East, all those issues, have made me feel very, very uncomfortable. Muslims used to always feel—educated Muslims—that we had, in Jews, friends, because at the end of the day we have very similar religions, where our religions are Semitic in nature. Well, so is Christianity, but Christianity you associate with Europe, northern Europe. And Judaism, recently you associate with Europe, but still Jerusalem, Middle East. So you've got Christianity. You've got your Southern Baptists' conservative agenda. First they were after the Jews because the Jews killed Christ, right? So that was the enemy. Jews battle really hard, work their way up, and make it into the mainstream, right?

And now what's disturbing is that they're after Muslims, and you have this unholy alliance between very aggressive, very conservative Jews and Southern Baptists, because Southern Baptists have this apocalyptic vision of messiah coming. And so they support, unabashedly, anything that is pro-Israel or anti-Arab/Muslim. This is a perception that I have, or that many in our community have. And then you have people like Pat Robertson and then Billy Graham's son saying, "Islam is an evil religion. Prophet Muhammad was a wicked, wicked man." Something snapped in me. I'm not particularly religious but I felt a deep, deep fear and deep pain, deep anger, very deep, because I'd never heard that before.

And I felt like this is just like when African Americans came up from the South to the industrialized North, thinking that you had the Underground Railroad and you had all these liberal people who had fought on behalf of them, and then [up North] they realized that, you know what? Down [South], people called them the "N" word, and up here people treated them the same way, but didn't call them the "N" word. And I felt it the same way that people [in the United States] are now coming out of the woodwork, showing their real attitudes toward Muslims. I'm not saying it's all religion-based. To be fair, a lot of it is race. Muslims are dark. We're Middle Eastern. We don't necessarily fit in all the time. And a lot of it is that Muslims belong to a poor part of the world and this is America's time. America is a dominant power and you have people like Saddam Hussein and the Saudis, who are idiots, representing our religion.

My point is that in the last twelve months I've seen a change in attitudes on the political level [and] in day-to-day conversations about people. Even well-meaning people. Someone at work asked me, "I'm just curious. Do you guys have a lot of fascism?" I mean, a very honest, open question. I don't have a problem with it. But the fact that it's being asked suggests that someone is telling people "[Islam] is about violence, intolerance, and killing." So all this stuff has made me really upset, to the point I don't even read the paper anymore.

One other story that makes this more real: This friend of mine—he's thirty-five. He was born in Buffalo but he is of Indian background, Indian meaning the subcontinent, South India. Father came to America, went to Harvard [University], educated family. I met him in Poughkeepsie, New York, in 1987 when he was a headbanger. He had hair down to his shoulders. And then all of a sudden he changes his life. Something happens. He meets someone and he accepts Christ in his life. Okay? No problem with that. He straightens his life out, ends up going to Colgate [University]. So I follow him there because we're friends. He's older than me and I end up going to the same school. We were housemates, and then he graduates, has a very successful career. Goes to business school. Guess what? I also go to business school. I went to his wedding. He sends me cards of his kids, so we're in touch but we haven't seen each other. So he pops up in New York [last week] and looks me up and says, "Hey, let's hang out." And I've known his views. He's a very good person. I respect him a lot. But he is, and he considers himself, a born-again evangelical Christian. So naturally we started talking about terrorism.

The good news is that we had an open conversation, which is what I expect of him. But he said a couple of things which betray, in my mind, exactly what Christians are being taught. He's like, "It's very tough for my wife and me to [understand]. We know Islam is a great religion, blah, blah, blah. But if 80 percent of Muslims are terrorists or aggressive, then what does it say about the religion?" Very well-articulated question, a fair question, but again, the subtext was that someone in his Bible studies [probably] brought that issue up.

Take another example. He's like, "Many of us also believe that the Koran teaches Muslims to kill infidels." And I could not believe this shit. I told my friend when I was responding to his questions, "What's sad is that you don't understand that you cannot be a Muslim if you do not believe in Jesus." We have the same prophets. [But] Muhammad is number one, because he's the last [prophet]. We believe it's the same word of God, same message; it just happens that Muhammad is the last prophet. So we have Muhammad and then we have Jesus. Literally, he's number two. I said, "You guys don't realize that for us, Jesus is a huge part of our religion, yet, for obvious reasons, Muhammad is nothing to you guys, because he came after your religion."

But anyway, we agreed that on matters of faith it's all opinion at the end of the day. I mean, we laughed about it. I said, "Look. We can agree to disagree and we can't argue people's beliefs." I said, "The important thing is, let's focus on the common ground." I said, "The reality is that you are very pious, and as such, you probably raise your children in a manner that's probably very similar to the way I'm going to raise my children. Whether or not your kids believe in Jesus and mine believe in Allah, it doesn't matter. The fact is that we'll probably teach them the same things, right? Don't do drugs. Don't kill anyone. Don't hurt anyone."

So to me there's been a triangulation of attitudes that makes me feel very angry and upset. That's, I guess, the point of what I'm saying and I think that is a direct outcome of 9/11. But not just that. I think it would be letting people off the hook if we attributed [all of] this to 9/11. September 11 created an atmosphere where people felt more comfortable voicing these otherwise very extreme viewpoints. The point is that they've always been there.

I remember the first time we spoke you talked about that concern and I think you wore a baseball cap or something right after September 11 and I was wondering if that continues to be on your mind.

It's on my mind, not because I want it to be, but it's thrust in my face whenever I travel. I mean, it's a joke. I swear, I'm personally not offended by it. I'm not offended by being singled out for checking [at the airport]. It's a pain in the ass but I'm not offended by it. Because you know what? It's always been the case for me. Forget 9/11. I mean, terrorists have been around for a long time. I was always checked at Heathrow, any airport. So that's nothing new to me. What pisses me off is, don't call it random. "Oh, you're being randomly selected." Hello? Don't insult my intelligence. I went to Phoenix two weeks ago. And it's a game now. I stand in line and I see people ahead being checked and I say to myself, "Let's take wagers. Will I get checked or will I not?" And nine times out of ten I win my own bets.

[When] you are in an environment where you perceive that people are hostile [to you] there are a couple of ways you could view it. One approach has been, for a lot of people, to sort of disavow who you are. So you wear the [baseball] cap, you tone down your name. You change your name or you call yourself something else and you totally separate yourself [from your original identity]. You apologize for who you are, right? "No, no, no, really, we're very good people." So that's one extreme. The other extreme is to be very defiant. "F-you. This is who I am. Kiss my butt." But that's an extreme.

However, I've found that I'm becoming more steadfast about my own identity. I've never questioned it. No one calls me Sal, right? It's Salmaan or Sam. I'm very clear on my identity. But now I feel like I'm making an extra effort [to express that identity]. Like, we had the month of Ramadan, which is the month of fasting. I didn't keep all of them, for work reasons, but I kept a whole bunch of them. I kept sixteen, seventeen, eighteen fasts out of twenty-eight, which is pretty good. I did a lot of things. And why? Because I felt like, "You know what? I want to do it. This is who I am."

JUNE 21, 2005

I've talked about being from a different culture. I've talked about my grandfather being West and East at the same time—myself having that real luxury of growing up that way. Well, [making sense of 9/11] is the ultimate test. You're living in a Western society, with Western freedoms, Western outlooks. But you have a deep, innate understanding of some of the angst and some of the issues that people overseas are facing. As a rational person you understand that killing people is morally abhorrent, especially innocent people. But as we know, the world is seldom black and white. It is a bunch of shades of gray. But when it's shades of gray, and you yourself are impacted by it, then it poses a problem because personal loss *is* very black and white. The idea of losing a father—there's no gray area. In my case I almost thought I had. It's less raw with the passage of time. But that was a huge, huge source of conflict.

As someone who has lived all over the world—particularly in the Middle East and Pakistan—I continue to understand where the resentment and anger [toward the West] comes from. I understand it because I know the cultures. I understand how it feels to be impacted by certain policies. But I also struggle with the fact that I no longer live in an environment that has violence in it. Gone are the days where I'm in Karachi and I'm seeing carcasses in the road, or a bomb exploded down the street, or there's violence. I'm not used to it anymore. I live in a society where, yes, there's a lot of gun violence, but I don't see it. It doesn't impact my life directly. So the massive loss of life and the manner in which it happened posed a conflict. I guess where I'm at now is, I struggle with having the fortitude to say that when you kill people who are not directly involved with a conflict, that it is completely wrong. And that's my point of view. I do believe that.

But I also struggle with what I think about it intellectually. What has more significance, suffering of people here or suffering of people there? Why is it that we are able to talk about the onetime suffering of the families of 2,800 people who died? And as one person who almost experienced it, I understand how immense it can be. So is that less painful, or more painful, than people who deal with this sort of violence on a daily basis? Or who have lost many, many multitudes more people over a period of eighteen months? What's worse?

To me a loss is a loss. Every person's loss should be equally important because it is equally painful. But I think we have bathed in sort of some self-pity over the last three years, where we've focused a lot on the continuing loss and the pain suffered by people here in Manhattan, and perhaps a little bit less to the suffering and pain—and loss of life, by the way—for people who are impacted by our policies overseas. So it's a struggle. I struggle with it.

17.

Sandra Hernandez

Community Organizer / Activist

Interviewed by Amy Starecheski

Sandra Hernandez was born in 1952 in New York City. Hernandez had a difficult youth and sometimes lived on the streets. After finding refuge in a church, Hernandez turned her life around. She overcame her own struggles with drugs and alcohol to found the Freedom Community Center in her South Bronx neighborhood. Located in the basement of the building Ms. Hernandez lived in, the Freedom Center serves the Mott Haven community with housing for domestic violence victims, space for Alcoholics Anonymous meetings, HIV testing, and youth programs. Hernandez was also the founder of Casa Atabex Aché, an empowerment organization for women of color in the South Bronx. Hernandez died of cancer in 2007.

OCTOBER 23, 2001

My name is Sandra Hernandez. My mother's name is Carmen Gitarre. My father is Joey L. Hernandez. My father at that time was an alcoholic and he died at the age of sixty-five of cirrhosis of the liver. My mother, after that, married someone else. My mother was also a beautiful woman, but within the four kids, three took to the streets. Even though I went to school and tried to do the right thing, going to communion and confirmation, I started in the wrong track of hanging out in the street and being in gangs and taking drugs and drinking alcohol and sniffing glue and all that stuff.

It's been about fifteen years that I've cleaned myself from the drugs and the alcohol. Those things just came from being sick and tired of the lying and of the stealing and then crying over the money and being hungry and living in the street and being part of the problem of the city instead of what I'm doing now, "finding a solution." I've changed my life considerably because I see more clearly now. Before, I used to say this system is what did it. But it wasn't the system. It was just me, not seeing life the way it was supposed to be. Even though I have my mother and my sisters that were there for me, and my beautiful sister Violet that was helping out when I was young, I would never listen to them.

At that time, in the seventies, that's when the Bronx was burning down and the landlords were paying us to burn buildings down. There was a lot of things going that was very ugly at that time. I see New York the way I'm being brought up. I never went to anything out of the Bronx. Me going to Manhattan was like me going to Puerto Rico. So when you only see the ugly side, you don't see that there's another side so beautiful.

Now since I've stopped at 140th [Street], it has changed my life considerably. When I came to St. Peter's [Church] at 140th, the people at St. Peter's treated me so different than everybody else. They never looked down on me. They respected me for who I was even though I was still getting high. I kept praying every day to get me out of this mess because I was tired. At that time I was sleeping on the roof even though I had family that would give me a place to go. So I just continued living in the streets, surviving the best I could, with me and my husband. Then my first husband died of alcohol.

Finally, I got myself on welfare. I got myself in the methadone program and I got to find out that the methadone program was the best thing that I ever did in my life. Between that and seeing everything that was happening in the Bronx and everywhere out there, I got involved in the church, and I started giving myself more to the community because I knew where all the hurt was. I knew where the drugs were. I know where the hunger is. I know where all the empty lots are broken because I think I found them all in the South Bronx getting high. I was tired then.

I live in a basement, yes. I've been fixing it little by little. But I live next to my church that's given me so much. I live next to my community—for twenty-four hours they depend on me. I have in my house people coming over looking for [help with] problems, asking me questions about world affairs. I've absorbed so much information that I never thought I could in my little mind. I'm still learning, and it's a process. I never thought that I would be able to come as far as I have.

When September 11 came, it changed my way of thinking. But I had already been thinking, "What if it ever happened? What if? What happens if it [war] ever gets close to home? What will we do? Do we have to get the cannons?" I always pictured myself in that what-would-happen scene. But reality hit us. At ten minutes to nine I was debating about getting up. Do I want to go to work? I would get there late. If not, don't worry about it. I'll call the office. I'm sitting up in bed and I always watch *The Maury* [*Povich*] *Show.* I was sitting down and I see a building [on TV] and it just hit.

I screamed all over the house because I didn't know where to go. It's just like, "Oh my God, a bomb." I realized I was talking to myself. I was trying to talk to my daughter but she was sleeping. But I didn't know where to go in my house. I just couldn't believe that right there in front of me this was happening. I started crying when I started seeing people just flying out the window.

I wanted to jump in the TV and see if maybe you could grab the air— maybe stop the airplane. Because you feel so helpless when you can't do anything. That's the thing about the TV, that now you can see the shelter blowing up in front of your face and you could see that it's a dramatic thing, but knowing that you're standing there and you can't do nothing, you can't reach it, you can't stop it. It's like a standstill. Ten minutes after that I just ran out in my street, tears in my eyes. I just went into the community because I've been working here for so many years. Everybody knows me. I said, "Did you see what happened? I can't believe it." I was crying up and down. I felt like the doors were just clicking, one after the other. Even though you couldn't hear it, but the way everybody just came out. There was like this serene [moment] in this block. As a matter of fact the Bronx is not even a tip away from the island, so could you imagine the effects if they would have just turned a little bit, it could not have just taken a building, it could have taken the Bronx itself.

The people here, they didn't take it as bad as I thought because reality hadn't set into them yet. I don't know if I understood why it happened because we have taken things for granted in the United States. These kids [in the neighborhood] have been brought up to think that the United States is bad. They have been brought up to believe that the United States is the one that's causing them hunger, death, and all that. We have been so safe for so long that it is like an accident. You go back to sleep. It's okay. Then you wake up and are scared and confused. But going to another country to kill and bomb, and then other people are dying. Just to get one guy. That just doesn't make sense. An eye for an eye I understand . . . but so many people are dying. Even if some people believe it is necessary, and you kill him, there's always another.

JUNE 22, 2005

Sandra, I wanted to know if September 11 and the aftermath had affected your fund-raising efforts here at all?

We had a lot of grantors that sent us applications for 9/11, asking us if we wanted to work with them to give workshops and send the kids to their programs to see how they got affected. But we're only two people, three people here at Freedom, and it's so hard to do the writing. But, yes, that was a very big issue, 'cause the grantors were only looking at 9/11 and they wanted to give money to do things in that area.

So was it harder then to get money for non-9/11-related stuff?

Yes, because 9/11 was all they were focusing on. 'Cause everybody was looking for money to go give to the people on the aftereffects of 9/11, how it affected the school kids. They wanted organizations like us to get involved and we didn't do any fund-raising because I didn't want to make money on somebody else's life just so I can give Freedom [money]. I'd feel like I was using people again and I wanted to stay away from that. It would dirty the memories. I wouldn't do that, no.

In a community where there's so much need, very basic needs for food and housing, medical care, do you think there's any resentment of all the money that's gone to . . .

Yes, you hear all that. The first conversation that you hear is: "They had all this money, certain people didn't get it, certain people got it. Some of the Hispanic people that were there couldn't reach any of the money." That's been the gossip up until now. So everybody forgot about 9/11; they concentrated on where all the money from the funding went to. None of the small organizations are going to get that money; we're not even [able] to write out a thousand pages [of grant proposals] just to get a couple of thousand dollars, and that's the way it goes. [Laughter]

At that time, when it hit the [World Trade Center], this community was hurting. And it was the first time that everybody got together and we talked—people that we didn't even usually talk to, didn't even say hello to, managed to say hello to us, and strike up a conversation about 9/11. And that was very weird. So we activated this [program] with another agency. Before 9/11, I picked six sites to do a collaboration with other organizations and I decided to do a block party. But then because of what happened on 9/11, we did our second annual on 9/11, on 139th Street. We called it "In Unity There Is Strength," which some of the people here put together and organized. And we had a beautiful block party. We had a health fair, activities for the kids; we gave books and pencils, and mugs; helmets we gave away; we had an HIV site there for testing. We had rides for the kids, we had arts and crafts, we had painting, we had balloons. We had five hundred frankfurters to give away that day, with sodas. It's exciting because, when you come to put it in words, I didn't realize how much we did. The Federation of [Protestant] Welfare [Agencies] collaborated with us and help[ed] us put the function together. So every year on 9/11 we do an annual festival which is called "Unity in Strength," because of what happened. People have gotten together more on the block. We did prayers, we did candle vigils, and we went to church. People that we hadn't seen for five or six years were in church that day. We got some of the senior citizens that don't get out and let them see us and know who we are. We have one bash before school starts, so we can give books and pencils and things like that.

Did you see any difference after 9/11 in people's food needs, any shortage?

Yes, it got even bigger. We have a shortage now at the church. Maybe their food funding got cut down. Okay, I'll tell you the truth. Ever since 9/11 all the [regular] programs are being cut and money has been diverted into different areas. We are going to see the outcome, in another year or two, of people sleeping in the streets again. The food right now is very scarce. I thought I would stop seeing people eat from the garbage but I'm seeing more of it now than any other time. We shouldn't have this because people are more educated about the community, and empowerment. But the food scarcity here—you are seeing senior citizens being hit because of the shortage of checks. By the time they pay their rent they have no money. You will see them every week. And they will go from here to the pantry at St. Benedict's. You get people from Grand Concourse, Fordham, all the way down there that get here at five thirty just to get on line. By nine, when the pantry opens, they have been standing on line for three to four hours, whether there's rain or snow or not.

I don't turn anyone down when they come down [to the Freedom Center] for food. But I have been starting saying: "I am not here to feed you. I am here to take the hunger off until you find your program, where you can go." And the kids who come, usually they will get their juice or snack, or we buy french fries and cook some chicken. That's what we do every day. That's how we survive. I know it looks like a basement to everybody but the kids love it. They come down here and we work hard and this is what Freedom is about. It's about putting all that love in here with no money. Nobody gets paid. We continue giving back and I live for that. I'm giving back the help that's been given to me, and the knowledge and the education. We need to give that back to the community, to empower the kids.

I'm still here. No one's going to take me out because my kids are here. This is where I started Freedom, and for a person that didn't get her GED I'm very proud of where I've come. I want to get my GED. But for now, I think I've done pretty good.

18.

Robert W. Snyder

Historian and Journalist

Interviewed by Mary Marshall Clark

Robert Snyder is a historian, journalist, and documentary filmmaker who directs the graduate program in American Studies at Rutgers University. Snyder was born in the Bronx in 1955. He earned a BA at Livingston College, Rutgers University, and his PhD in American history at New York University. He has written extensively on New York history and culture and has consulted on many museum exhibitions. He is the author of The Voice of the City: Vaudeville and Popular Culture in New York; Transit Talk: New York's Bus and Subway Workers Tell Their Stories; *and the co-author of* Metropolitan Lives: The Ashcan Artists and Their New York. *On September 11, 2001, Snyder was commuting to Newark, which required catching a train at the World Trade Center.*

I grew up in a small town in North Jersey called Dumont. My mom was a native New Yorker and my father was born in Hartford, Connecticut, and had moved to New York in his childhood. My dad's parents were Jewish immigrants from Russia. His father was a painter. They moved down to New York City in the twenties and really lived through the depression, on the hardest edge of it. My grandfather, in addition to being a painter, would be like a one-man rehab team for a building. They would move in, and in exchange for free rent he would fix up the whole building for the landlord. So he was a native New Yorker that way, grew up in New York, served in the army in World War II, came home, and eventually went to work for the Moses Safe Company as a mechanic. My father was a very highly skilled mechanic; he was like a safe cracker—a legitimate safe cracker.

The morning [of 9/11] began very, very normally for me. My wife and I walked the kids over to school and dropped them off at Public School 290 on East Eighty-second Street and then we headed back to the Lexington Avenue line. On the way I said, "Maybe I should vote later. Maybe I should vote at the end of the day. I'll get to the school early."

She goes, "No, if you go to vote at the end of the day it's going to be crowded, let's vote now."

So I said, "Okay, we'll vote now." Round about Fourteenth Street the train started running very funny. It stopped between stations. It got really pokey. I asked myself, "What's going on? Why are we not running right?" And I couldn't figure it out. And then there was this very elegantly dressed guy on the train, wearing a $2,000 suit with a Rolex watch and he is fuming. And I am sort of laughing, watching him get mad and sort of making eye contact with this other guy on the other side of the aisle, as if to say, "Can you believe this guy in a $2,000 suit and how angry he is that he's being delayed?"

And eventually the train picks up again and it goes further south, but then it goes to Fulton Street and it doesn't stop. Which was odd because

Fulton's a normal stop. Then it goes to Wall Street and the squawk box on the train says something incomprehensible. So I get [out] and I'm sort of disoriented for a minute, then I walk and make a left onto Broadway. And I start thinking I'll walk up to the World Trade Center complex and then swing down to the PATH line like always. So I'm walking up and then I look up ahead and I see a crowd of people standing on the east side of Broadway up across from Liberty Plaza, and I think, "This must be it. They must know what's going on." So I walk up, and I look up, and then I see the World Trade Center, both towers on fire.

Next to me is this man saying in this utterly anguished voice, "Oh my God, did you see that? Oh my God. Oh my God. Oh my God." I didn't know what he was looking at. Later, I realized he was watching people jump. I didn't see people jump. I wasn't looking for that. I was looking at the debris being spit out from the fire and I'm thinking to myself, "We're only two blocks away from that building. And there's a couple hundred people here in the sidewalk. If one of those pieces of sheet metal comes down here, it's going to go through us like a buzz saw. This is not a safe place to be. I've got to get out of here."

I was watching and thinking. I was thinking about my friend Frank, who was up there [in the towers] and I said, "I've go to think about what am I going to do next." And I was close to making a decision when suddenly the building erupted. The top third of the building just seemed to erupt in a mushroom cloud. I didn't wait another second. I took off. And I instinctively thought that the best thing to do was run east. The people standing there on the east side of Broadway with me started to run too. There were police officers standing on Broadway with their backs to the building, not watching the building, trying to keep us from getting into Broadway. They wanted to keep Broadway, I assume, free for rescue vehicles. Nobody thinks this thing is going to come down. And suddenly, crack, the mushroom cloud stops and the very top third of the building looks like it's going to fall on top of us. In other words, it starts to fall at an angle, like the top third of a tree falling down on the loggers, right?

So I turn around and I start to run and other people run too. And I notice that some people are running even faster than me. The big fear I had in the back of my mind was the whole thing was going to come down like a tree, and for thousands of feet just obliterate everything to the east of it. People were running like mad. Although I was one of the very first people to turn and run, I wasn't really at the front of the crowd. I would call myself, like, in the back third. I didn't like that.

[Chuckles] I wanted to be as far as I could from this falling stuff as possible. So I started to really run fast. Everybody's trying to not panic. People weren't shoving each other. They were trying to be orderly. [Hesitates] But I wanted to run faster because I was about a third of the way back in the crowd, so I start running and dodging as fast as I can. I was a very fast runner, always. When I was a kid I was a really good sprinter. And I just start running.

To the side of me, I see people starting to fall, because they're clumsy, because they hit something. I see one person go down, and then another person stumbles over them, and then another person stumbles over them. A couple of times, as I'm running now, I'm seeing off to the side of me these piles of people, arms and legs, sticking out, flailing in every direction. The last thing I want to do is wind up in one of those. So I'm running and I'm running, and now I'm getting faster and faster, and I'm really starting to break out of the crowd. It's almost like running in a football game, right? I'm almost breaking through, I'm almost in the open, and then I see off to the side of me this one woman go down, falling, and as she falls her ankle twists or something. So she falls on her back and she is shrieking in terror and in pain. I mean her mouth looked like an open wound, she had makeup on, and she's screaming at the top of her lungs.

For a fraction of a second I thought, "Maybe I can pull her up." I knew from when I was a garbage man, you wouldn't believe it, but you can pick up an enormously heavy load on one arm if you cock your arm right. I know how to do it. I see her, I think maybe I should sort of cock my arm, like jam it under her arm, yank her to her feet and keep running. But I think to myself, "Boy, you're going to end up like all those people in the pile." So I kept running. And I felt bad afterward that I hadn't been able to save her.

I look over my shoulder now because I'm hearing this rumble behind me and I look and the whole horizon is now obscured by this huge roaring rumble of debris and smoke heading east. It seems to be gaining on me. I thought I was done for. I thought that I was going to get crushed, and it was obvious the building was falling right on top of us, and that it was going to kill me. And I thought, "That's absurd, I'm on my way to work! Clara's at work. The kids are at school. They're living normal lives. Why is this happening to me now? They're going to feel so bad when I'm gone. And it's going to be so hard for Max. He isn't going to grow up with a father. This is so terrible."

And I ran faster. At this point I was really at the very front of the crowd. I had gone from being about a third of the way back, weaving and dodging and spinning. I am now flying as fast as I can to the east, expecting that any second my head is going to be split by a falling steel beam. And then suddenly, completely stunning me, everything goes black. I felt myself buffeted a little bit by wind or something, but I couldn't see. I tried to look. I opened my eyes. I couldn't see an inch. I could not have seen my hand in front of my face.

I hear this voice off to the side of me, "Stay low. Stay low. The air will be better." And I say to myself, "The hell with staying low. If I get down on my hands and knees I'm going to get trampled. There's at least two hundred people behind me. They're going to step all over me." So I go into a crouch. I get as low as I can but stay on my feet. I try to breathe and it's just like gravel and crud goes down my lungs, and I start to cough and I think, "Shit. This is it. It's like a fire. It's not the flames that get you, it's the smoke."

I yank off my hat and I put it over my face and I take a few breaths and I look around. I see nothing. And this is taking a while. I don't know how many minutes I was down there. And then slowly, gradually, almost like the sunlight comes at the end of the night, the vaguest outlines of streets and buildings begin to come clear to me. I can see the glow of a light inside a window. I can see the rough street wall. And I can start to make out directions. And I said, "East, I've got to get further east. If I get further east I'm going to be by the river. There are lower buildings there. If any of those buildings go down they're less likely to cause a catastrophe like this. And by the river the air is going to be cleaner, cause it's going to be swept by breezes. And, goddamn it, if I have to I can swim across the fucking East River and get to Brooklyn, and get out of here."

I start heading across this plaza. From my left comes this man wearing a suit, briefcase, and he's walking along just shaking, rocking his head from side to side, in a total daze. I grab his arm. I said, "Come on, we're going to get out of here. We're not going to die here." And he clutches my arm as if I had awakened him from a nightmare. So he's on one arm and we head down off the staircase and we start heading through the streets, which are still obscured by the dust. And there's this other guy sort of wandering along, in much better shape. I said, "Come on. Stick with us." So I grabbed him and the three of us are sort of walking arm in arm down the street. I figure three guys have a better chance of surviving than one guy or even two.

We're headed down this really narrow street and suddenly somebody throws a door open and they're shouting, "Come on. Get in here." I hesitated for a second. Being inside a building struck me now as the most dangerous thing you could be in. I could see atria and buildings filling up with people. And who wanted to be inside a building? You could get crowded and crushed in the buildings. The buildings could come down. I didn't want to be inside a building for a million bucks, but these people said, "Quick, come in here. You can breathe better. The air is clean."

So I said, "All right," and jumped in. It's these McDonald's workers. They pulled us into the door; they slammed the door shut behind us. I haven't even said a word and this woman hands me a soaked towel to put around my face like a gas mask. Another person hands me a big container of water and says, "Here, wash your throat out." It's totally confused, but these people, McDonald's workers, were all helping us, you know? And I rinsed my throat out as much as I can. I splash water in my eyes so I can start to see again. Everybody else is doing the same thing and the workers are helping everybody. And there was a somewhat older guy, my age, and I looked at him and I said, "Terrorists?"

And he said, "Yeah, it's all over the news. It was an attack."

And I'm like, "Shit. This is for real. This is for real."

[Snyder borrows a phone to let his wife know he is okay. Then he makes his way home to Brooklyn on foot. Crowds of others are doing the same.]

We headed up into Chinatown, and E.B. White has this wonderful essay about how New York is so big, and so complex, and the neighborhoods so dense and insulated that there could be an earthquake in one neighborhood and in the next neighborhood you don't know what's going on. And this is the living truth when I get to Chinatown. There are sidewalk construction crews smoothing out the cement. [Laughing] It was sort of reassuring. And I go past the Church of the Transfiguration, and there's this family there, and they were all dressed up, and the kid's in a dress. It's First Communion. And they had these very nervous smiles on like, "Are we here on the wrong day?" [Laughing] And clearly they knew something was wrong but they didn't know exactly what was wrong. And so much of the routine was going on as if normal, right? The stores are still open.

As I got further up in the East Fifties, it's a strange scene. There are throngs of people headed north in the streets like me that look like refugees out of movies about wars and catastrophes. And yet there's a lunchtime crowd watching us too. And I see this restaurant. And all the people who work in the restaurant are sitting in the window looking at us walking by. And I just sort of knock on the door and I go, "Excuse me, can I have some water?"

And they go, "What?"

And I sort of pantomime, "Water—drinking."

They said, "No."

I said, "No?"

And they said, "No, we're closed."

I said, "Come on."

They said, "We're closed."

I go, "Fuck you!"

And they go to me, "Fuck you," as if, "Who are you to be offended at us for turning you down for a glass of water?" You know it was so grotesque.

I go, "All right, next shop."

There's a place called Jameson's Pub next door. I go up to the bar. The bartender's down at the other end. I'm trying to get his attention, when a guy next to me says, "Hey, buddy. I think you need this." And he slides his drink down the bar. [Laughs] And it was perfect. Scotch and water on ice.

I gulped it and said, "Thank you. I needed that." I drank it and I kept walking north.

[*Snyder made it home. In the days that followed he found out that his friend Frank had survived and reflected on his footrace from disaster.*]

I was haunted by that woman who fell. I felt bad that I somehow couldn't save her. And I talked to my friends about it. They're all saying to me, "Rob, that's crazy." One of my friends who'd been in the air force said, "Rob, a soldier's first duty in the battlefield is to stay alive. That's what you did, and you can't berate yourself because you didn't save somebody." And basically they all said, "The death tolls are really low, initially. You were standing among hundreds of people. If a significant number of them died you would have heard about it already." I'm sure she got away. But I felt very bad that I hadn't been able to save her. I mean, if I had stopped to pick her up we could have wound up like those tangles of arms and legs getting trampled and then we might have not made it. [Hesitates] I kept thinking, "Was there somebody I could talk to who had been through this?" Because I was telling my story and the stories that I was getting back didn't fit in a way that helped me make sense of my own.

And then I went to soccer that Saturday. My kids play in the West

Side Soccer League and I ran into one of my favorite of the soccer dads, this guy Gary Joy, who had been my son's coach. His friend was being evacuated [from the World Trade Center] with a colleague when the debris was falling. We'll call Gary's friend Bill. And the colleague sees all these bodies on the plaza. The colleague says to Bill, "We gotta help these people."

Bill says, "They're dead. We can't help them. We have to get out of here." And they're sort of having this conversation, argument, as they head across the plaza. Bill says, "No, we can't help these people. They're already dead. We have to get out of here."

And the colleague kept saying, "But shouldn't we do something? Can't we help them? Maybe some of them are alive."

And they're talking, and they're maybe six feet apart, when another body comes down and hits the colleague and kills him. And at that point a police officer comes over and grabs Bill and hauls him away.

Gary says, "You know Rob, Bill has just been sitting, staring at the wall ever since."

And I thought to myself, "Right. Bill understood what was going on. If the colleague had only listened to him, the two of them might have been alive today." And so I knew what was going on too. And I did what I had to do to stay alive that day.

I think the firefighters who went up into the building are heroes. And I've watched the film footage. There's no swagger. Most of the guys' shoulders are stooped and they're facing this awful duty. And they're going to do it anyway. So I don't feel that I'm entitled to call myself a hero. But I do think that, in a strange way, on that morning whatever I had to pull up from inside me to survive, and think it through as I was doing it, and run as fast as I did, and figure out the angles and directions and how to help people, that was me. That was me. I was as fully realized on that morning as in any other moment in my life, as I've been in any of the other things that have mattered to me profoundly, like my marriage and being a father, and my writing, any of it. I was as fully realized on that morning as any other time in my life. And yet that knowledge comes with direct experience of the most awful horror. Boy, I would have forgone that knowledge of myself in a minute [laughs] if we only could wind the tape back and not have the planes crash into the towers.

And so, for me after 9/11, the big question became, "What should our country do? What should our response be?" And it surfaced first in the debates around the war in Afghanistan. I had some friends and colleagues who had been comrades in different causes who thought that the war against Afghanistan was completely indefensible. I thought it was an ugly necessity. I had problems with the way it was fought. I thought that the reliance on U.S. airpower inevitably would mean that innocent people were going to be killed—that we ought to, however horrible it was, accept greater American casualties if it meant reducing civilian casualties on the other side. But I thought it had to happen. I thought it had to be done. I thought we couldn't allow the Al-Qaeda network the run of a country as a staging base. I remember being very wary going up to colleagues and talking about this. I didn't particularly want to talk. I didn't want to argue about it. It was not something I felt comfortable debating with people because it immediately brought up roaring emotions with me about September 11. And so I felt really comfortable among the ones who felt like I did but I didn't want to argue with people.

And I came away, as times passed since then, with this difficult wrestling match going on inside my own mind. I had been very active in the American support groups for the Israeli peace movement. I'm still active in that. So I still haven't become a hawk. But what September 11 convinced me [of] is that there are really horrible people out there that would do terrible harm to many people, me included, and they have to be put down the way you put down a mad dog. How you do that, where you do that, when you do that is an enormously complicated question—one that requires vastly greater subtlety and intelligence than the president has displayed in Iraq. But I've become sort of a reluctant "National Security Dove," I call myself.

[*Snyder describes returning in December 2001 to lower Manhattan and seek-ing out the McDonald's workers who helped him.*]

I went back to the place with a friend of mine just to look them up. And we were standing outside the door that was thrown open and this man was having a cigarette break. He turns around and sees me and he goes, "Hey, it's you!" And we were all hugging each other and he said, "Come on in."

The ladies said, "We remember you." And I was worried about them because they had to go through not one firestorm but two. And I guess the final thing I'd say is that for all the heroism of the uniformed workers [on September 11] we cannot forget that ordinary people, who were not wear-ing uniforms, helped out too. I was saved by women wearing McDonald's uniforms. Those were the uniformed people who saved me.

19.

Ghislaine Boulanger

Psychologist

Interviewed by Mary Marshall Clark

Ghislaine Boulanger is a clinical psychologist and psychoanalyst in New York City. She specializes in treating survivors of violence. Boulanger was born in England in 1942. She is the author of Wounded by Reality: Understanding and Treating Adult Onset Trauma *as well as numerous journal articles. Boulanger is on the teaching faculty of New York University's Postdoctoral Program in Psychotherapy and Psychoanalysis.*

JUNE 24, 2005

My father was French and my mother was English, hence my name. I was raised mainly in England. At a certain point in my late teens, I decided that England was not the place for me. France was far too bourgeois and I wanted to come to America. In America, I got a job in publishing, then became an editor. The books I commissioned were usually about psychology, and I thought, "I'm kind of a vicarious psychologist here. Maybe I should actually become a psychologist." I trained in clinical psychology at Columbia University.

While I was at Columbia, I was looking for a topic for my dissertation and there was a sociologist in the Social Psych program who described to me a number of the projects that he was working on. One of them was with Vietnam veterans. As I now know, those vets were actually working with Robert J. Lifton and Hy Shatan starting the self-help groups, the veteran "rap" groups that became legends. They wanted epidemiologists to start to look at what was being called post-Vietnam syndrome. What they generally wanted was to look at the veterans' adaptation to post-combat life, and I said, "That's it!" I had been active against the war and felt that at the same time I had failed to understand the issues of the veterans themselves. I think many of us did at that time. So I said, "That's it. I'd really like to do that."

We started with three hundred people, mainly from the New York area—both combat veterans and people who had been in Vietnam and not in combat, which meant designing a combat scale, and civilians who had never served in the military. A lot of the early research had not made a distinction between combat and noncombat vets, which is, of course, crucial. We added another thousand men, so we had thirteen hundred interviews—again, matched samples, as I described. We had a sociologist, we had a political scientist, we had a social psychologist doing the analyses. People were looking at marital adjustment and the incidence of divorce. People were looking at education and how vets were using the educational benefits. We were looking a lot at drugs and alcohol, because Vietnam was supposed to be the big laboratory in which everybody became drug addicts. I said that I, personally, was interested in this post-Vietnam syndrome, and I was lucky enough to have available some of the papers that subsequently were used for the diagnosis of post-traumatic stress disorder [PTSD]. I read those; I immersed myself in the early literature: Abraham Kardiner's work, *Men Under Stress* by Roy R. Grinker and John P. Spiegel, these World War II classics and classic papers—and from this I extrapolated a list of symptoms that I thought measured the syndrome.

And indeed it did. If you controlled for combat, then measured what I had come to call "long-term stress reactions," you found a clear distinction between those who had been in combat and those who had not. But what I was particularly interested in at the time was if there was a predisposition to this stress reaction. Surely, I said to myself, there must be. Nobody would just fall apart like this. This is the way people thought in those days, and in some ways still do. I also made a scale to measure predisposition, looking at early history of any psychological problems, looking at any instance of instability in the family of origin, looking at patterns of friendships, looking at school performance. I found, to my astonishment and excitement—and it really has changed my life—that at the highest level of combat, predisposition made no difference. In other words, as they said after World War II, "Every man had his breaking point." I was just flabbergasted. And I said, "My God, how do we understand this? We have to understand this phenomenon: what happens to people, as adults, even if they really have their act together, that alters them in such a way that they can't apparently put their lives back together again after a massive trauma?" So that was what brought me here. I remember the guy who had been the director of the Bronx Veterans Administration Psychiatric Department for many, many years coming up to me and saying, "Honey, I've never seen a case of post-traumatic stress disorder yet." How do you argue with that? He's constructed the world in such a way that he's not going to see it.

I'd like to hear you talk about the clinical work you do, the kind of people you work with around these issues of traumatic stress.

I should say first I hope no one has a practice devoted entirely to working with people who are massively traumatized. It's extremely punishing work. The whole issue of vicarious traumatization is something to really be contended with. So, much of my practice is just a normal practice at this point. But I normally carry in my practice three or four people who have had some massive trauma, and sometimes it has happened absolutely unawares. One of the horrible things, the insidious things, about massive psychic trauma and its results is that people feel very much alone with what's happened to them. They don't feel comfortable volunteering the symptoms.

One of the things I've done that I've been chastened by, and learned an enormous amount from doing, is assessments of people who have been tortured and are seeking asylum in this country, and really having to tolerate listening to and thinking about the consequences of being tortured. And then the horrors of coming to this country, as an illegal alien, seeking political asylum, and ending up in [detention]. I gather they're about to close it, but the [United States Immigration and Customs Enforcement's] Wackenhut Detention Center in Queens [New York] or the detention center in Elizabeth [New Jersey] often repeat, one hopes without the actual torture, so many of the elements of what led asylum seekers to leave their country in the first place. It is just horrible to see them being re-traumatized. And, of course, more recently, I have a number of people who were very close to Ground Zero on 9/11, or who were among the first responders. So that's become, I can't say in any way a focus of my practice, because, as I say, to focus only on this is just too difficult, but it's certainly become a large component of my practice.

Could you describe for us your own personal experience of the day of September 11, and following?

It was a Tuesday morning and I was seeing patients, as usual. I was expecting a young woman to come over to help me with some office work. She called me and left a message for me saying, "A plane has just gone into the World Trade Center. I'm just watching it on TV. I'll be there soon." This was obviously the first plane. It was between patients that I picked up this message and didn't give it a moment's thought. Obviously, we all thought it was a small plane. Then I think I saw my second patient and the secretary reached me between patients and said, "A second plane has just gone into the building." My next patient was sitting outside my office. I said, "My God, this is terrible."

She said, "I'm not going to come up."

So I found out from her. I brought my next patient in and we were having a regular session. I live way uptown. My office is on 101st Street. I started to hear ambulances and alarms and things, so my mind went back to this again. I had been concentrating on my patient, I'm listening to my patient, and I'm thinking, "Someone told me that they've just gotten a job high up in the World Trade Center." And I started going through this mental Rolodex, saying, "I know it was a woman I'm very close to. I knew where I had been when she told me—I was in my kitchen." I thought, "Who was in my kitchen recently?" And then I said, "Oh, my God. It's Betty," who was my next-door neighbor. She lived, actually, in the apartment above us. I said to my patient, "I'm sorry. Do you know what's happening?"

She said, "Yeah. A plane's gone into the World Trade Center."

I said, "I've just thought about something. Would you give me a moment?" I went into my bathroom. I had some water and I just said to myself, "She's dead." I don't know whether I couldn't bear to live with not knowing, which, I have to say, I did, after that, but I just pulled myself together, went back, and completed the session.

Betty was a woman in her early sixties who had been a nightclub singer—vital, fun. She came from New Orleans and was a jazz singer who was now working for Cantor Fitzgerald. That morning none of us knew the name Cantor Fitzgerald. It's now engraved on our hearts. I had the card of Cantor Fitzgerald upstairs in my kitchen. She had left it with me that Saturday. We had been roaring with laughter, about how she basically conned this guy into hiring her, not that she wasn't a wonderful secretary but she needed to twist his arm a bit. So I called our tenants who were friends of hers too, to say, "Do you know how Betty got this job? We have to find out what floor she was on." They were stunned. The guy was still in the apartment. His wife was actually coming home from work because of the attack. She was five months pregnant and she was walking home from Midtown. We all sat together in our living room, eating sandwiches. The first thing I did was to make sandwiches, which is, I know, so many people's response. Michael, my neighbor, said, "I'm going to go and donate blood."

And I said, "I'm going to go to the Red Cross to see what I can do." I went to the Red Cross building and there were thousands of people, milling around outside. I went up, rather tentatively, to one of the guards and said, "I'm a psychologist and I wonder if you can use me."

He said, "Third floor."

I went up to the third floor, and again, there were by now hundreds of people milling around. I saw some friends and one of them [Todd] knew that this was my expertise and he said, "Oh, Ghislaine, let's work together. Work with me."

I said, "Sure." I was very glad to have him, because he was a bit more pushy than I was.

He went up to this woman and he said, "This is Dr. Boulanger and she's worked with massive trauma." Of course, everybody was claiming this but it was more helpful if he said it than if I did.

They called us over and they said, "Will you work in the morgue?" I said sure. I did have to think about it for a moment. They said, "You don't have to go into the morgue. You just take people there, and you wait for them."

I thought, "No way I'm waiting for them. I'll go to the morgue. I'll go in with the people." So Todd and I went downstairs and they took us by some Red Cross vehicle down to the pier that later became the family center [the New York City Family Assistance Center at Pier 94 on Fifty-fourth Street and Twelfth Avenue]. I was so impressed at how organized it was. The cops already set up these lines. There were no people there but they designated lounges where people would be. The building where the bodies would be taken was next door and we walked that walk, just to see. That was the first time that I could actually look down and see the plume of smoke and that the buildings weren't there, which was just so shocking.

It was like that feeling of when you've had a tooth out and you put your tongue in the gap. It's unfamiliar, but you familiarize yourself very quickly with it. We're waiting for the ambulances and we were sort of suspended in no-man's-land here. It was a beautiful day, and we're waiting, and nothing happens. Finally, about nine o'clock, they call us and they say, "Can we call you back?" I don't know that they knew why nothing was happening. I don't think anybody understood that there weren't bodies. It was too inconceivable. You have to allow these ghastly facts to kind of come in slowly. You can't take it all in. So I went home.

It's funny how little things get to you. I remember getting on a bus on Amsterdam Avenue and the guy put his hand over the fare box and he said, "We're not charging." And I thought, "It's always these little kindnesses that get you." I didn't cry at the time. I was too in survivor mode and in I-must-be-strong mode. I got home, got immediately onto my Listserv, and told people what there was to be done. Many, many, many, many people I knew had already been at the Red Cross. Many people had not been deployed as I had. Many people had actually gone down to Ground Zero and done things there.

As the week went on we did decide that we had to have some kind of memorial for Betty on the Upper West Side. We got one of these big candles and flowers and we put them on the stoop, outside the door to the building. People came and put flowers there. What was fascinating to me was that some patients would come and say, "What's happened? Are you all right?" It felt important not to burden people with this. But I could say, "A neighbor died. A friend died." Others didn't notice.

On Saturday I went to the Armory with a man who had been a student of mine. He's had much more experience than I do in working with massive trauma and we decided we'd go together. By now the Red Cross was really organizing themselves and you needed certain credentials to get in. I had not had the Red Cross training because it had never seemed necessary. Tom could present his VA credentials and get in. I had my Columbia University professor's badge and they let me in with that. And I thought, "My God! You shouldn't be doing this. You'll be getting people from the English department coming in here. This is outrageous." I didn't tell them that. I just came in. We were assigned to a table where we were going over the lists of the people who were in the hospitals, who had been identified. Families were filing through, coming to us, and we would look through the list of names and then say, "I'm sorry. That name isn't on this list."

I remember at some point Bill and Hillary Clinton came around and it was such a pain. I thought, "Don't come!" I suppose they really wanted to see and touch things and sort of get an idea of what was going on. It felt so disruptive to this work that was so intense, and our needing to say to people, "Okay. We can't find the name on the list. What are you going to do? Have you brought hair samples? Maybe you should go home and bring a hairbrush."

I remember one man saying, "What do you mean?" Absolutely not ready, in any way, to accept—five, six days later—that his wife might be dead. He was taken out by his brothers-in-law, the brothers of the woman who was clearly not there. We were sometimes able to send people to counseling centers set up by companies. Cantor Fitzgerald, of course, had a counseling place. This was in the Armory on Lexington Avenue. Already they were starting with this memorial wall, which was very moving. Some of the photographs we saw on that wall were the same photographs that people had brought to show us, to say, "This is the person. This is the name. Are they on the lists?" At the end of that day we were taken, again by the Red Cross, and sat on the staircase somewhere and got debriefed, and talked about what was difficult. Then it was safe for volunteers to cry.

So that day was engraved in my mind. And many days of going to the pier and finding people to talk to. Once I was pulled aside by these young girls in their mid-twenties who were on Giuliani's staff and had not had a day off since it had happened. I'll never forget this. By now the city had produced little urns full of ash taken from the pit. And people who came for these little urns had to endure a ceremony that was being conducted by these twenty-five-year-old kids. These kids said to me, "This is very, very difficult. Could you help us do this?"

I said, "Sure. I'll come over." So I sat there and watched them do it. And they had to have the flag folded in a particular, ritual way, then hold on to the flag, place it on top of the urn, then read a little statement about how important this person's sacrifice had been and how the city mourned their death and here were their ashes. And, of course, these girls were stumbling over the lines, which seemed so unnecessarily formal. Nonetheless, they were scared to deviate from them. And the people who were getting the ashes were clearly confused. Some of them were in such a dissociated state that I think you could have said, "Humpty Dumpty" to them, and it wouldn't have meant anything. I think I was probably among the first to say, "Look. We're going to have to talk about how to do this." And we managed to sort of humanize the experience a little bit.

I would talk to the people who came for the ashes first and say, "Who is it? Who's died? What's this like for you? The mayor's office wants to make a formal presentation of these ashes. Will that be okay? Can you accept them?" This went a lot better. I have no idea how many of those little urns we gave out that day. But what was also important was to be able to talk to these kids who had just been lost in the system. All the attention paid to the first responders and, of course, to the survivors. But these kids on the staff had really been shattered. Talking of vicarious traumatization, they had seen a lot, they'd heard a lot. They were scared. So those are all my associations to the immediacy of 9/11.

How is it for you now, over time?

It's interesting that my mind goes to this first, and I think it's an important thing. It was so extraordinary, on that day, to be both personally implicated and professionally implicated. We have Betty's picture in the stairway in our house, so I see her every day. It is so much a part of my everyday life. I had started to write a series of psychoanalytic papers before 9/11 about the necessity for psychoanalysts to be able to understand what I call adult-onset trauma. Now I'm writing a book. It's not a 9/11 book, though, of course, the book has many 9/11 stories to it. So when you ask, "How is it for me now?" It's part of my everyday work. Not all day, but it's very much a part of my everyday consciousness.

I believe that massive psychic trauma comes because you are directly confronted with your own death, annihilation. I don't mean symbolic death. We psychoanalysts talk a lot about annihilation anxiety, how it echoes through our lives. How it comes up in infancy. I don't mean that kind of symbolic death. I mean actual death. When you're faced with that, in some ways, you do die. I believe that the personality basically shatters, comes apart, and it cannot be seamlessly put together. Now, I'm not saying this happens to everybody who faces this terrifying moment but it happens to many of them.

I think of Susan J. Brison. She's a philosopher who wrote about having been raped in France and left for dead. It was a brutal, brutal rape. She found herself, a year later, as she writes in her book saying, "I was murdered in France last year." People who experience this kind of trauma will often feel, in some ways, that they are dead. It's not that you think you're almost dead—you have to convince yourself that you're alive. I think I can name it in almost everybody I've worked with who has been massively traumatized. This will also come up for those who are exposed to the sight of violent death, the horror of the pit, the horror of those body parts, those awful things they saw. The sense of physical cohesion comes under attack and the feeling of the immediacy of death becomes real to these people too.

If I just confine myself to 9/11 for a moment—we were all terrified, and some people felt that they were in danger of annihilation. Yes, it was a terrifying experience. But I do want to make a distinction between those who were right there—who saw it, who experienced it, who ran from it, or who may have lost someone, or first responders who went in and started seeing these awful things—and those who watched it on television. I don't believe the TV constitutes massive traumatization. You may well have re-petitive thoughts and what I call vicarious traumatization. But it hasn't got the same impact.

For those who don't understand what the symptoms are of post-traumatic stress disorder, could you explain them? And then also talk about the concept of PTSD and how it's being used today?

Rather than give you the list of symptoms, what I'd like to do is try to talk about the experience. The most remarkable symptoms are these instances of intrusive memories. They can take the form of thoughts or bodily sensations. They can take the form of repetitive dreams. These intrusive feelings—memories, images—will come up sometimes in response to something that's happening outside. If it's a beautiful blue day you'll think of a plane going in, if that's what you saw. Or a body falling, if that's what you saw. I can remember a Vietnam veteran, in the early eighties, talking about how it was becoming increasingly difficult to come to work, get to work, because more and more Korean greengrocers were opening up, and the smell from the Korean greengrocers took him right back to Vietnam. And he just panicked. The smell elicited the memory of the experience. So you have this intrusiveness.

Then there is a way of trying to escape from it. So people's lives will become more and more and more circumscribed. "I don't go near the Korean grocers." Or "I don't go downtown." Or "I don't watch television, because I don't want to see planes flying over. I don't read newspapers, because I'm going to see events about 9/11."

There is a kind of numbing, a reduction in the intensity of feelings. There is a sense that what has meaning to other people doesn't have mean-ing to you, because what has meaning to you is this event that you went through two weeks ago, two years ago, or ten years ago. There is a reduc-tion in ties to other people, sometimes, because other people don't under-stand. So I think I've captured the syndrome and how it removes people from being citizens of the world.

Could you describe, for those who experienced this catastrophic trauma, the dialectic between knowing and not knowing?

On some level, I knew that Betty was dead. On another level, I couldn't yet come to terms with it. There are ways in which your knowing is dissociated so that it's not hooked up with feelings. It might be hooked up with an intense understanding of the phenomena but somehow you don't let your feelings know. And sometimes the feelings are so overwhelming, they feel so powerful, yet you don't let yourself know the details of what happened. Knowing and not knowing, Lawrence Langer uses that expression in terms of the Holocaust. Dori Laub does too. If you really let yourself know about these horrors is there a way that you can go on? So maybe the only way to actually live your life is to put them in the not-knowing place.

I think of a very famous psychoanalyst, Wilfred Bion, who was actually quite a hero in the First World War. As he was preparing for battle he would read out the coordinates in this absolutely obsessive way, as a way of reducing the terror. After the trauma, you find that your mind really doesn't move much beyond this kind of obsessiveness. It's sometimes very hard to start to be able to think creatively again. I think the most striking evidence of this is in the dreams that, time and again, are repeating exactly what happened to you.

Is there some fundamental need to tell that we should respect more, that we can do more with, after these catastrophic events?

I think the need to tell is all about bearing witness. And I think we have to be very clear that we are bearing witness to our own experience when we really are able to put together a coherent narrative. Those narratives of yours that I've read from the oral history program have been strikingly fluid to me and are coherent in a way that, very often, when people first come to me and talk about a traumatic event, they are not able to give such a story. As I read your narratives and thought about the demand characteristics of your interview, you basically tell people, "These interviews are for history.

They have great significance." I believe this helps people mobilize them-selves, at least at that moment, to tell that story. It really makes me think twice about the privacy that we analysts and therapists generally promise our patients. In the preface to Anna Akhmatova's poem "Requiem," about state-imposed violence in the USSR, she writes of a woman who is clearly suffering, approaching her to ask, "Can you describe this?" And when Akhmatova says she can, "something like a smile passed fleetingly over what had once been her face." Knowing that there is a witness to the hor-ror brings this woman peace.